IMAGES
of America

CASCADE PARK

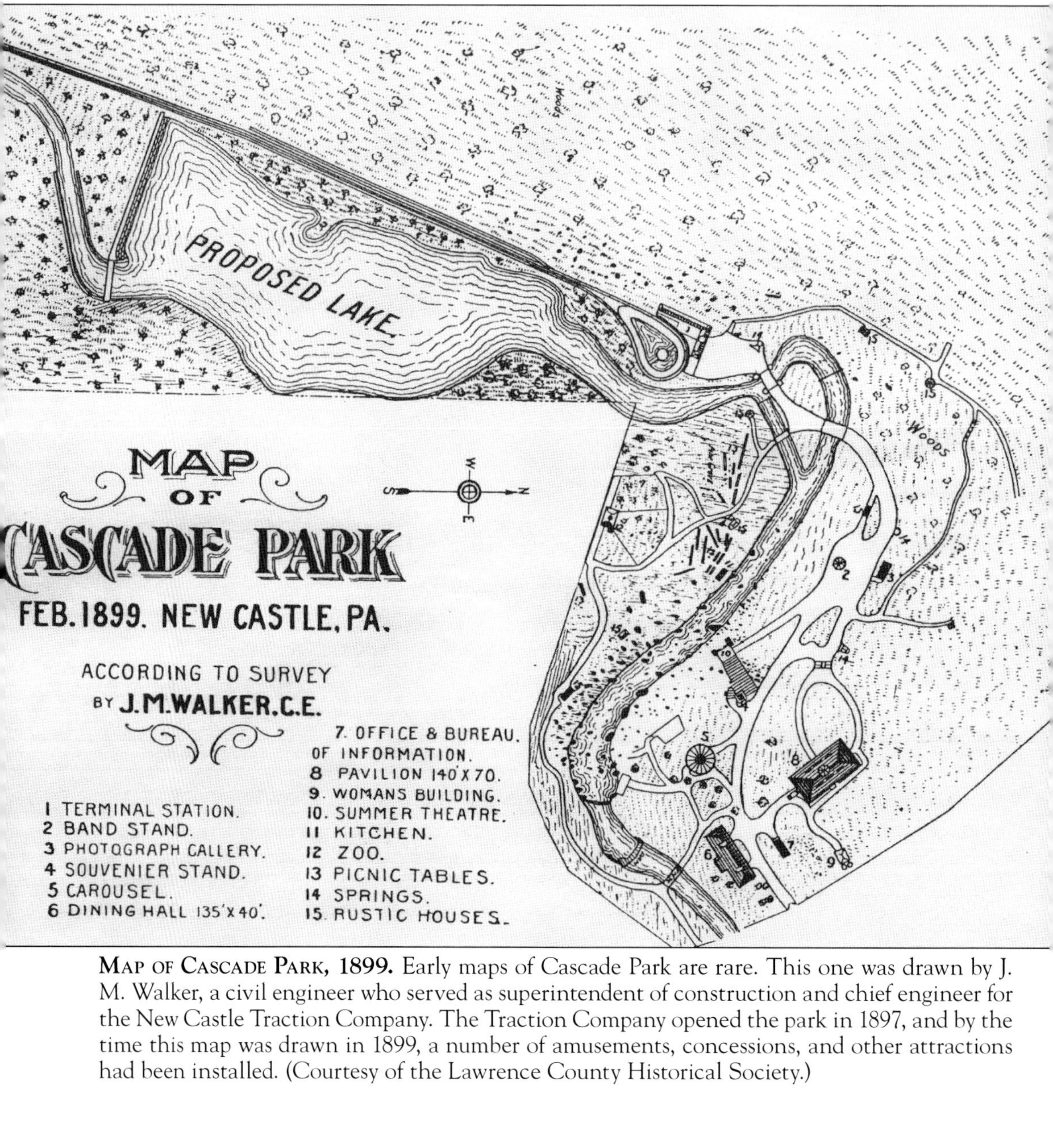

MAP OF CASCADE PARK, 1899. Early maps of Cascade Park are rare. This one was drawn by J. M. Walker, a civil engineer who served as superintendent of construction and chief engineer for the New Castle Traction Company. The Traction Company opened the park in 1897, and by the time this map was drawn in 1899, a number of amusements, concessions, and other attractions had been installed. (Courtesy of the Lawrence County Historical Society.)

ON THE COVER: CASCADE PARK LAKE. Cascade Park Lake, once called Crystal Lake, was one of the park's most popular attractions. Over the years, its 15 acres offered visitors rowboats, a motorized launch, fishing, swimming, boat races, and, in the winter, ice-skating. In the lake's later years, a riverboat, complete with sternwheel, entertained crowds. (Courtesy of the Lawrence County Historical Society.)

IMAGES
of America

CASCADE PARK

Anita DeVivo and the
Lawrence County Historical Society

ARCADIA
PUBLISHING

ISBN 978-0-7385-7316-8

Published by Arcadia Publishing
Charleston, South Carolina

Printed in the United States of America

Library of Congress Control Number: 2009942981

For all general information contact Arcadia Publishing at:
Telephone 843-853-2070
Fax 843-853-0044
E-mail sales@arcadiapublishing.com
For customer service and orders:
Toll-Free 1-888-313-2665

Visit us on the Internet at www.arcadiapublishing.com

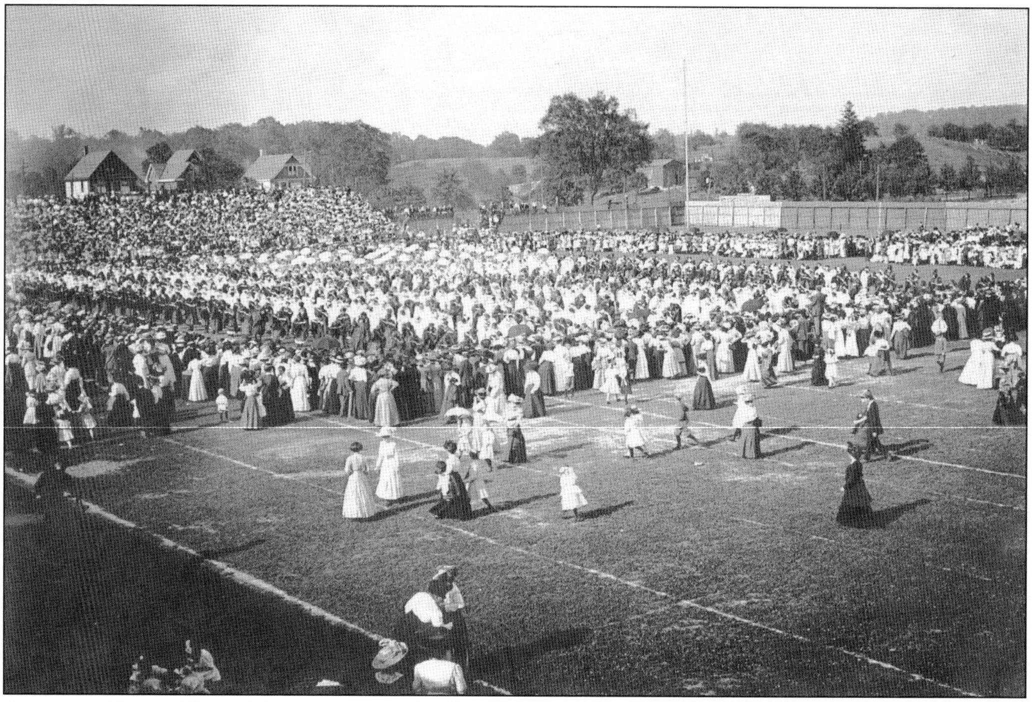

Cascade Park Ball Field, c. 1906. As passengers on the Hamilton Street Trolley line approached the Cascade Park lake, they could see the ball field on the right. The field had a $12,000 grandstand that held 3,000 spectators; the bleachers held 300. The event pictured here is probably the first annual outing of the Uniform Rank of the Knights of Pythias, July 11, 1906. The outing drew Pythians from Beaver and Mercer Counties and points west to compete in drills, relays, and other exercises. (Courtesy of the Lawrence County Historical Society.)

Contents

ACKNOWLEDGMENTS

The photographs, postcards, and ephemera that make up the major part of this book are from the collections of the Lawrence County Historical Society (LCHS) and the society's John Hitch Collection. Other photographs included here are from the generous people mentioned in the courtesy lines that accompany their contributions.

The authors thank the following people for reviewing the manuscript: Sandra Bumgardner, whose father, Claude Crill, was a Cascade Park employee in the park's heyday; Anna Mary Mooney, LCHS administrator and archivist; Adam Pivovar, technical expert; Lynn Slovonsky, journalist; and especially Beverly Zona, whose book *All the Summers Were Golden* was an invaluable reference.

The authors thank the following people and their offices for information and reference material: Anthony Mastrangelo, mayor, City of New Castle; Chris Fabian, New Castle Public Library; Frank Gingras, Lawrence County Planning Office; Janet Falotico, Lawrence County Tourist Promotion Agency; Joann McBride, Lawrence County Tourist Promotion Agency; and Joe Temperato, Community Development Office, City of New Castle.

The authors thank the following people for technical and research assistance, reminiscences, and reference material: Carly Bouwman, Dwight Copper, Sally Daytner, Jean DiTullio, Gene Duda, Tony Elisco, Chris George, Sam Gunnett, Mandy Kendall, Dan Martwinski, Leslie S. McCracken, Angelo and Kay Nocera, Staci Olson, Debbie Schukert, John Small, Debbie Smock, and Tom Zumpella.

Introduction

Ask local people to name their favorite memory of Cascade Park, and most of them will say "French fries with vinegar." Not the gorge, not the lake, not the merry-go-round, but French fries with vinegar. That might surprise the people who operated Cascade Park, the owners, concessionaires, and grounds people. They worked hard to keep the rides and other attractions appealing. Who could have guessed that tastes would change so radically over the years. The rides were an exciting novelty when Cascade Park was new. Today they are just another piece of nostalgia.

At this writing, Cascade Park in New Castle, Pennsylvania, is 113 years old. It has had three owners. First was Col. Levi C. Brinton, who in 1891 saw the potential of 70 acres or so of natural beauty on the south edge of New Castle. He paid $5,000 to create Brinton Park, a modest amusement park with a carousel and a dance platform.

In 1897, Arthur Kennedy and Richard Quay bought Brinton Park for $15,000 and shortly thereafter sold it to the New Castle Traction Company, which they owned, for $46,000. The Traction Company had big plans. First, they built a trolley line to get people to the park. Then they installed rides and other attractions: a roller coaster, a carousel, a theater, a lake, a dance pavilion, a ball field, picnic grounds, and a zoo. The park was magnetic—crowds poured in by trolley, train, and automobile.

By the 1930s, the novelty of the park was not enough to keep the crowds coming. People could go places by car now, and they could find entertainment elsewhere. And of course, the Depression changed the entertainment they could afford. The New Castle Traction Company had also undergone changes. The trolley company was now part of what had become the Pennsylvania Power Company.

The power company was not in the amusement park business. In the early 1930s, Penn Power sold Cascade Park to the City of New Castle for $1. Matters were now in the hands of Mayor Charles B. Mayne.

Over the early years of city ownership, the park stopped trying to attract tourists as the traction company had. Instead, it promoted community support. One of the first events, even before the deed was signed, was a community day. According to the *New Castle News*, the mayor issued a proclamation declaring July 26, 1933, a "legal half-holiday" and urged all businesses to close at noon so that everybody could participate. The *News* also announced in a smaller item that a "community picnic is expected to attract thousands of persons on July 26; and on August 7 there will be a big crowd of colored people, as that date has been designated as 'Colored Day.' "

With the city in charge, much of the activity of the park remained unchanged. Churches, clubs, companies, families, labor unions, and other groups continued to hold their picnics there. Women were still meeting in "kensingtons," small social groups, often enjoying tureen dinners.

In the 1940s, buses replaced streetcars. Families' needs were changing with the demands of wartime. The park now had a kiddies' day, Mondays, when rides were half price. The infrastructure of the park was beginning to show age, the swimming pool filters needed attention, the lake dam had broken, and the lake ran dry. New attractions, such as Swing Lobby in the summer, were introduced.

And then came Vesco. In the 1950s, the park got new energy. Paul Vesco formed the Cascade Amusement Company. He introduced new attractions and installed new rides, particularly a new roller coaster. With the postwar boom and the baby boomers, a new generation of young people fell in love with the park.

The French fries made their appearance. So did lemon ice and meatball sandwiches and sausage sandwiches. The park was in its second heyday; it was a destination again. But a drama was playing out down at the lake. Silt had taken over, and community leader Jack Gerson spearheaded efforts to save the lake. By 1958, the lake was restored, but the efforts were in vain. First, more silt and a broken spillway slowly began to drain the lake. Then the dam broke, destroying the lake completely. The pleasures of fishing and boating disappeared with the water.

The city's fortunes were not looking better than the fortunes of the lake. It seemed that no sooner was one area fixed, then another needed repairs. Although a new swimming pool was installed in 1979, the dance pavilion had begun to deteriorate. And when the local square dance group stepped in and raised funds for restoring the dance pavilion, a tree fell over the roller coaster's tracks and ruined them. Then vandals discovered the park and made off with carousel horses and the restaurant burned down.

Through all of this, the park retained its beauty. In the 1990s, the Lawrence County Garden Club restored the flowers and other plantings. A Cascade Park Development Commission had the old blacktop removed from the midway. The Rotary Club restored the carousel building.

In 1997, Cascade Park celebrated its 100th birthday. Ceremonies took place accompanied by band concerts, fireworks, plays, and picnics. By that time, most of the amusements and rides had disappeared. In 2000, the swimming pool closed. And yet, through all of that, the city was able to maintain the grounds. Picnics were still held in the grove. Kids could still use the playground. Square dancing, classic cars cruises, and ethnic days could still take place at the park. And let us not forget Old Timers Day, almost as old as the park itself.

In 2007, the 100th Old Timers Day took place. The pavilion was filled with senior citizens, many of them in lightweight and colorful summer clothes–a far cry from the elaborate long dresses and heavy suits of the first Old Timers Day. The Grand March took place as usual in addition to the waltz contest and the competition for the titles "Oldest Person" and "Traveled the Farthest."

So for all the changes at Cascade Park, some things never change. Not Big Run, not the falls and cascades, not the boulders and rocks, not the memories and echoes of the past, and not the little rush of anticipation one gets when entering the park, even if one is an old-timer.

In the pages that follow, the first two chapters illustrate the history given in this introduction. Chapters three and four show the rides and amusements and how some of them changed over time. Chapter five tells the story of the dance pavilion, the oldest building in today's park. Chapters six and seven show some community groups and events that have figured in the history of the park. And the final two chapters feature the beauty of the park and demonstrate why its natural setting continues to be a local treasure.

One

Brinton Park

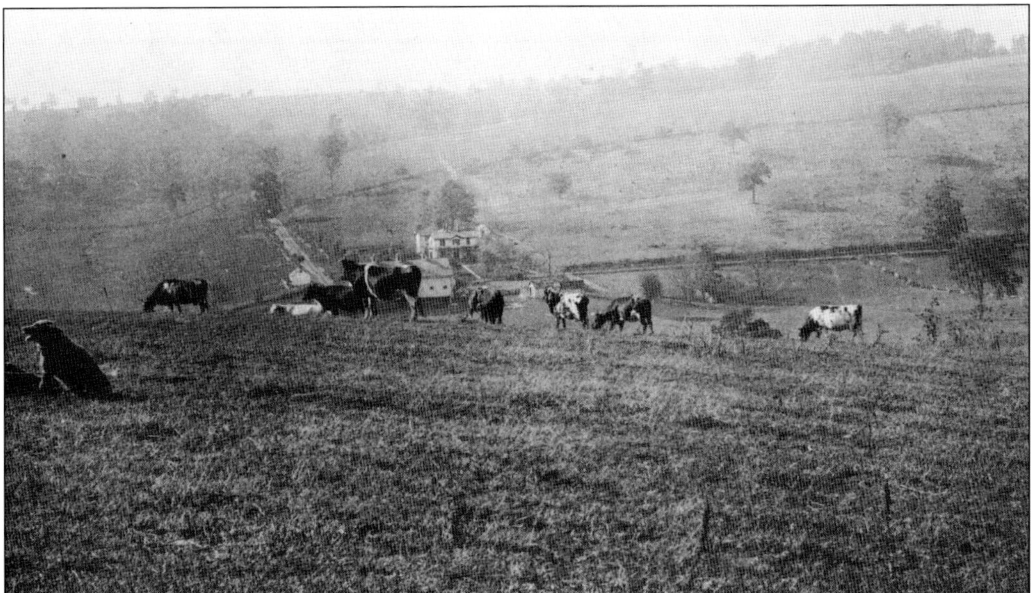

Brinton Farm, c. 1894. In the 1800s, this acreage in Shenango Township just outside of New Castle was known as "the Patterson property." In 1892, a later owner, H. L. Palmer, sold 65 acres to Col. Levi C. Brinton for $5,000. Brinton was a Civil War veteran who had fought at Bull Run, Fredricksburg, Antietam, and Vicksburg. (Courtesy of New Castle Public Library.)

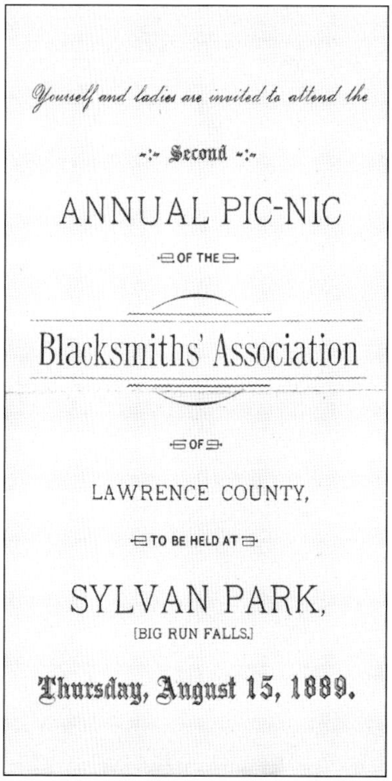
Yourself and ladies are invited to attend the

-:- Second -:-

ANNUAL PIC-NIC

OF THE

Blacksmiths' Association

OF

LAWRENCE COUNTY,

TO BE HELD AT

SYLVAN PARK,

[BIG RUN FALLS.]

Thursday, August 15, 1889.

AN INVITATION TO SYLVAN PARK, 1889. The land Brinton bought was known as Sylvan Park, but most people called it Big Run Falls. As evidenced by this invitation, the area was often used by locals as a gathering place. During this time, the blacksmiths of Lawrence County were numerous enough to support an association. Among them were John Miller, behind Kirk's hardware store; John Wesley Bagnall; J. H. Vogan; J. E. Emery; Al Shaffer; Charles Waddington; and many others. (Courtesy of Sandra Bumgardner.)

BIG RUN, C. 1894. Fallen trees, bushes, brush, rocks, and the falls in the distance led the original publisher of this photograph to entitle it "Where the Groundhog Seeks Its Shadow." Often described as wild and romantic, the scenery of Big Run Falls is dominated by countless boulders left by the Wisconsin glacier. (Courtesy of the New Castle Public Library.)

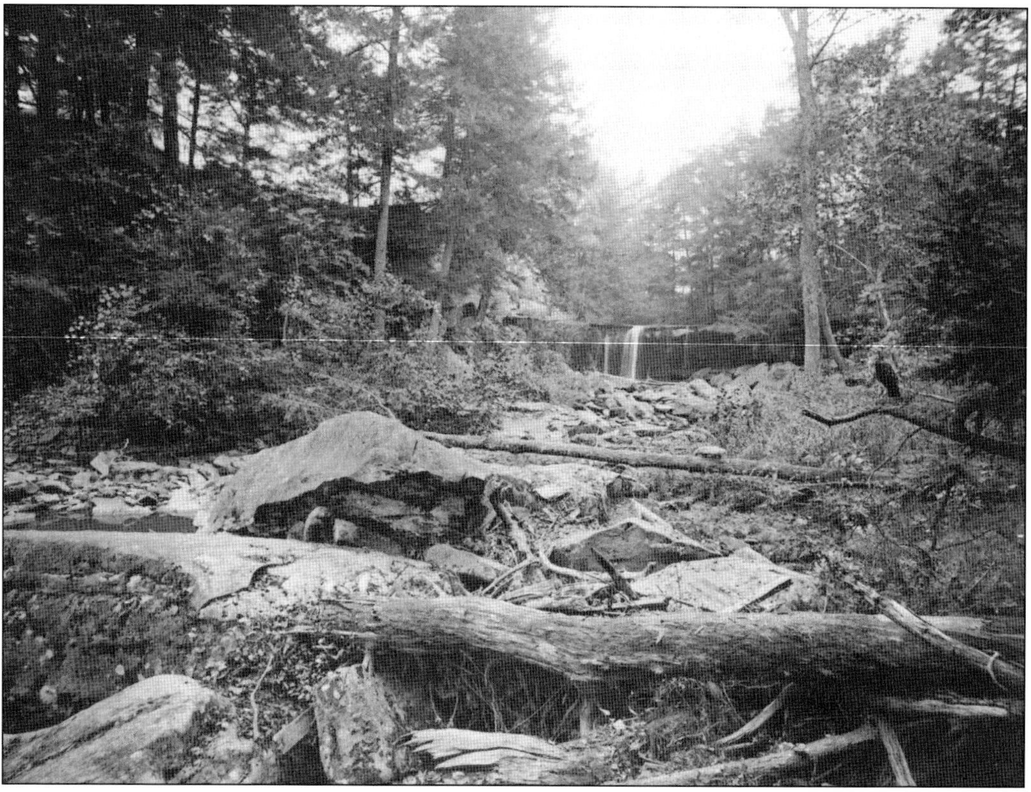

Col. Levi C. Brinton. After Brinton acquired Big Run Falls, he named the property Brinton Park. Pictured here in full uniform with his veteran's medals, Brinton continued to use the title "Colonel." He did not earn the title in active battle but acquired it later as a member of a reserve unit.

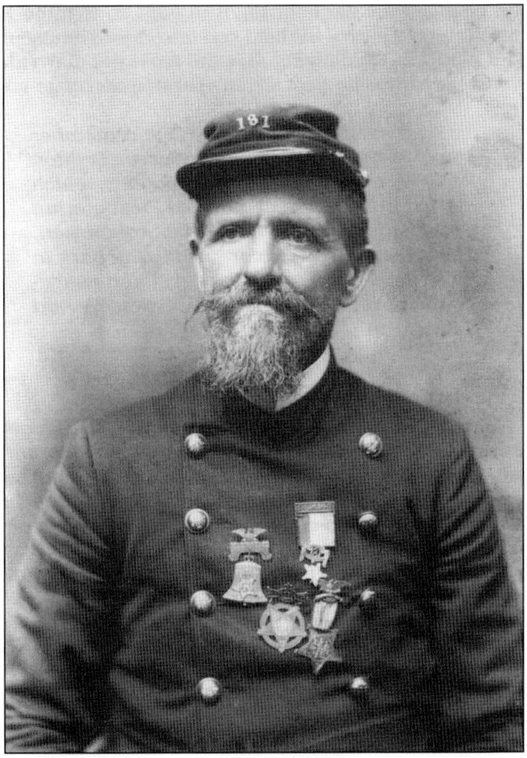

Under Big Run Falls, c. 1894. The coolest place in Brinton Park was under the falls. Originally 20 feet high, the falls lost some height when surrounding rock was blasted in order to cut a race for a sawmill. It is said that some farmers washed their sheep under the falls, and that the face of a Native American princess is carved on a huge boulder just beneath the falls.

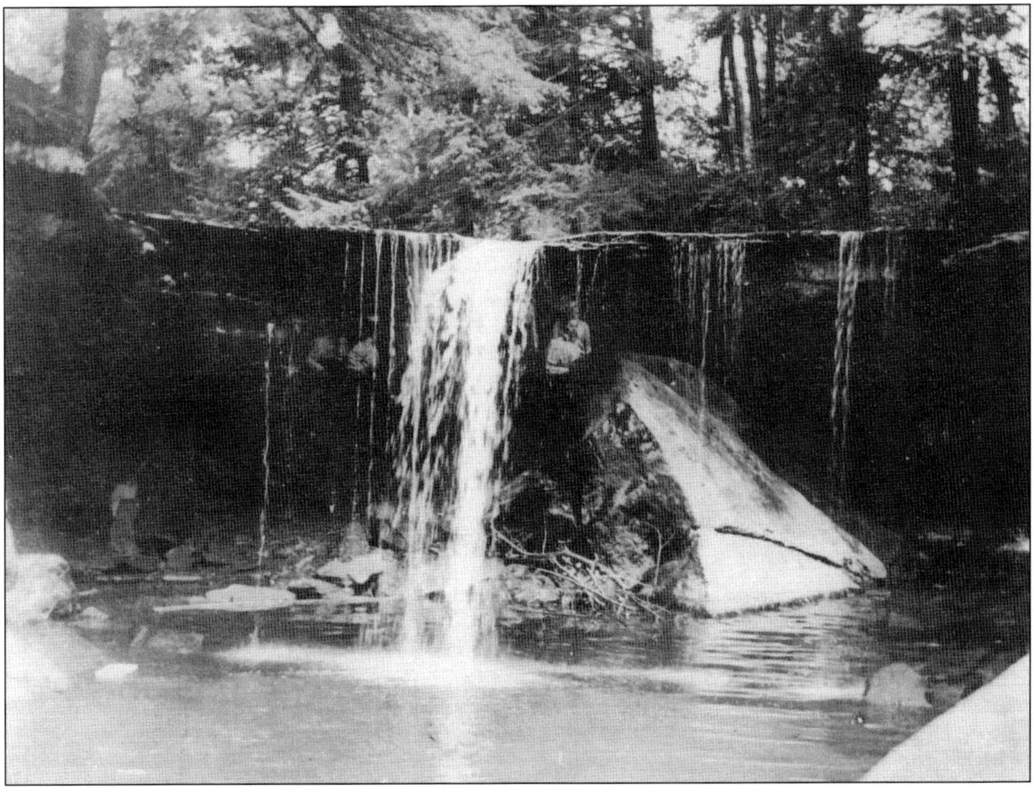

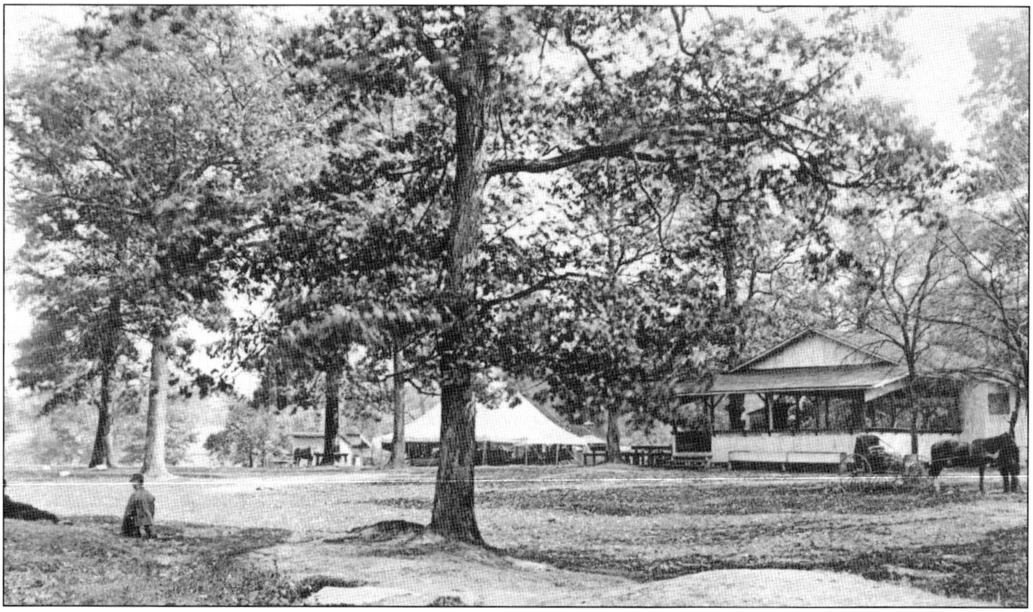

Merry-Go-Round at Old Oaks, c. 1894. The new park offered picnic grounds, fishing, swimming, and other recreation. Brinton installed a platform for dancing and a steam-driven merry-go-round with a canvas top. Then, to bring more people to the park, he began to build a trolley line. Lacking a charter, he was forced to shut it down before it was completed. (Courtesy of the New Castle Public Library.)

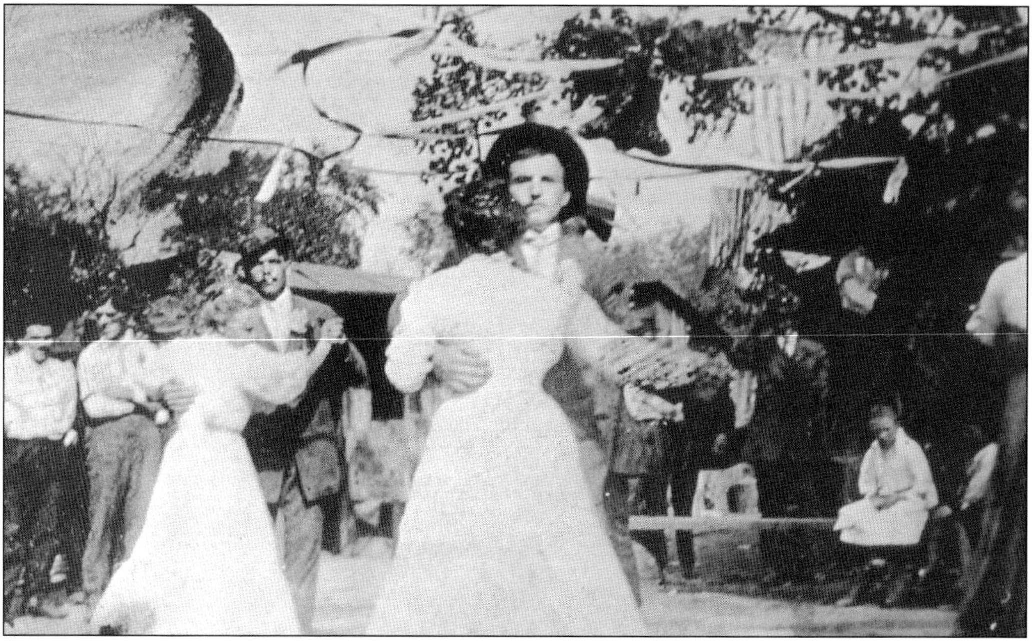

Outdoor Dancing at Brinton Park, c. 1895. It has been said that nature did most of the work for the park at Big Run Falls. For dancing, Levi Brinton improved on nature, installing an outdoor dance platform in the area later known as the midway. There was plenty of space to park horses and buggies, and dancers and musicians had their choice of shade trees when the music stopped.

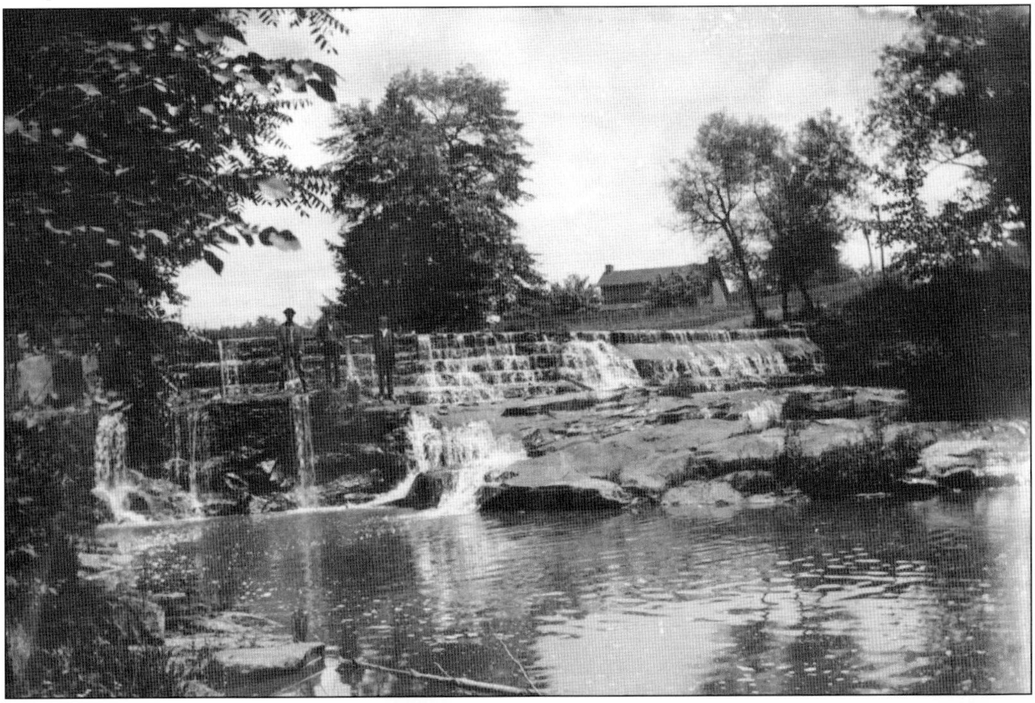

DAM ON BIG RUN, C. 1890S. Before Colonel Brinton acquired Big Run Falls, a gristmill and a sawmill operated on Big Run for farmers living in surrounding areas. The dam shown here was constructed so that the water of Big Run could be used to power the mills. The irregularity of the rocks around the dam created the picturesque cascades.

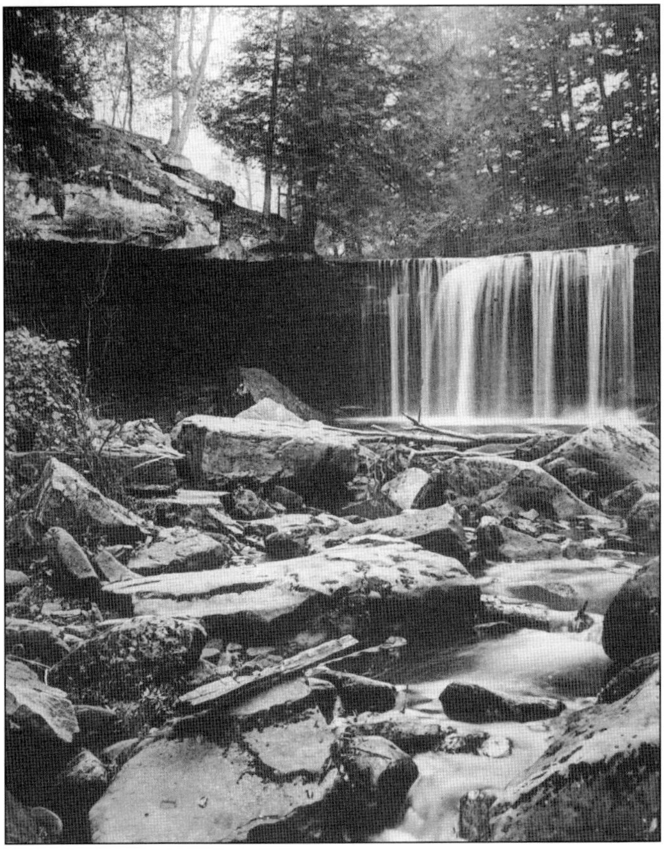

BIG RUN FALLS, C. 1894. The sound of falling water, the movement of the air around the falls, and the view from the ledge above drew people to the falls. The scene changed from day to day as the speed and volume of the drop changed with the weather. (Courtesy of the New Castle Public Library.)

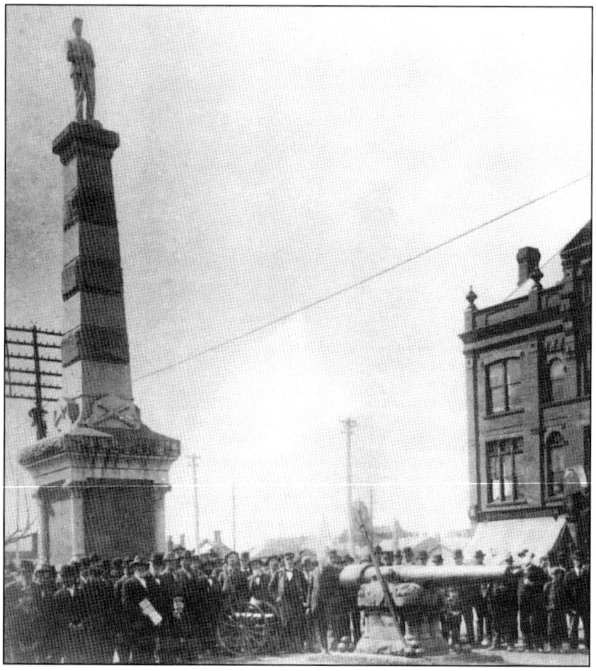

Dedication of Soldier's Monument, 1897. In 1891, New Castle's Ladies' Park Association decided to raise funds for a monument honoring Civil War soldiers. The monument would stand on the Diamond, New Castle's central square. To help raise funds for the project, Levi Brinton set up his canvas-topped, steam-driven merry-go-round in downtown New Castle. The marble soldier was placed at the top of the monument in December 1897, and it still stands there.

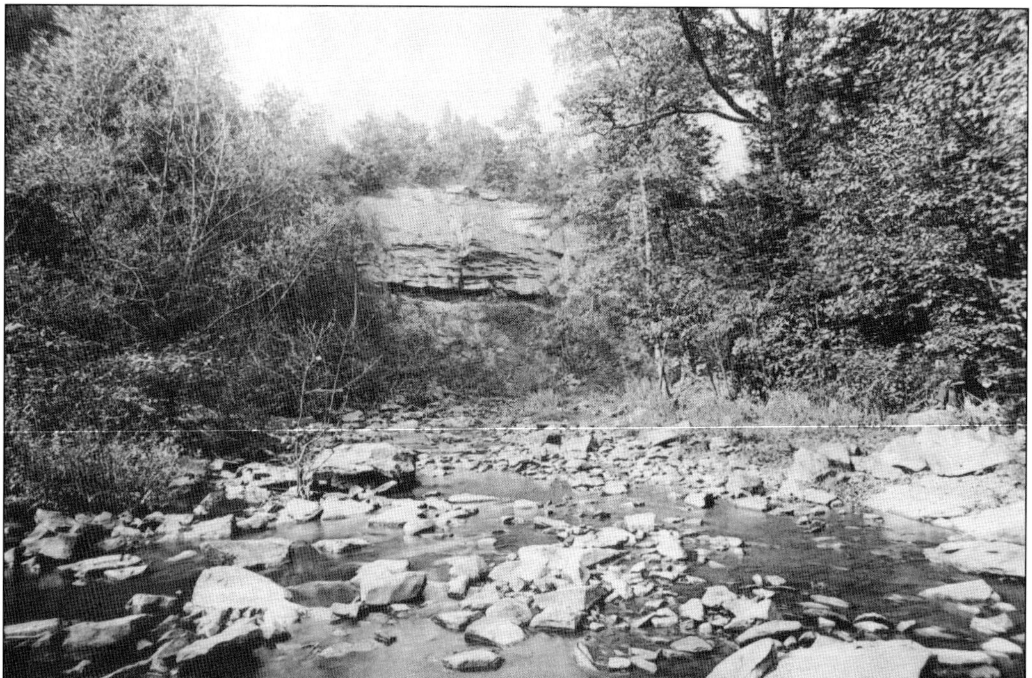

Cat Rocks at Big Run, 1894. In 1894, the Cat Rocks looked down on a 200-man contingent of Coxey's Army, the Randall Division, from Chicago. The men passed through New Castle as they headed for Washington, D.C., to protest widespread unemployment. Levi Brinton met the marchers at the western edge of New Castle and accompanied them to Brinton Park, where they stayed before resuming their march. (Courtesy of the New Castle Public Library.)

Two

Cascade Park

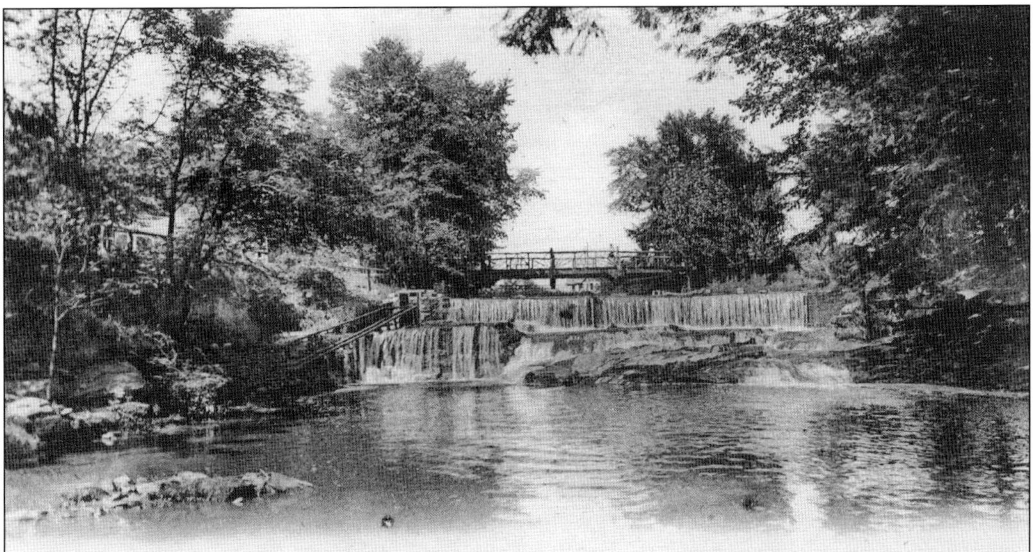

Cascades on Big Run, c. 1905. In 1897, cascades inspired 10-year-old Edwina Norris to enter "Cascade Park" in a Name-the-Park Contest. She won $10 for the winning name. This postcard shows some of the cascades at the dam that used to be above Big Run Falls. The new carousel can be seen on the left, through the trees.

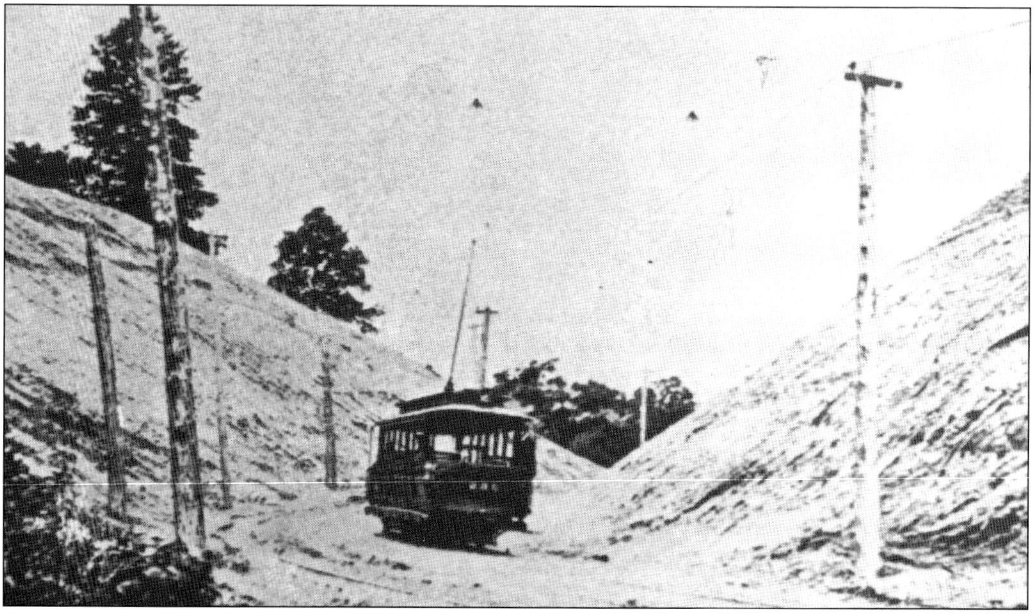

Streetcar on New Cascade Park Line, c. 1897. In March 1897, the *New Castle News* announced that the New Castle Traction Company had bought Brinton Park's 70 acres for $46,000. The company planned to build a streetcar line from Long Avenue, along Hamilton Street, to the park. They engaged the services of Frank Blaisdell, a landscape architect from Boston, to lay out the park.

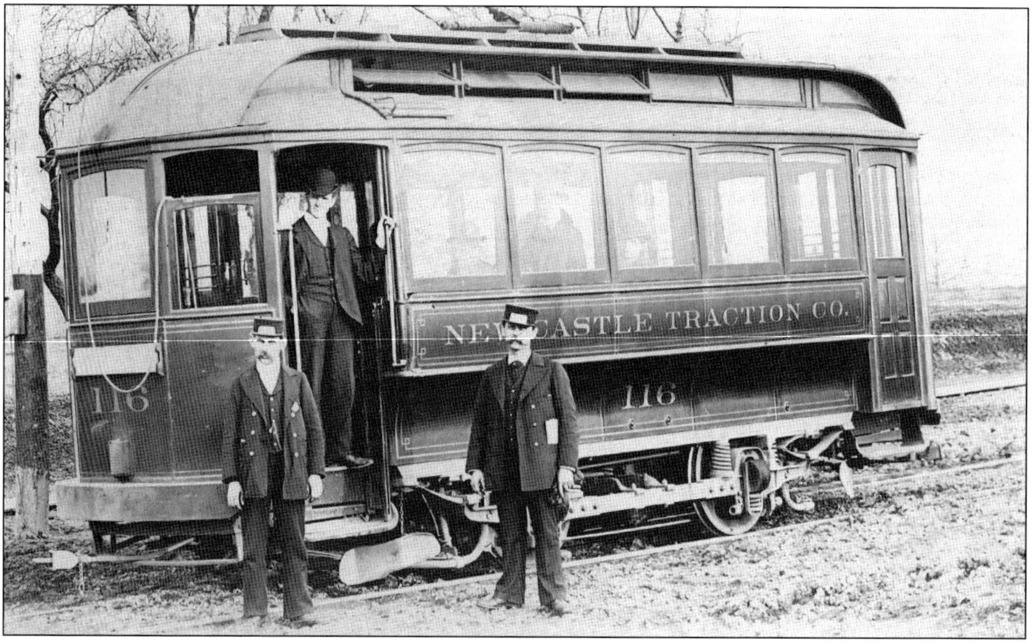

Streetcar and Conductors, Late 1890s. With the purchase of Brinton Park, the New Castle Traction Company joined other cities that were building trolley parks to bring in revenue. Nearby, Idora Park in Youngstown and Kennywood Park in Pittsburgh would also soon open. The traction company bought 15 new trolley cars to accommodate the crowds that were expected. Within a short time, five more cars were added.

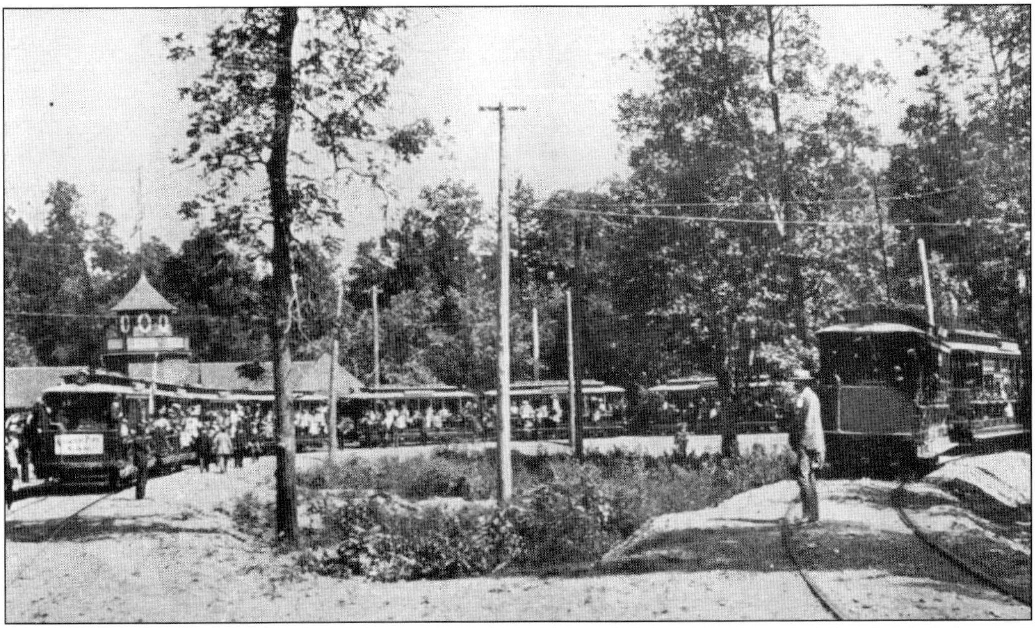

Crowds in Open-sided Streetcars, Late 1890s. More than 1,000 people attended the new park's opening day on May 29, 1897. At 3:00 p.m., the first official car to travel to the park carried the Citizens Band. The next car carried members of the press and traction company officials. The claim was that trolleys could leave a station every 30 seconds filled to capacity with 60 passengers, 7,200 visitors an hour.

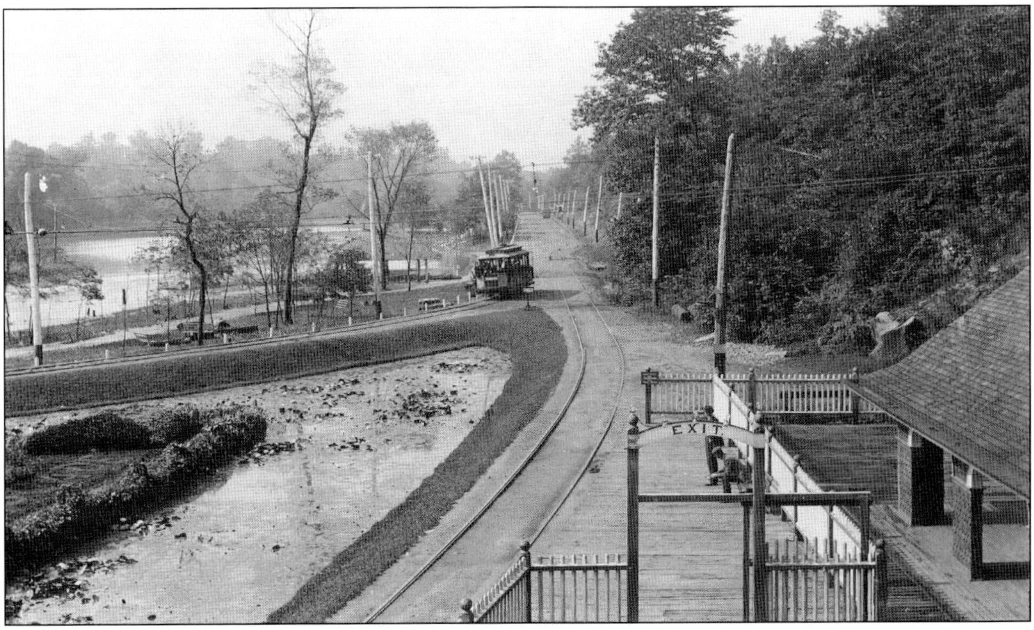

Hamilton Street Approach and Terminal, Late 1890s. The owners of the new park spared no expense in carrying out their plans. In this photograph, a trolley is arriving on the newly-completed Hamilton Street line, which, because of landslides during excavation, had cost two lives. Arriving streetcars circled the lagoon and deposited passengers at the new terminal. The picnic grove was a short walk from the terminal.

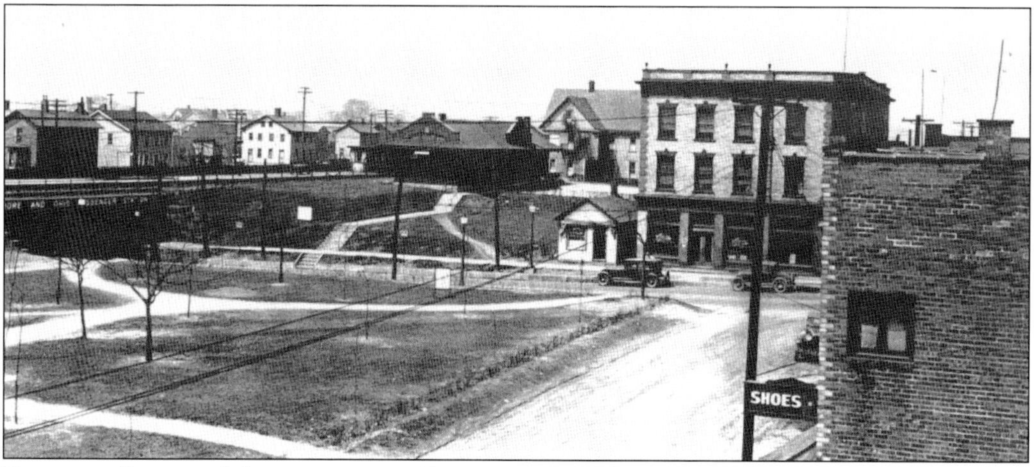

RAILROAD STATION, MAHONINGTOWN, EARLY 1900S. What was good for the traction company was good for the railroads. In Mahoningtown, Cascade Park passengers from the Pittsburgh and Lake Erie Railroad (P&LE) and Baltimore and Ohio Railroad (B&O) Stations (center) boarded streetcars, rode to Long Avenue, and transferred to the Hamilton Street line at Long Avenue. In Mahoningtown, three hotels were convenient to the station, the Arlington (behind), the St. Charles (center right), and the Wayside Inn (left, just outside the picture).

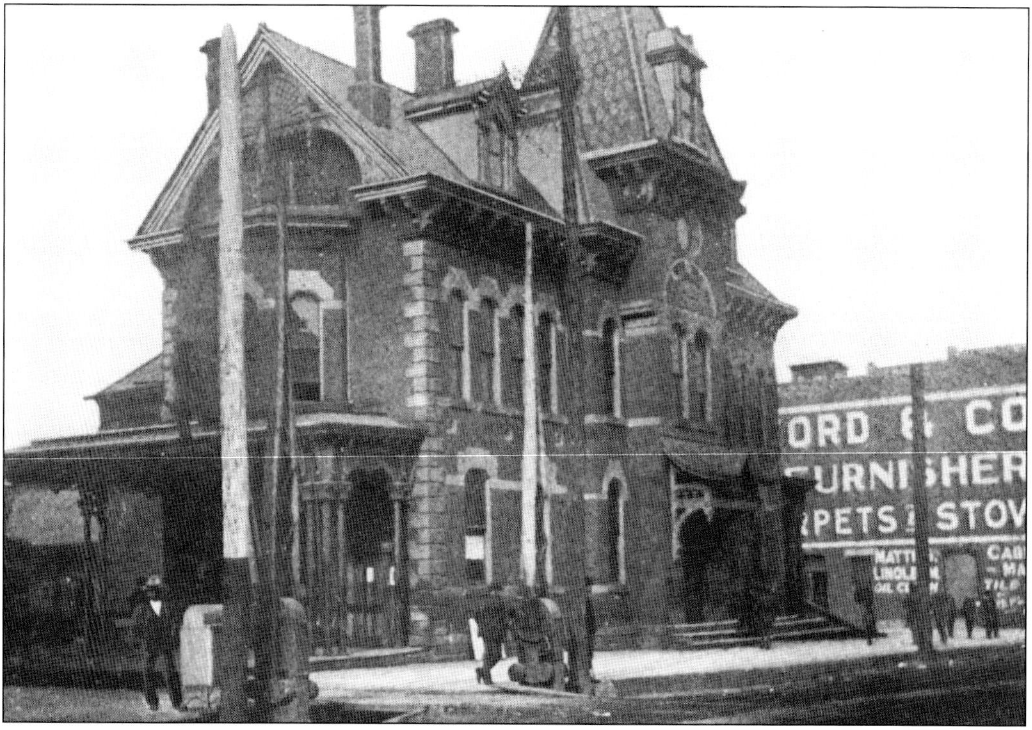

UNION STATION, PITTSBURG (EAST WASHINGTON) STREET, EARLY 1900S. More than 100 passenger trains went through New Castle every day. Many stopped at Union Station on Pittsburg Street (now East Washington where Clark's Studio is located) because it was convenient to the trolley line. Streetcars headed to Cascade Park lined up from South Croton Avenue to Mill and Washington Streets and filled quickly. They would proceed to Long Avenue, then take Hamilton Street to the park.

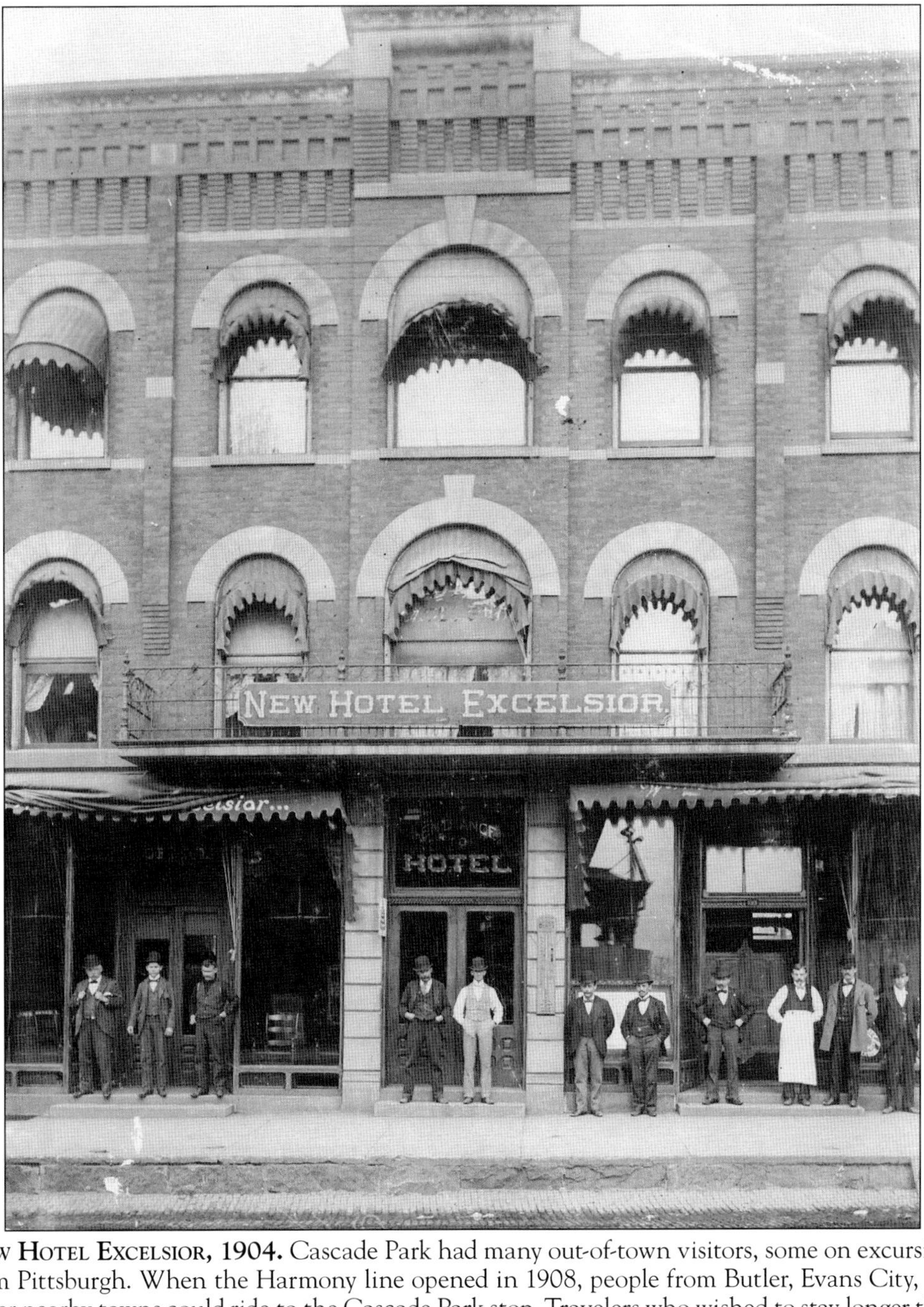

New Hotel Excelsior, 1904. Cascade Park had many out-of-town visitors, some on excursions from Pittsburgh. When the Harmony line opened in 1908, people from Butler, Evans City, and other nearby towns could ride to the Cascade Park stop. Travelers who wished to stay longer than a day could book a room at any number of hotels. This one was conveniently located at 37–39 Pittsburg Street, directly across from Union Station. The hotel was owned by Wilhelm Schmid, a prominent and well-respected businessman who was successful in the glass- and potmaking trades before entering the hotel industry. His first hotel, the Excelsior, was a house on the same site as the hotel pictured here. When New Castle's expanding commerce required more housing for travelers, he built the 50-room New Hotel Excelsior on the same site. In the photograph, the man in the apron is probably the bartender. (Courtesy of Caroline Winter.)

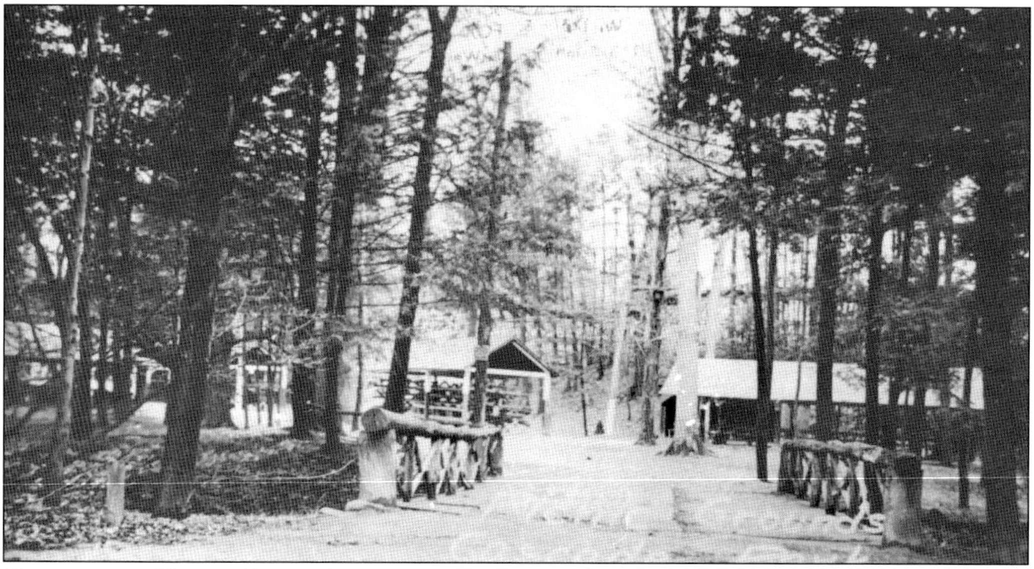

ENTRANCE TO PICNIC GROVE, EARLY 1900S. A typical rustic bridge leads the way to the picnic grove. Depending on which advertisement was being read, the grove could accommodate 2,000 or 5,000 picnickers. The rustic bridge is a good example of "twig architecture," popular at the time. Constructed for solidity, the bridge's unpeeled logs and entwined branches were harmonious with the natural setting.

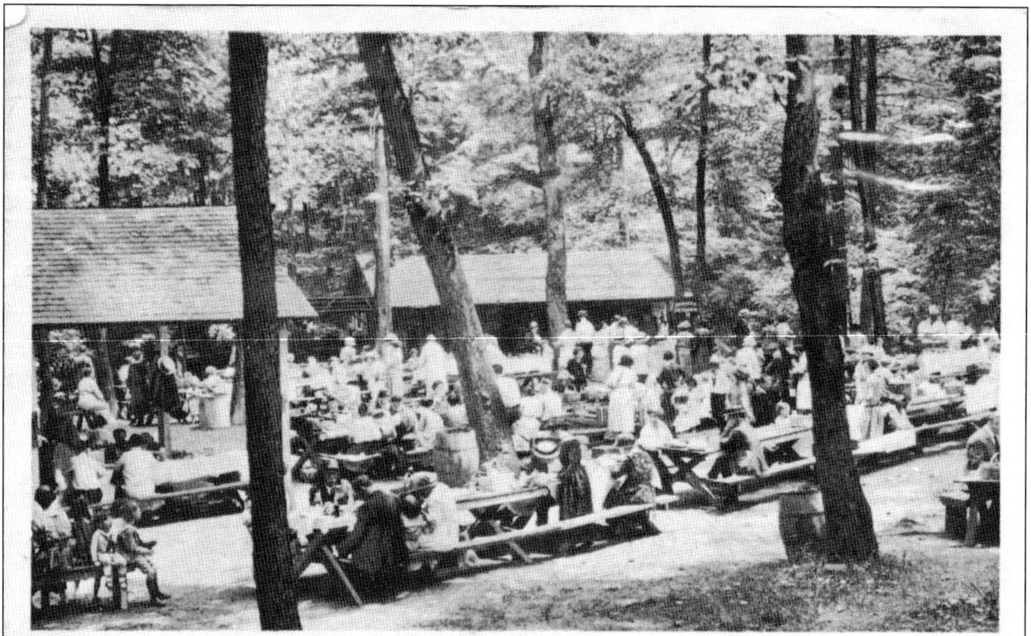

DINING GROVE, CASCADE PARK, NEW CASTLE, PA.

DINING GROVE, EARLY 1920S. Families and organizations toted bushel baskets of food from the streetcars to the grove, where they could have a picnic under shelters or in the open among the trees. Tables and trash receptacles were provided, and cooking facilities were available. The grove was a favorite for family reunions, employee picnics, and club gatherings.

VIEW FROM CAT ROCKS, EARLY 1900S. This view from the Cat Rocks shows the new 15-acre lake built by the New Castle Traction Company for water recreation. Many have speculated about the origin of the name "Cat Rocks" (sometimes called "Cat Rock"). One story told by journalist Bart Richards in his later years was that "wild cats and bobcats had been inhabiting there—and perhaps they were." (Courtesy of Pat Patterson.)

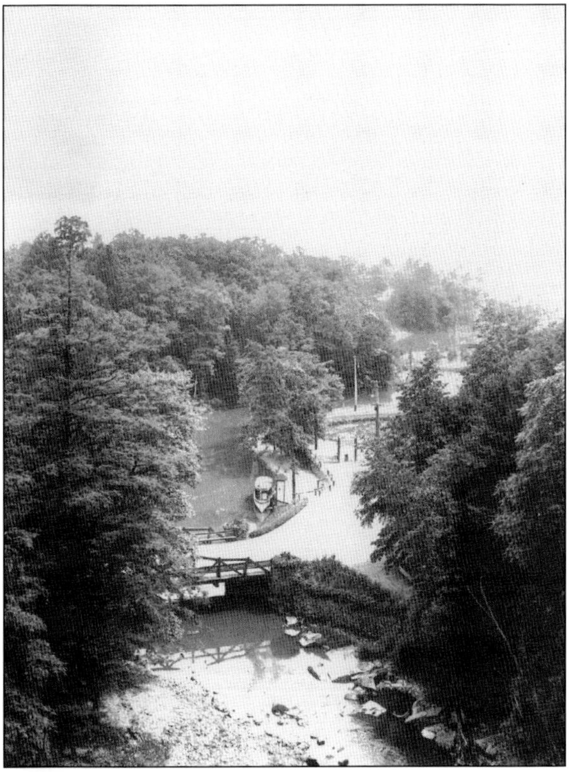

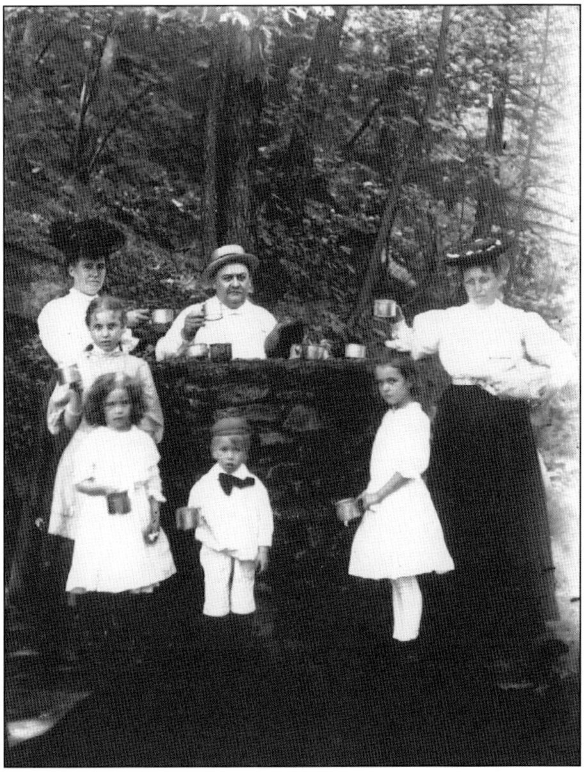

FAMILY AT A NATURAL SPRING, C. 1899. Nine natural springs scattered throughout the park provided clear, cold water. Tin cups dangled around the springs for the convenience of visitors. In 1914, a state law abolished public drinking cups. From then on, park visitors would have to carry their own cups or drop a penny into a slot to get a paper cup from machines near the springs.

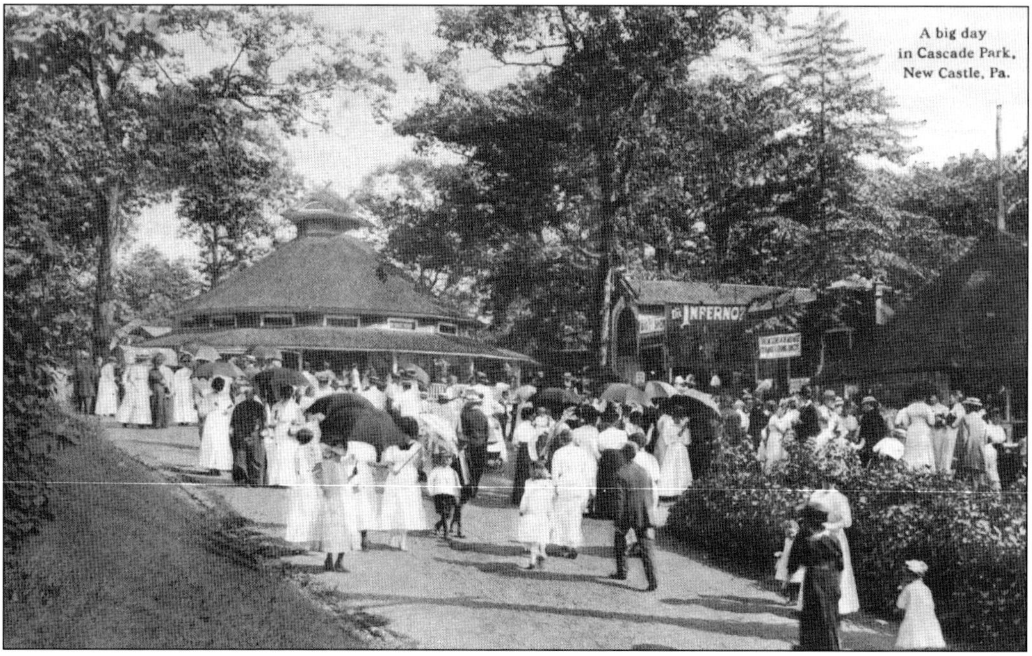

HEADING UPHILL ON THE MAIN WALK, C. 1914. This postcard shows a crowd walking uphill from the grove on what was called "the main walk." Along the uphill path were a tintype gallery, an outdoor theater, a bandstand, a souvenir stand, mineral springs, flowers, and greenery. The main walk led to the midway, where the carousel and other rides were located.

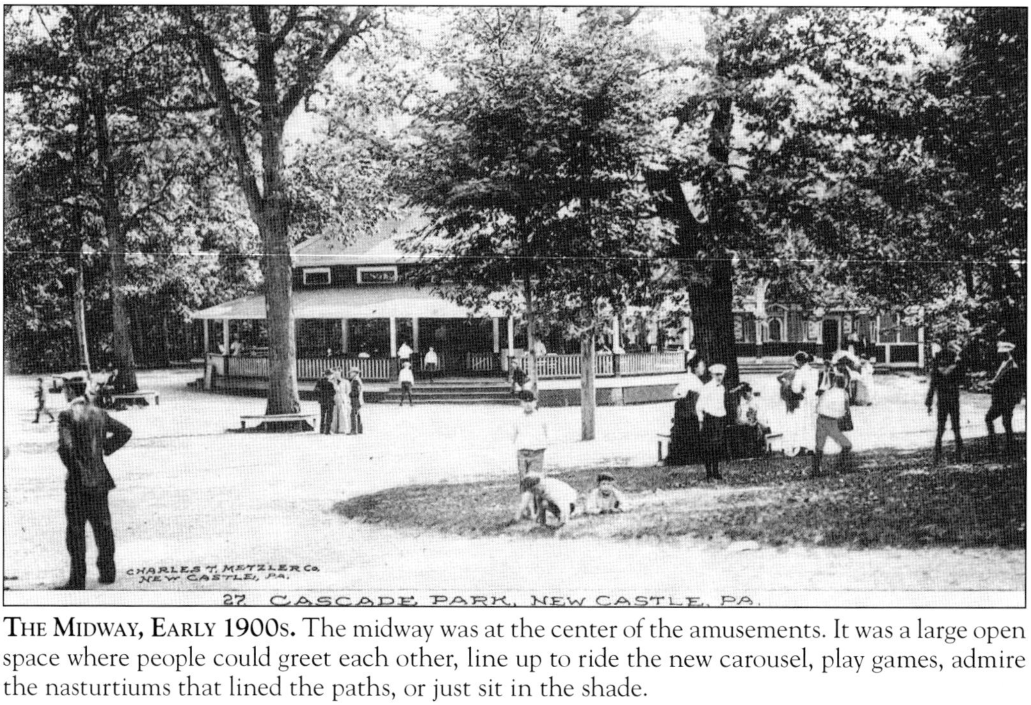

THE MIDWAY, EARLY 1900S. The midway was at the center of the amusements. It was a large open space where people could greet each other, line up to ride the new carousel, play games, admire the nasturtiums that lined the paths, or just sit in the shade.

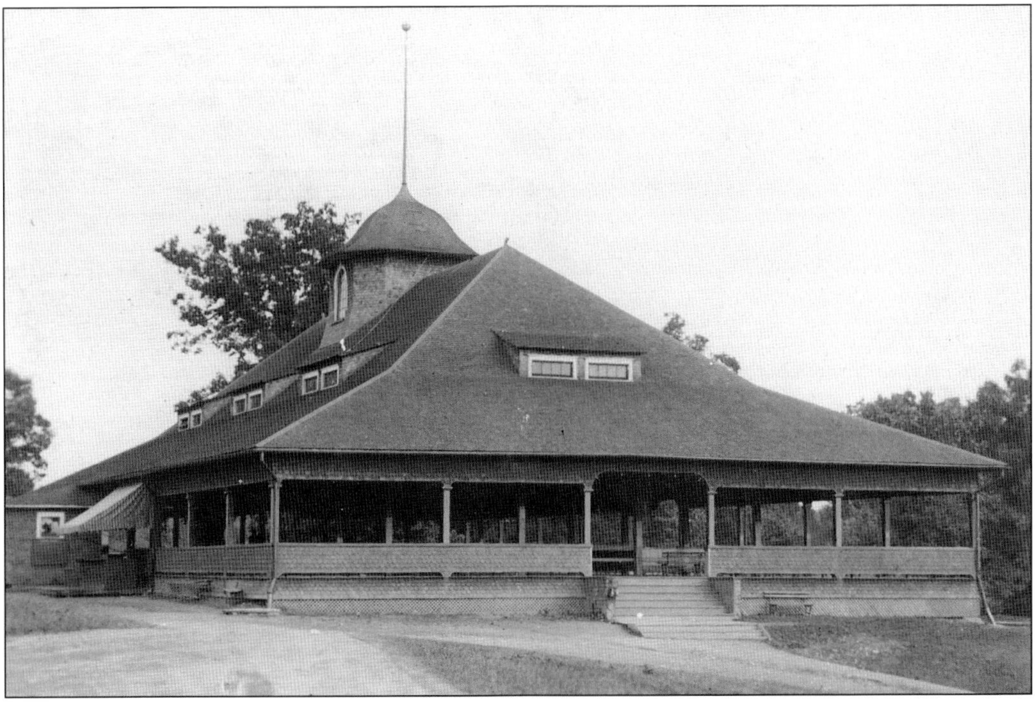

THE DANCE PAVILION, c. 1898. The open-sided dance pavilion crowned the entire park, rising on a slight slope above the midway. Dancers walking up the main walk could climb the flower-lined steps to the pavilion or approach from the midway or stop in from the roller coaster, which was behind the pavilion.

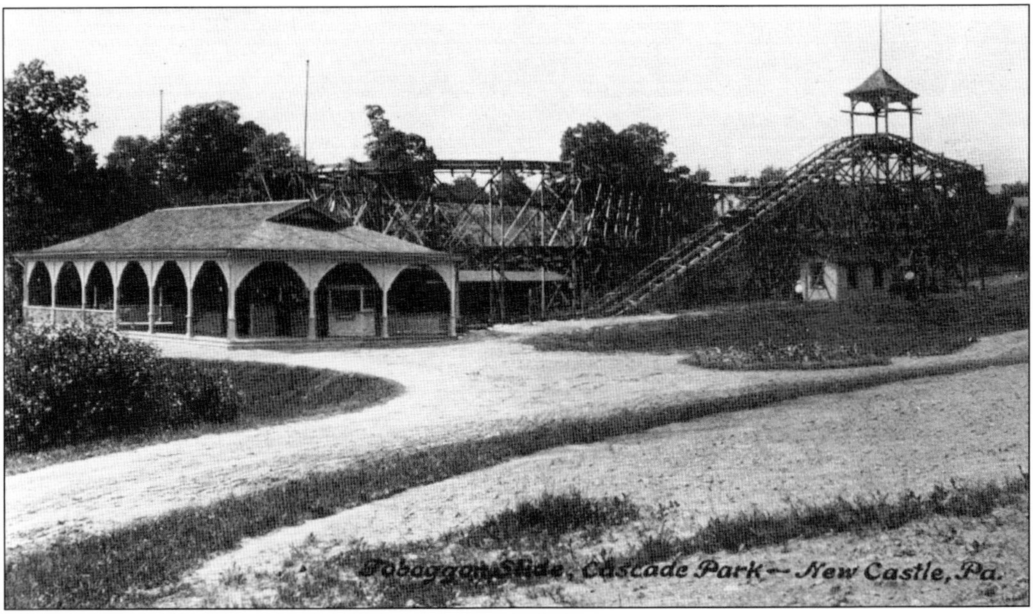

TOBOGGAN ROLLER COASTER, 1900. Cascade Park has had three roller coasters. This one, the first, was located behind the dance pavilion on the site of the present-day parking lot. Built for the trolley company by Fred Ingersoll, this coaster used the side-friction track system like most early roller coasters. It was 70 feet high and 225 feet long.

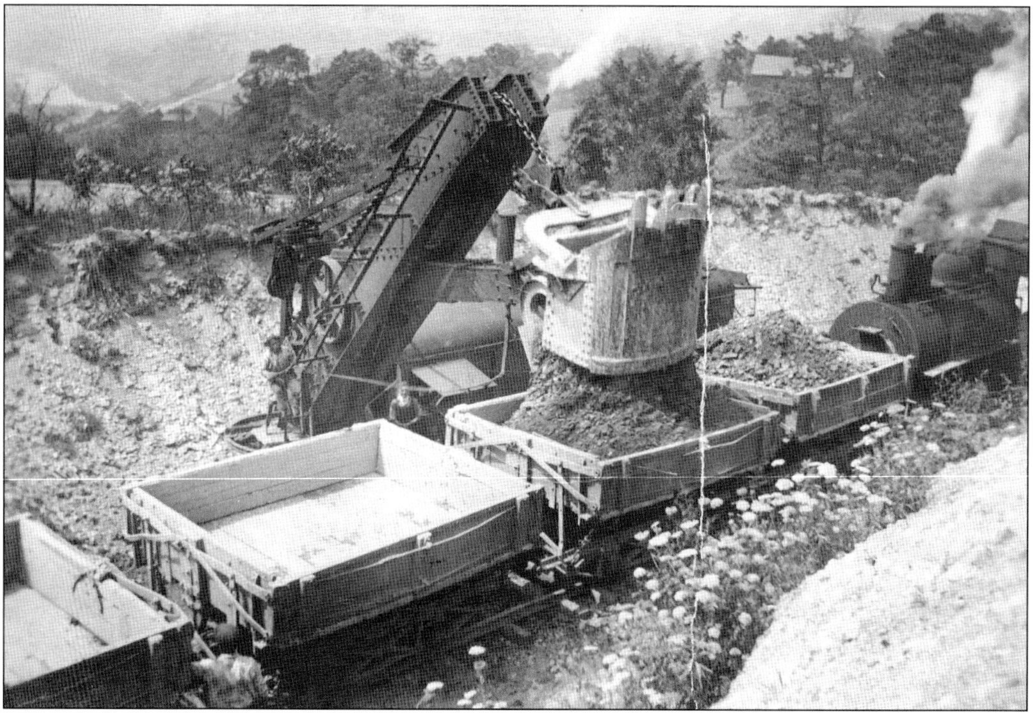

EXCAVATING FOR THE LAKE, 1898. Cascade Park's landscape architect included a 15-acre lake in his plan for the new amusement park. Located between the trolley terminal and the ball field, the lake was 14 feet deep. A wall measuring 400 feet long, 16 feet high, and 5 feet wide was built to retain Big Run's water.

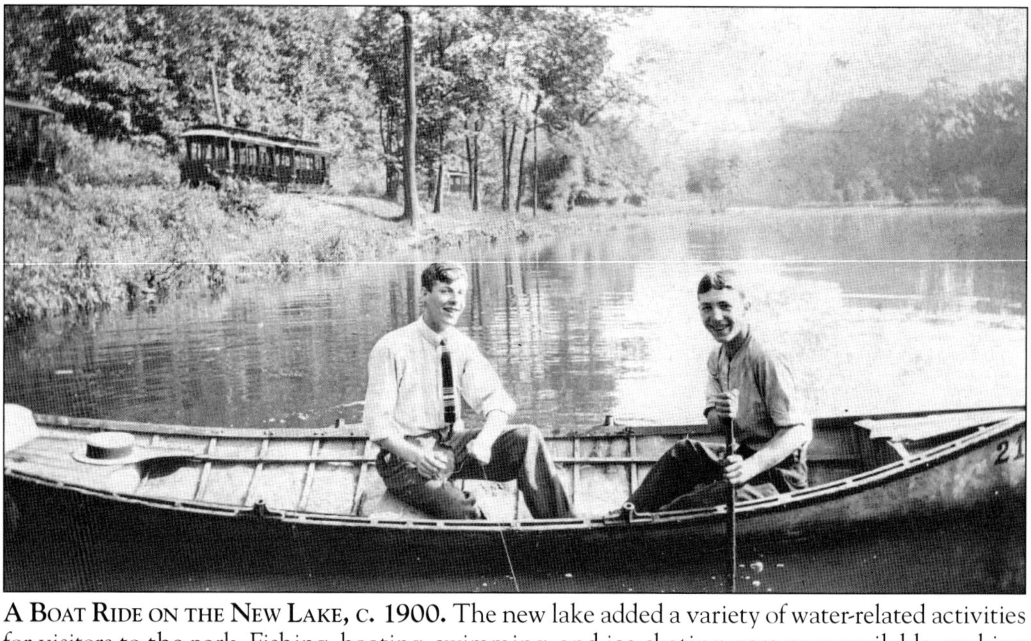

A BOAT RIDE ON THE NEW LAKE, C. 1900. The new lake added a variety of water-related activities for visitors to the park. Fishing, boating, swimming, and ice-skating were now available, making a day at the park more tempting, even in winter. These two young men are clearly enjoying themselves. (Courtesy of Jonathan Matis.)

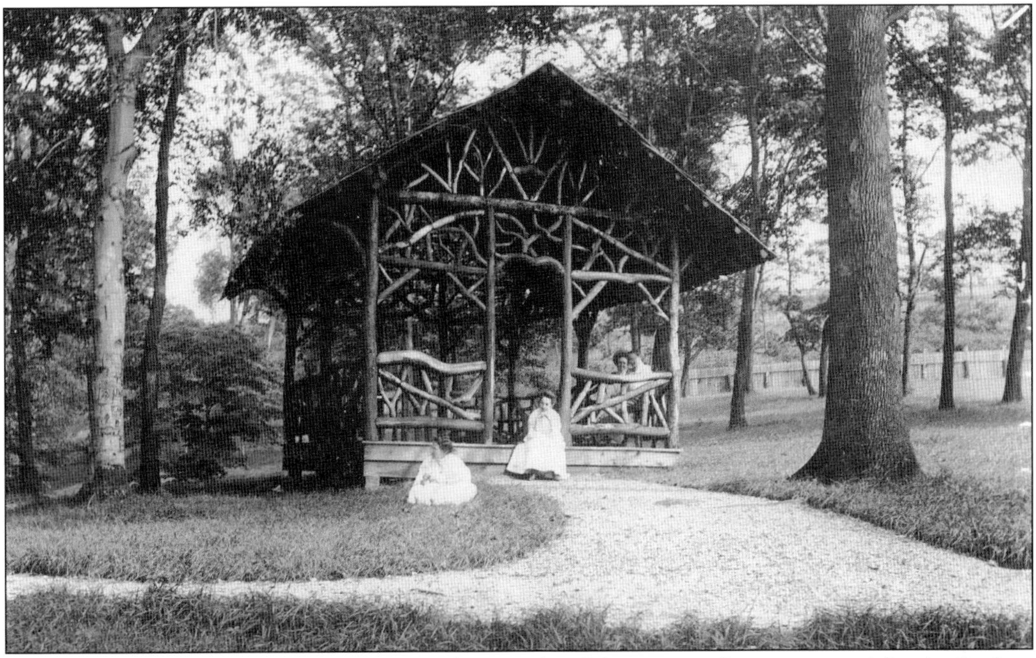

A Rustic House, c. 1900. This is a good example of the twig architecture used for the bridges and several open-air houses located throughout Cascade Park. This one is substantially built. Note the fence in the background of the photograph. The New Castle Traction Company fenced in the entire park.

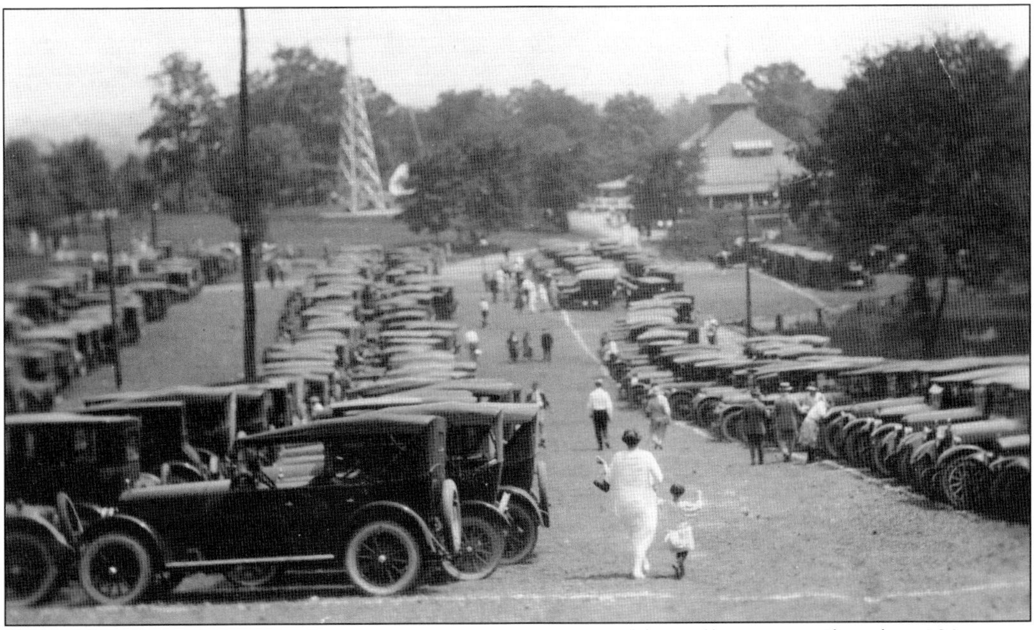

Parking Grounds, c. 1930s. By 1920, Henry Ford had sold a million cars. Thus, by 1930, many citizens no longer relied on streetcars and railroads for transportation. Cars had become affordable and comfortable. These changes brought about the need for parking grounds. In this photograph, the dance pavilion is in the distance, and the roller coaster has made way for cars, the new way to get to Cascade Park.

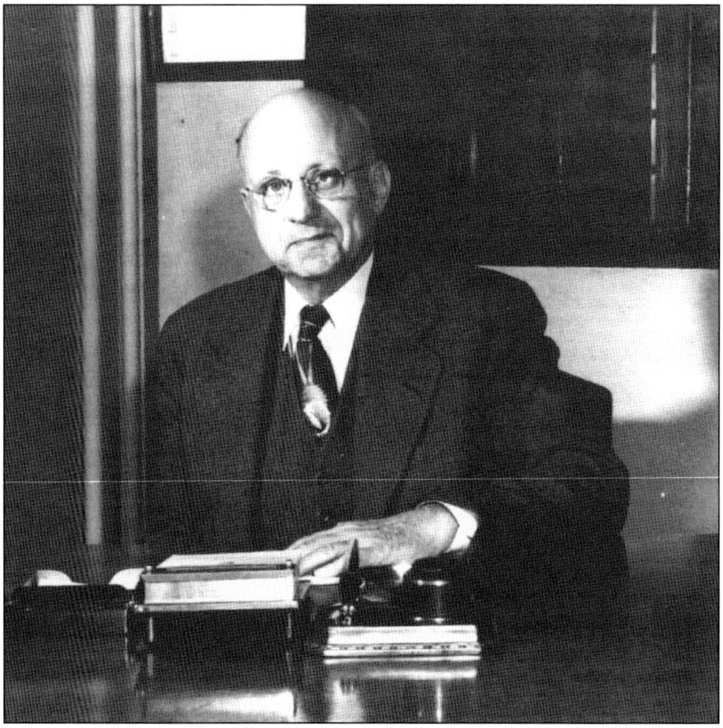

Louis B. Round, Penn Power Company. In 1931, the New Castle Traction Company and electric companies surrounding New Castle merged to form the Pennsylvania Power Company. Louis B. Round, vice president and general manager, ran the company in New Castle. At that time, between the Depression and the automobile, Cascade Park had become unprofitable. Round proposed that the City of New Castle take ownership of the park. (Courtesy of the Western Pennsylvania Conservancy.)

Deed ✓

Pennsylvania Power Company

To

City of New Castle

Ent. May 15, 1934.

THIS INDENTURE

MADE this 31st day of March, 1934, between PENNSYLVANIA POWER COMPANY, a corporation existing under the laws of the Commonwealth of Pennsylvania, grantor, and the CITY OF NEW CASTLE, LAWRENCE COUNTY, PENNSYLVANIA, a municipal corporation, grantee, witnesseth:

THAT WHEREAS, the Pennsylvania Power Company is and has been the owner of a certain tract of land situate in Shenango Township, Lawrence County, Pennsylvania, adjacent to the City of New Castle, and known as Cascade Park, which tract of land the City of New Castle is desirous of securing to add to the public park system of said city, and

WHEREAS, the grantor is willing to convey said lands and the appurtenances unto the City of New Castle, provided the same are accepted and actually used by said city for recreational purposes only, and the parties have agreed upon certain necessary restrictions for the use of said property.

NOW, THEREFORE, in consideration of the premises and in further consideration of the sum of One ($1.00) Dollar, lawful money of the United States, to it in hand paid by the said grantee at and before the execution and delivery hereof, the receipt whereof is hereby acknowledged, the said grantor does hereby grant and convey unto the City of New Castle, for the sole purpose of providing healthful recreation for the citizens of New Castle in particular and the public in general, as a part of the public park system of the City of New Castle, and for so long a time as it is used for said purposes and no longer, all that certain piece, parcel or lot of land situate, lying and being in the Township of Shenango, County of Lawrence, State of Pennsylvania, bounded and described as follows, to-wit:

Beginning at a point in the center of the Pittsburgh Road, which point is also the common corner of land formerly of William Vogan and the lands herein described; thence along the south line of land formerly of William Vogan, being the South line of the City of New Castle, South 89 degrees 31 minutes West, Fourteen Hundred (1400) feet to a point on the boundary line between land of the City of New Castle, formerly Cunningham, and the lands herein described; thence along the East line of said lands of the City of New Castle South 0 degrees 45 minutes East, Twenty-six Hundred and Ten (2610) feet to a point; thence South 89 degrees 6 minutes East, One Hundred Ninety and Twenty-five Hundredths (190.25) feet, more or less; thence North 47 degrees 26 minutes East, Ninety-seven (97) feet by lands of the Carnegie Steel Company to a marked tree; thence by same North 67 degrees 51 minutes East, One Hundred Ninety (190) feet to a marked tree: thence by same

Deed Transferring the Park to the City, 1934. Cascade Park was transferred in perpetuity to the City of New Castle for $1. One of the stipulations of the transfer was that alcoholic beverages could not be sold at the park for 10 years. In 1934, Cascade Park officially became part of New Castle's public park system.

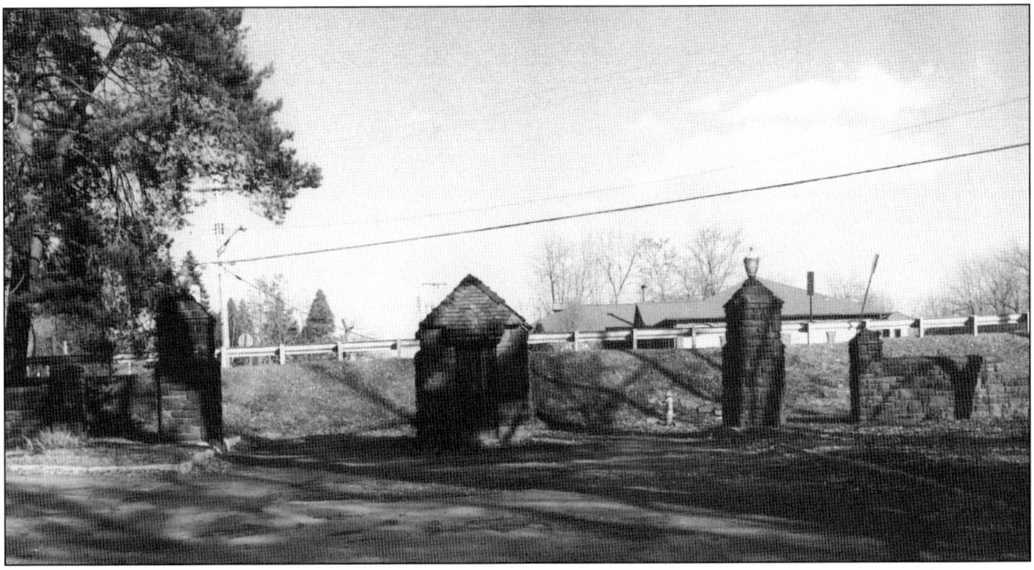

New Owner, New Entrance. Shortly after the city took ownership, it built a new formal entrance to the park on East Washington Street. The new entrance was to become the park's main entrance, replacing the lower entrance by the lake. The new entrance used beautiful stonework for its walls and gatehouse in a style characteristic of the 1930s. Cascade Park was now a destination for the trolley line on East Washington Street, and automobiles, more numerous now, could enter the park. From this new entry, visitors were enticed by an immediate view of the carousel, dance pavilion, and concessions. At first, the new entrance was level with the park grounds, but these 2009 photographs show changes. East Washington Street over the Stone Bridge was widened and raised in 1930 to allow for increased traffic. In the bottom photograph, the center of the pillar shows the dates of construction, 1933–1934. The inscription is still clear after 75 years. Tree lovers can find one of the park's few ginkgo trees nearby. (Both, courtesy of Adam Pivovar.)

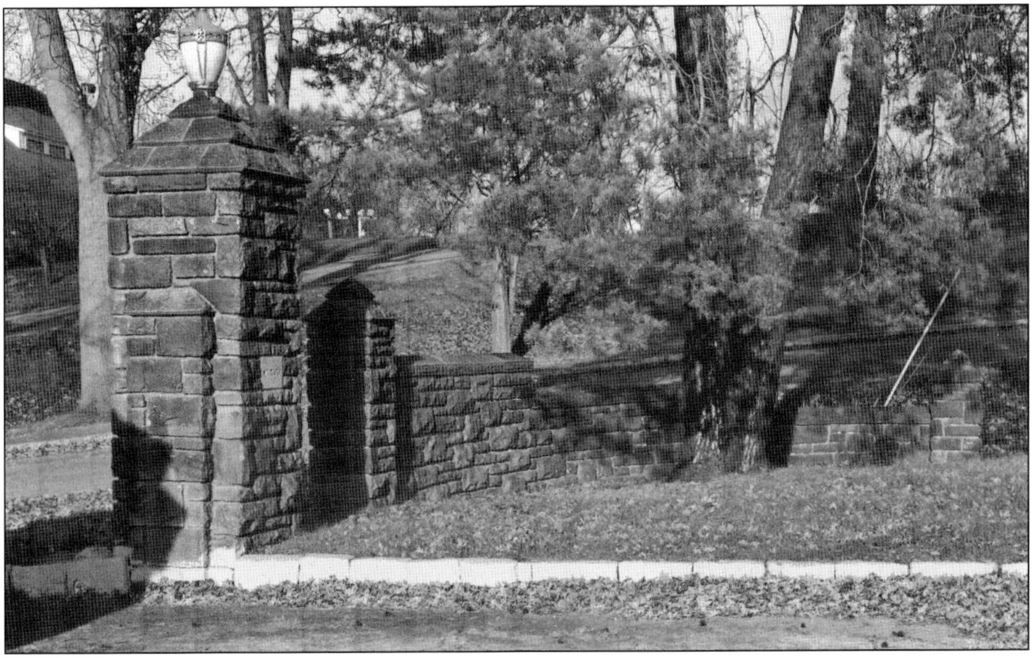

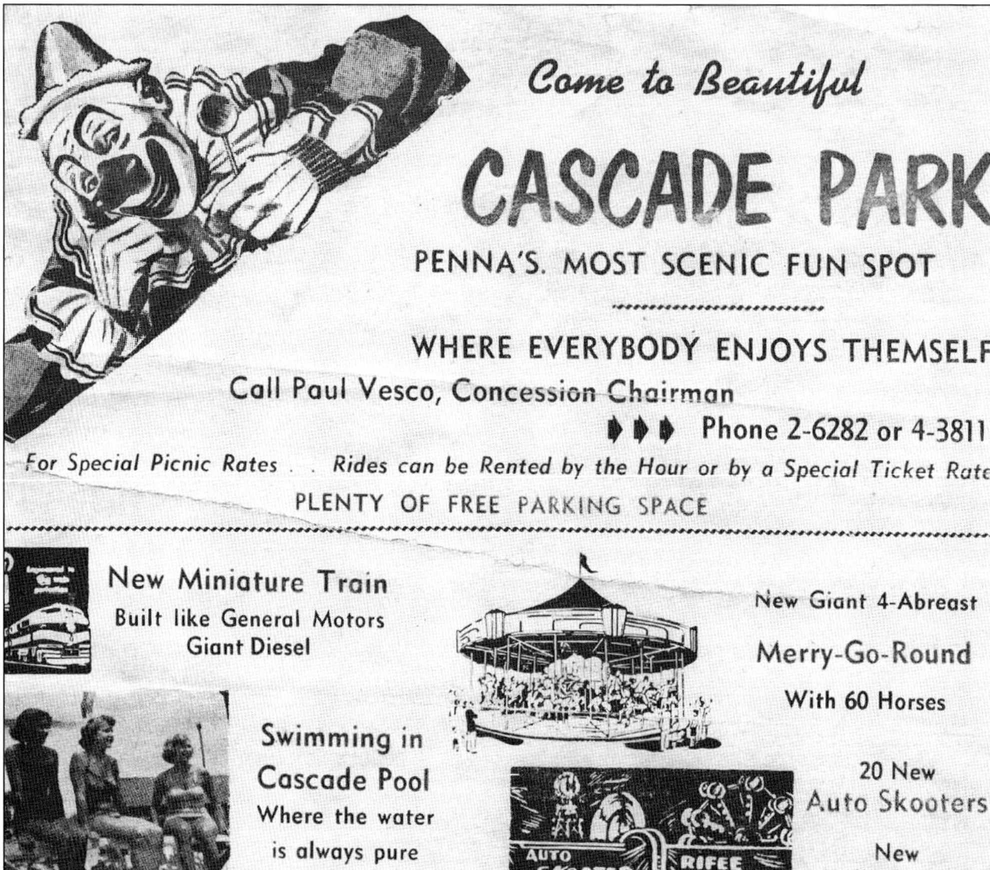

A New Era Begins. In 1952, Paul Vesco, a contractor who owned a music store, taught music, and performed, invested in some of the rides and concessions at the park. Over time, he expanded his holdings, constructing the Comet roller coaster and promoting the park's many amusements. The Vesco years came to an end in the 1980s; they are fondly remembered by employees and park visitors alike.

Three

Rides

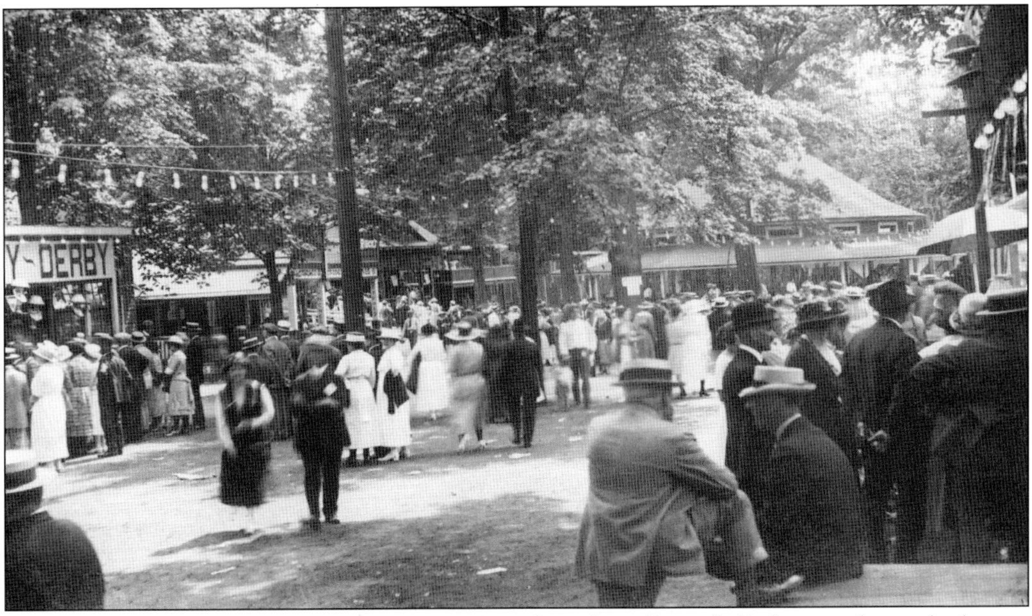

The Fourth of July on the Midway, c. 1920s. Crowds at Cascade Park were always the largest on the Fourth of July. Like a village square, the midway brought together the activities and the people. The carousel, the Dodg'em, the swings, and the refreshments were easily accessible, and other attractions were a short walk away.

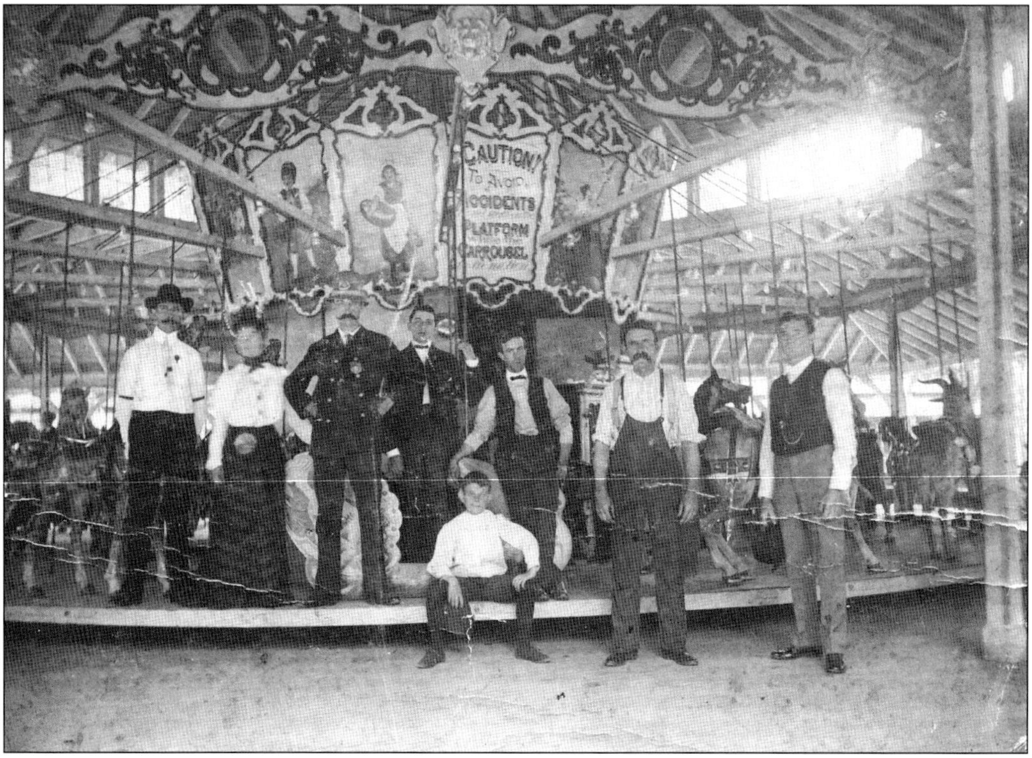

EARLY CAROUSEL, C. 1900. Cascade Park employees are part of the scenery on this colorful carousel. The first carousels in the United States were produced by Gustav Dentzel, a German woodcarver who went to Philadelphia to introduce to Americans the family carousel business. Dentzel trained a number of woodcarvers and essentially established the tradition of elaborately ornamented, well-crafted carousels.

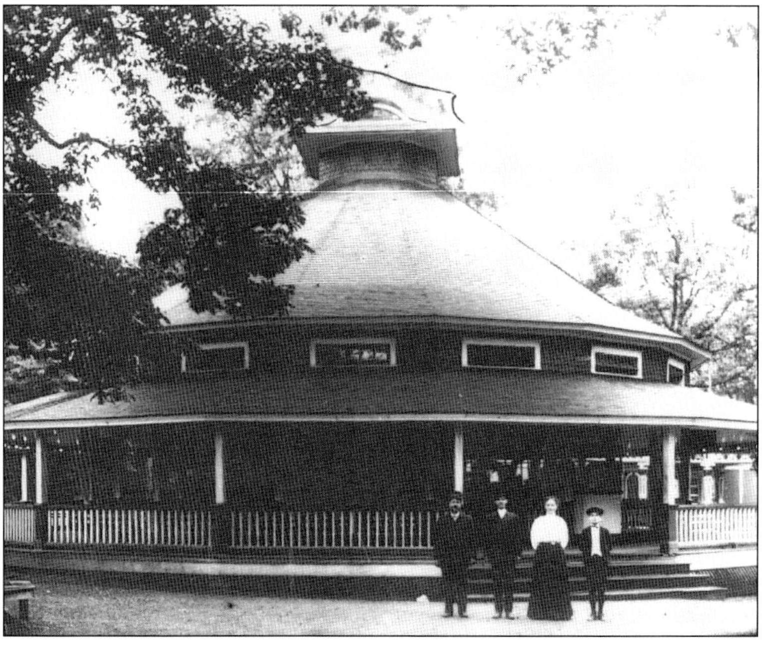

VICTORIAN-STYLE CAROUSEL BUILDING, C. 1900. According to a newspaper report at the time, Cascade Park's new merry-go-round "did service at the World's Fair." The report does not name the fair. The merry-go-round was 75 feet in diameter with everything attached to the center pole. In the early 1920s, substitutes for the carousel were proposed to take its place when it was dismantled, but they never materialized.

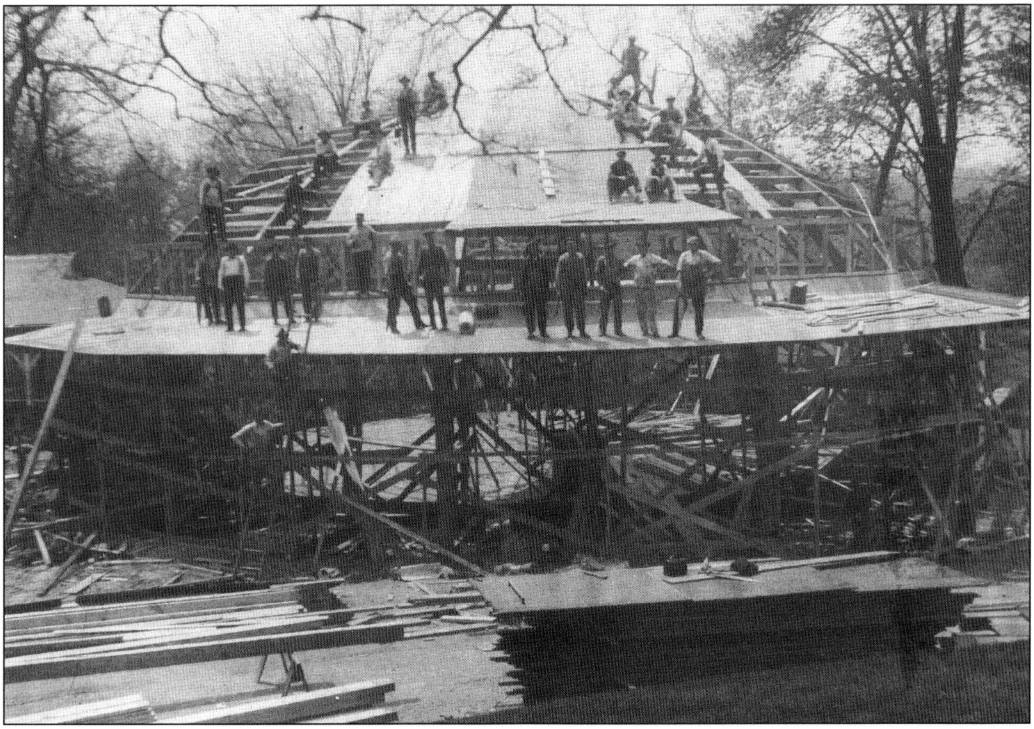

Building a Second Merry-Go-Round, 1921. The merry-go-round about to be installed here was one of the classic wooden constructions of the Philadelphia Toboggan Company, which made only 89 numbered carousels. The company had already built Idora Park's carousel, No. 61. Cascade Park's was No. 64R. The horses were both jumpers and standers, and the menagerie included a tiger, jackrabbit, and other carved animals.

The Third Carousel, c. 1970s. The carousel building remained, but the park's No. 64R was replaced in the 1950s by this carousel. Idora Park's No. 61 has survived, and it has a new home in Brooklyn Bridge Park in New York. In 1991, the Philadelphia Toboggan Company changed its name to Philadelphia Toboggan Coasters. It now makes and refurbishes roller coasters exclusively. (Courtesy of Jill Allerton.)

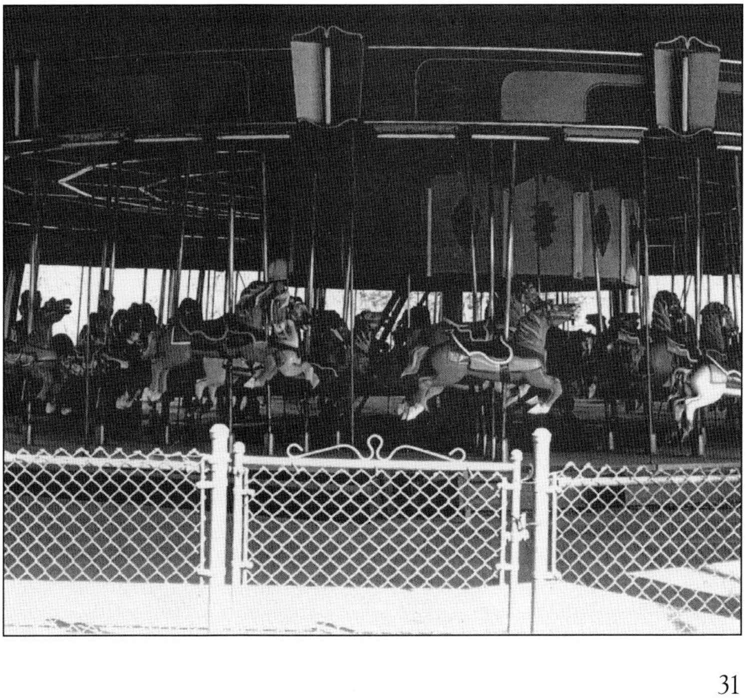

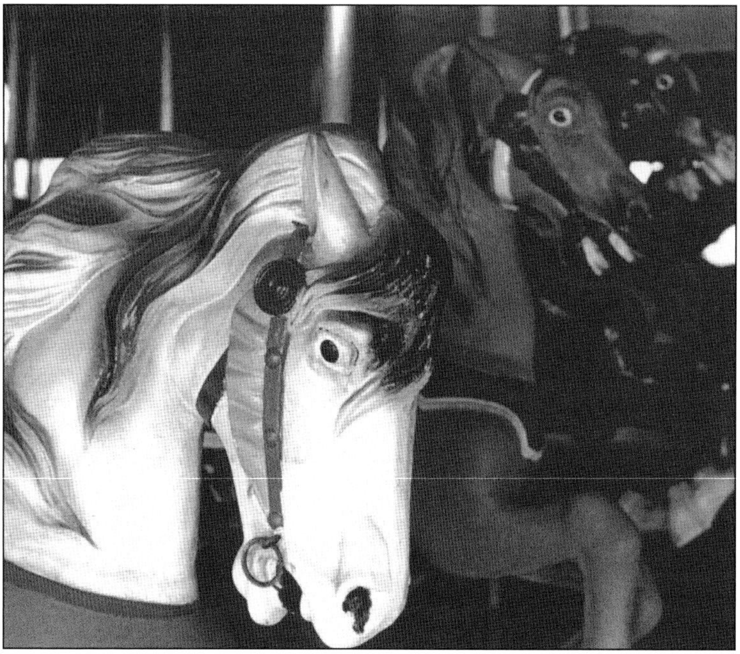

Close-up of Carousel Horses, c. 1970s. In this photograph, the horses seem to be running at full speed. With their bright lights, band-organ music, up-and-down steeds, and fantasy chariots, merry-go-rounds evoke gaiety and joy. Toy carousels, carousel music boxes, and even full-size carousel horses are widely collected, and perhaps for this reason, the Cascade Park horses disappeared sometime around the early 1980s. (Courtesy of Jill Allerton.)

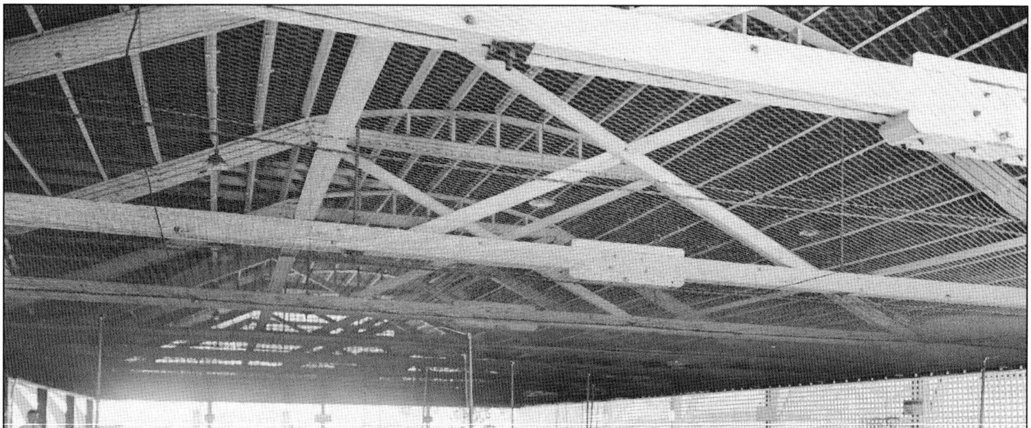

Bumper Cars, c. 1930s. The bumper car ride at Cascade Park was called the Dodg'em. Rods rising from the rear of the little cars made electrical contact between the metal floor and the metal ceiling. Pressing the car's accelerator pedal moved the car; releasing it stopped the car. This photograph of similar cars was taken at Glen Echo Park near Washington, D.C. (Courtesy of the Library of Congress.)

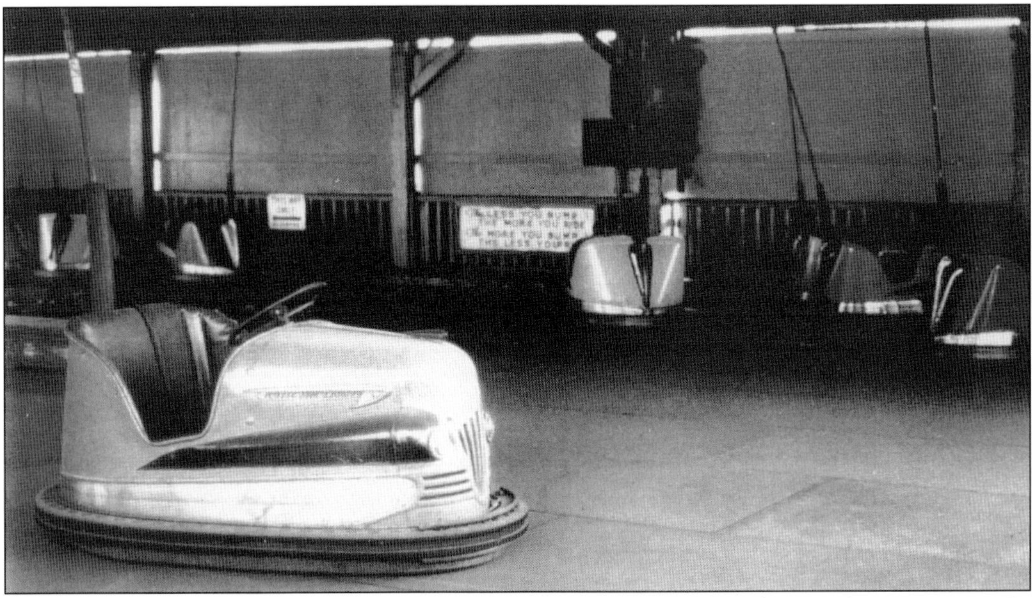

Dodg'em at Cascade Park, c. 1970s. The sign reads, "The less you bump, the more you ride, the more you bump the less you ride." In the 1930s, drivers could choose to bump a life-sized figure of comedian Charlie Chaplin who, at that time, was at the height of his popularity. This is the ride Paul Vesco bought in 1952, sight unseen, for $500. It was the first of the many amusements he later installed.

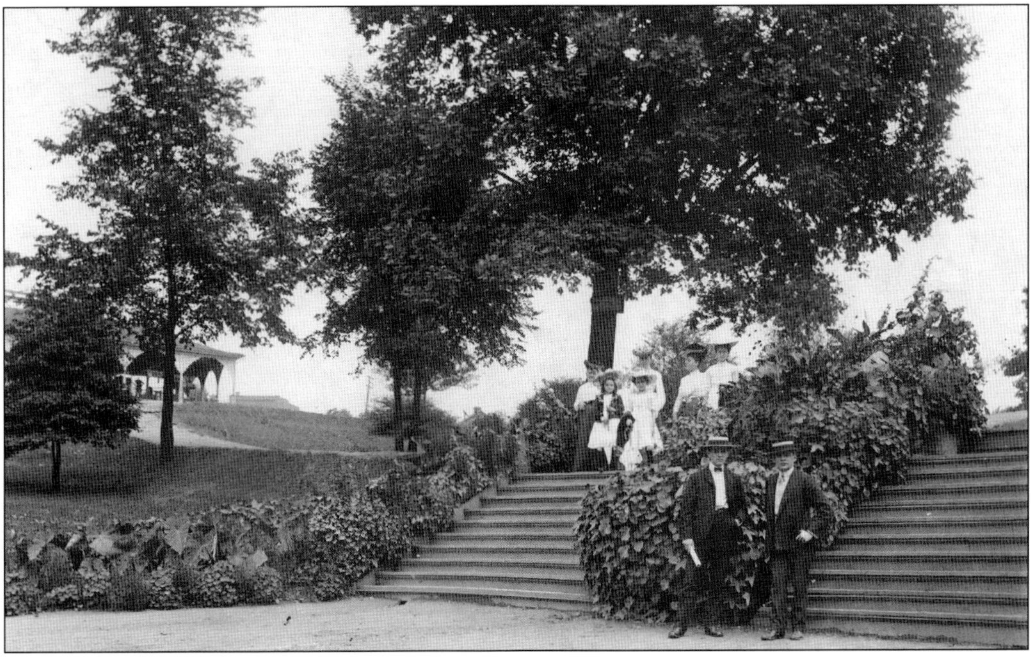

Floral Steps to the Roller Coaster, c. 1899. Climbing the floral steps was the easiest approach to Cascade Park's roller coaster. The first American roller coaster was actually a series of working coal cars on an inclined railroad track in Mauch Chunk (now Jim Thorpe), Pennsylvania. Starting in 1872, when the coal cars were idle, passengers could have a ride for 50¢. The Mauch Chunk Switchback Railway closed in 1929.

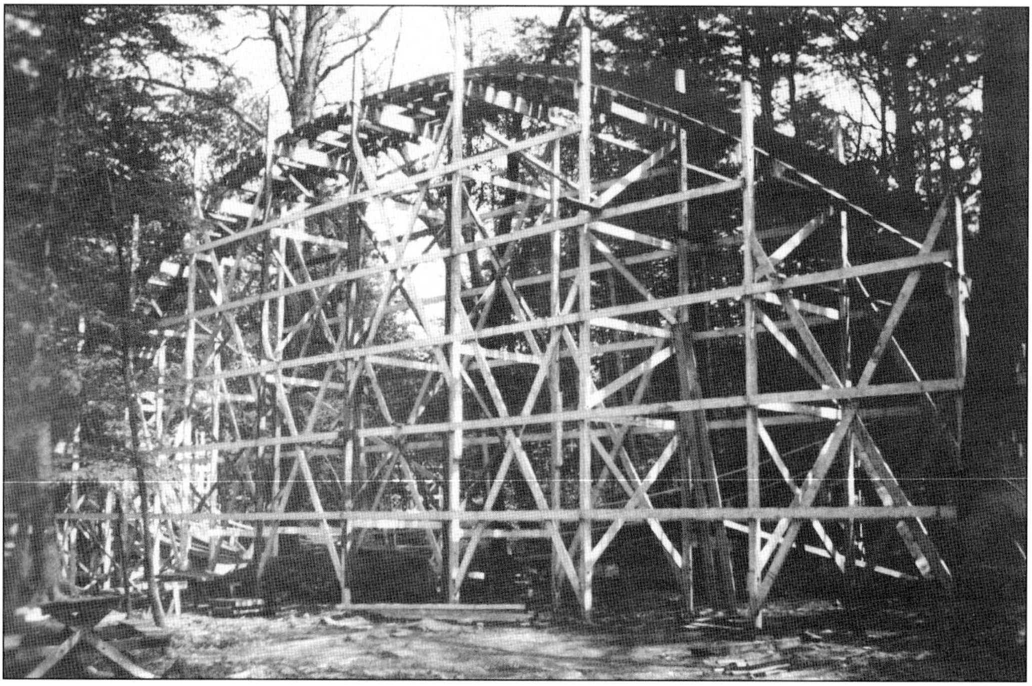

The Second Roller Coaster Takes Shape, 1922. In January 1922, a story on the front page of the *New Castle News* announced that Cascade Park's roller coaster would be dismantled because it was "antiquated." Described as a landmark, the coaster was one of the most popular rides at the park, but its aging wood was vulnerable to termites. The *News* promised a more modern roller coaster during the coming summer. Billy Glenn, a park concessionaire, undertook building the new coaster, engaging the firm of Miller and Baker to design it. He called it "the Gorge," a name that conveyed the idea that the new roller coaster offered a more thrilling ride than the old one that had only moderate speed and shallow dips. The new roller coaster would take advantage of the park's tree-lined gorge where the dips and curves were more exciting and the view of the park more memorable.

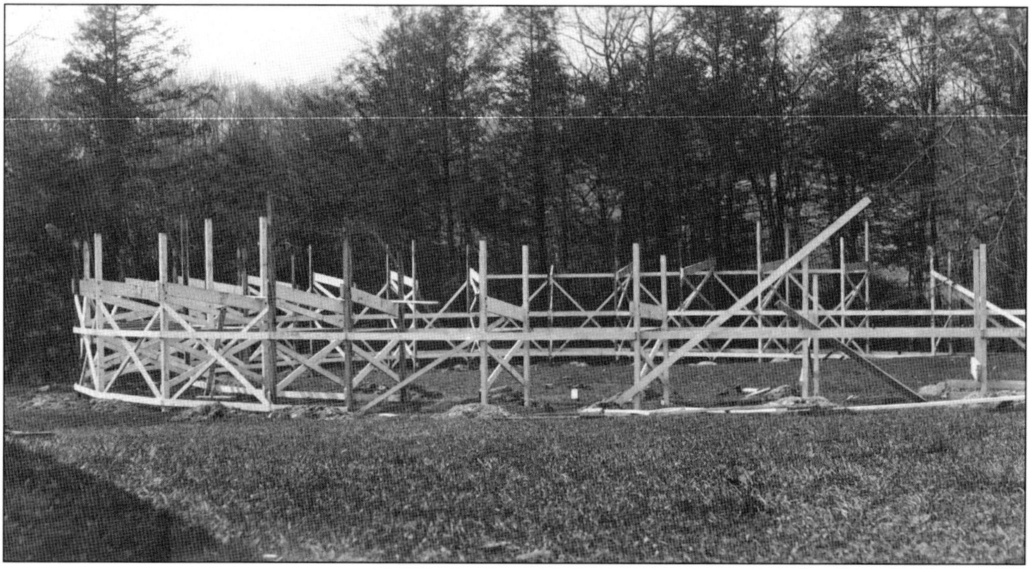

Construction Site, the Gorge, c. 1922. The height of the new wooden coaster was enough to impress the contractor, here with teenager Charles Lawson. When completed, owner Billy Glenn, builder Perry Barge, park superintendent E. D. McKibben, and engineer Stanley Treser inspected the job by taking the first ride. The coaster was found to work smoothly. (Courtesy of Donald Lawson.)

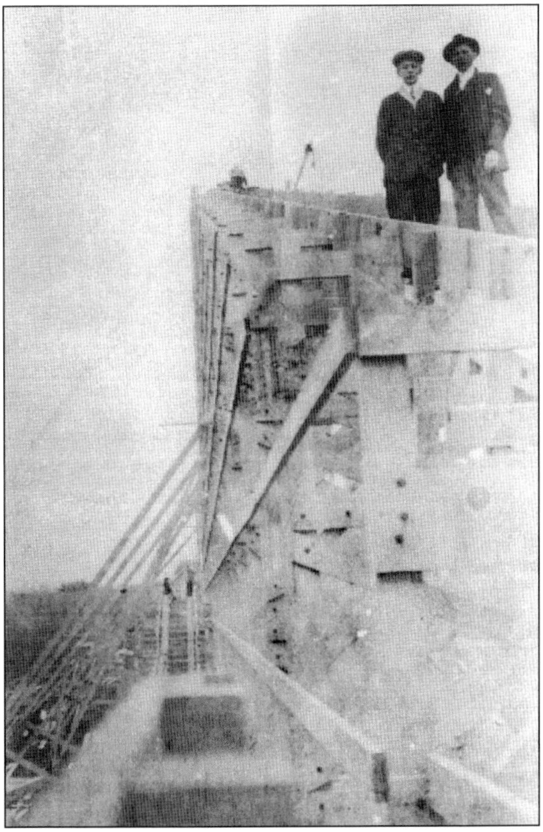

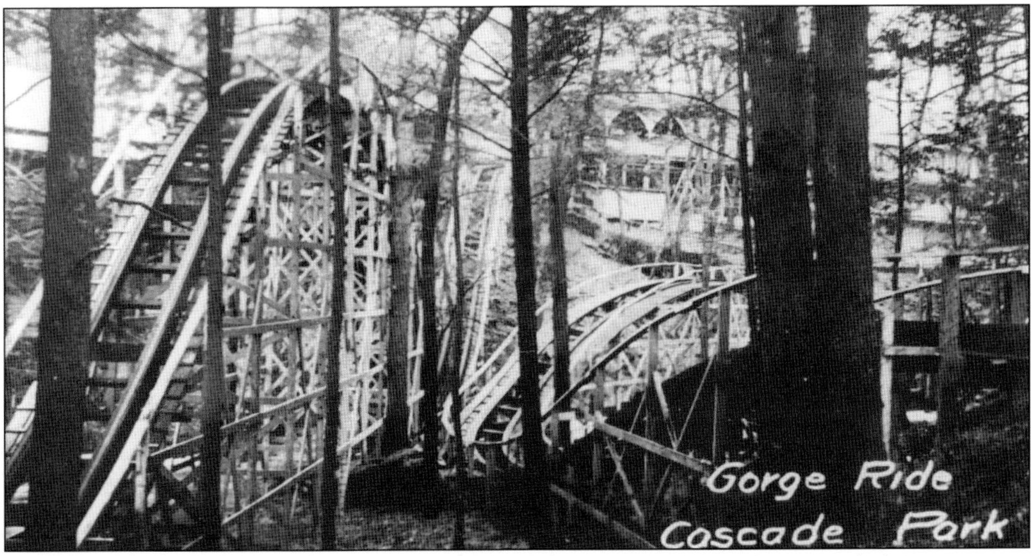

A Ride of Unsurpassed Beauty, mid-1920s. Many roller coaster fans travel the country to experience different roller coaster rides, comparing notes on the highest, the deepest, the fastest, and the most thrilling. The Gorge ride could probably have been called the most beautiful, surrounded by the lacy coolness of the park's many trees. (Courtesy of Pat Patterson.)

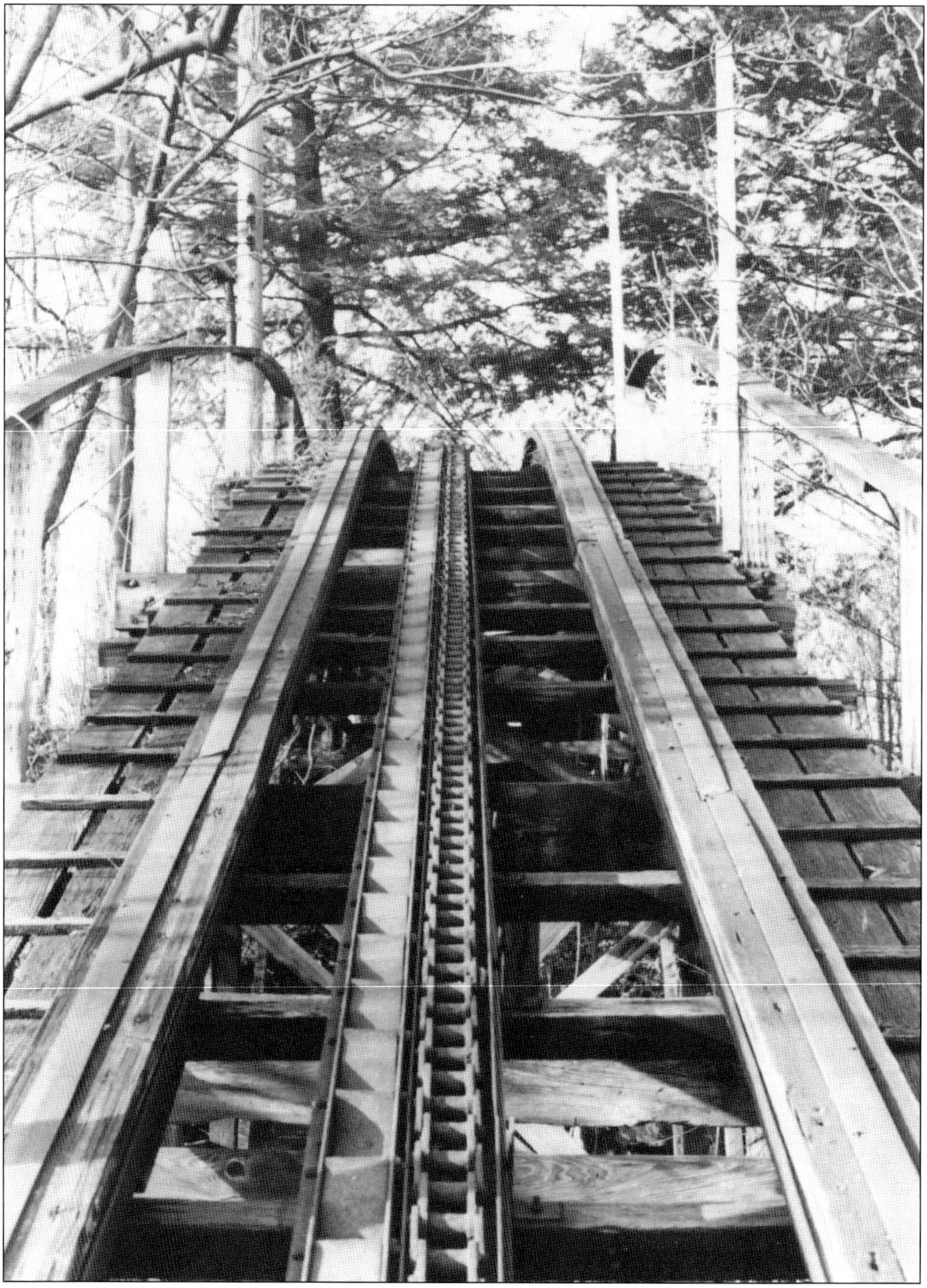

Close-up of Roller Coaster Tracks, c. 1980s. Passengers seldom see the ground from the height of the roller coaster cars. And passengers never have to climb the roller coaster tracks. Only the maintenance people regularly walk the entire circuit to check for safety. This photograph of the Comet shows the climb for roller coaster workers.

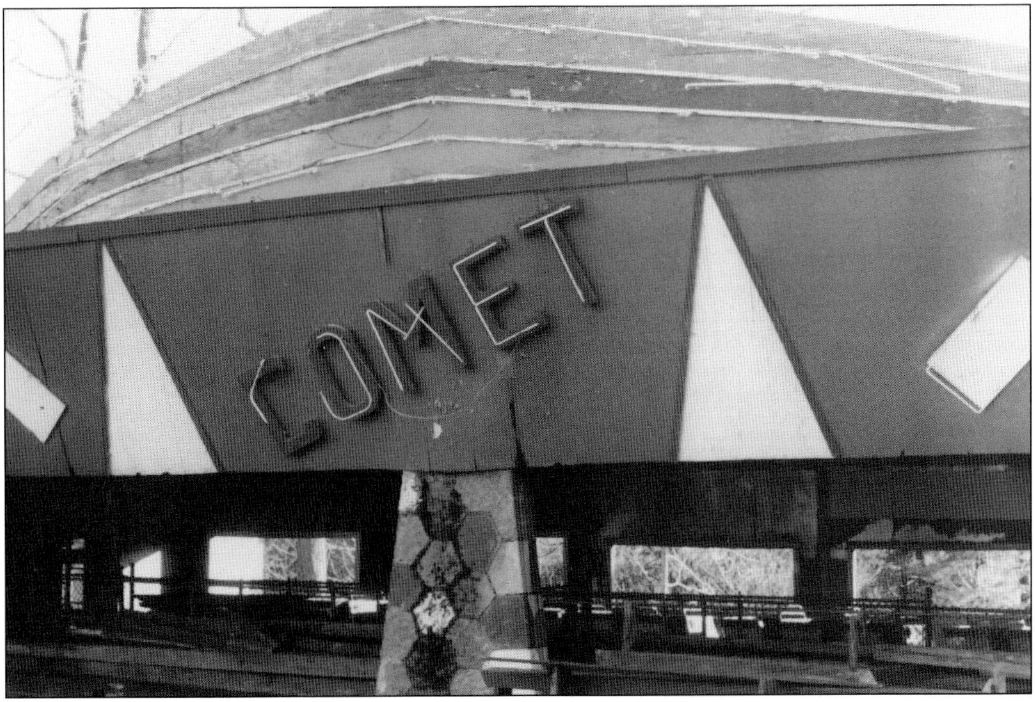

THE THIRD ROLLER COASTER, THE COMET, C. 1955. Concessionaire Paul Vesco built the Comet to replace the Gorge. The Comet was described as a "gully coaster," one whose trackwork makes use of the natural terrain and rides low to the ground. It was reported to be 65 feet high and 2,400 feet long. People who remember the Comet claim it was the most satisfying ride compared to other roller coasters.

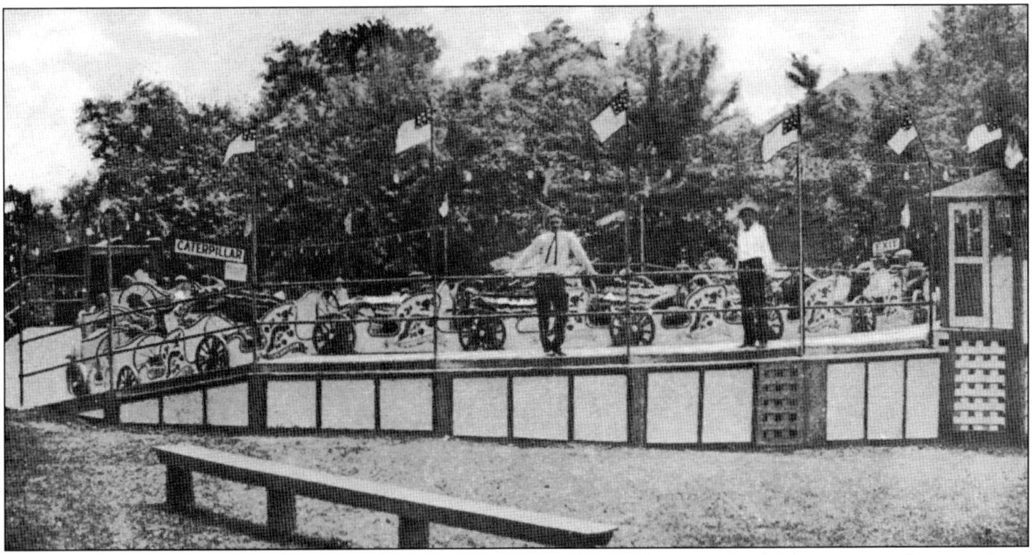

CASCADE PARK'S CATERPILLAR, C. 1925. The Caterpillar ride consisted of a string of cars riding on a track with humps. During the ride, a green canopy would close over the riders. This made the ride look like a giant creeping caterpillar. Some models of this ride surprised passengers with occasional blasts of air under the seats as they circled. Cascade Park's Caterpillar was located near the dance pavilion.

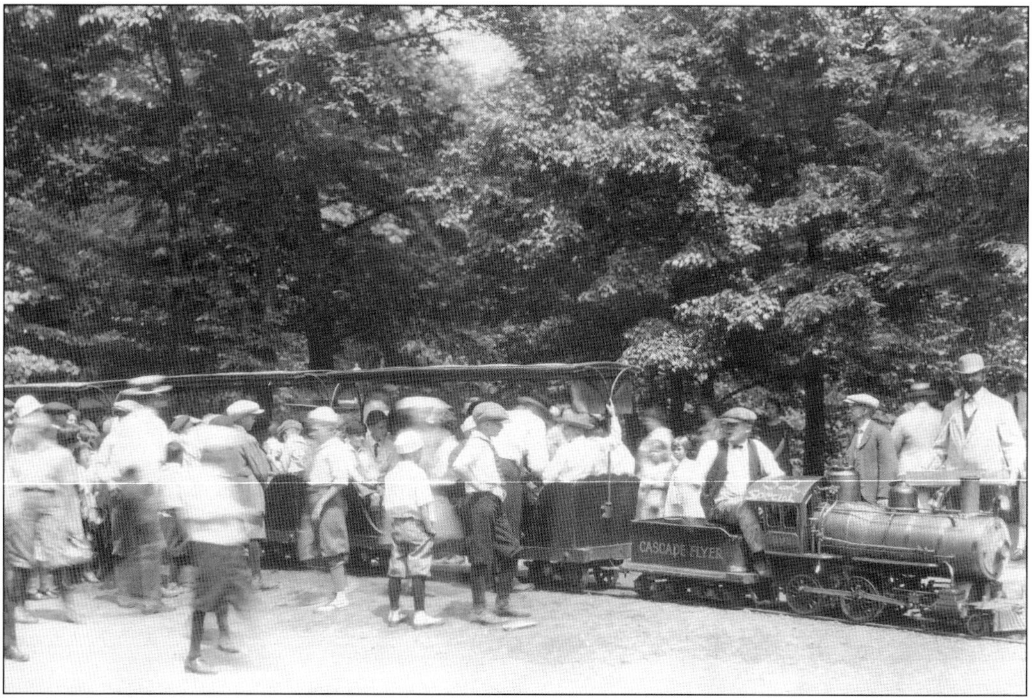

The Cascade Flyer, 1935. Excursion visitors to Cascade Park greet the miniature train pulled by a miniature steam locomotive. Little railroads intrigue adults and children, and at Cascade Park, the train ride was unlike any other because the luxuriant natural scenery changed from visit to visit. (Courtesy Mahoning Valley Historical Society, Mahoning Valley Regional Mass Transit Authority Collection.)

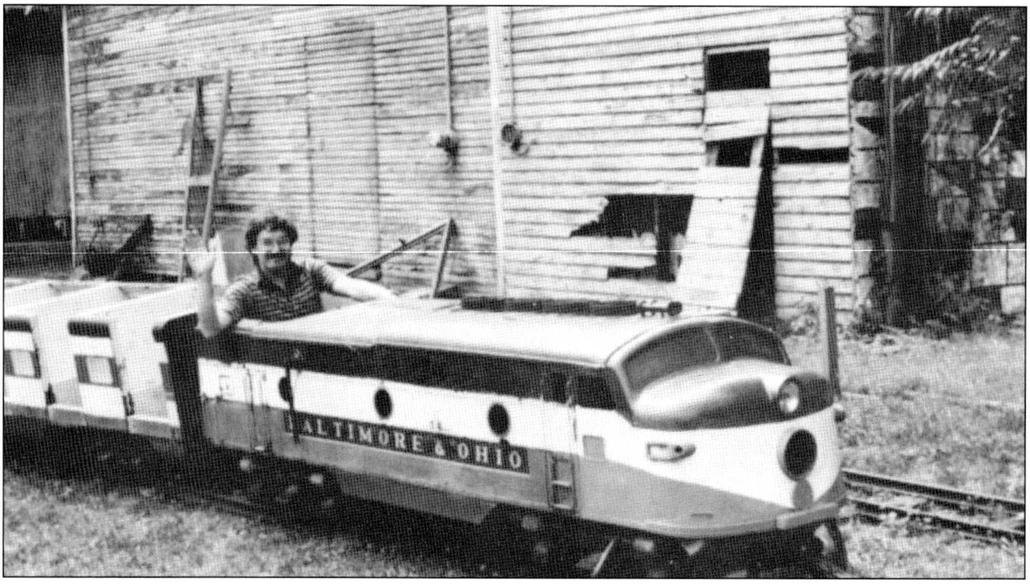

The B&O Miniature Train, c. 1955. This later train was made to look like the Baltimore and Ohio passenger trains that ran in and around New Castle. It had its own station between Big Run and the midway. It ran through the park, crossing a bridge and going through a tunnel along the way. The station is still at the park, serving as a platform for special events.

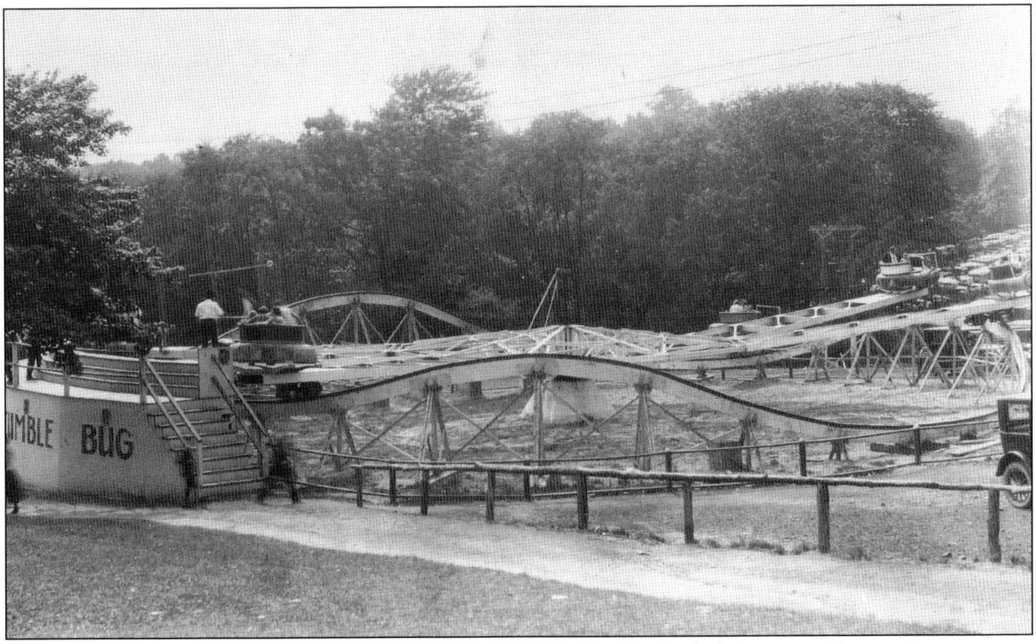

The Tumble Bug, 1935. This ride, installed in 1923, was made by Harry Traver Engineering of Beaver Falls. It got its name from the look of the cars on the undulating track. According to last reports, the Tumble Bugs at Kennywood Park and Conneaut Lake Park were the final two of these rides to operate. (Courtesy Mahoning Valley Historical Society, Mahoning Valley Regional Mass Transit Authority Collection.)

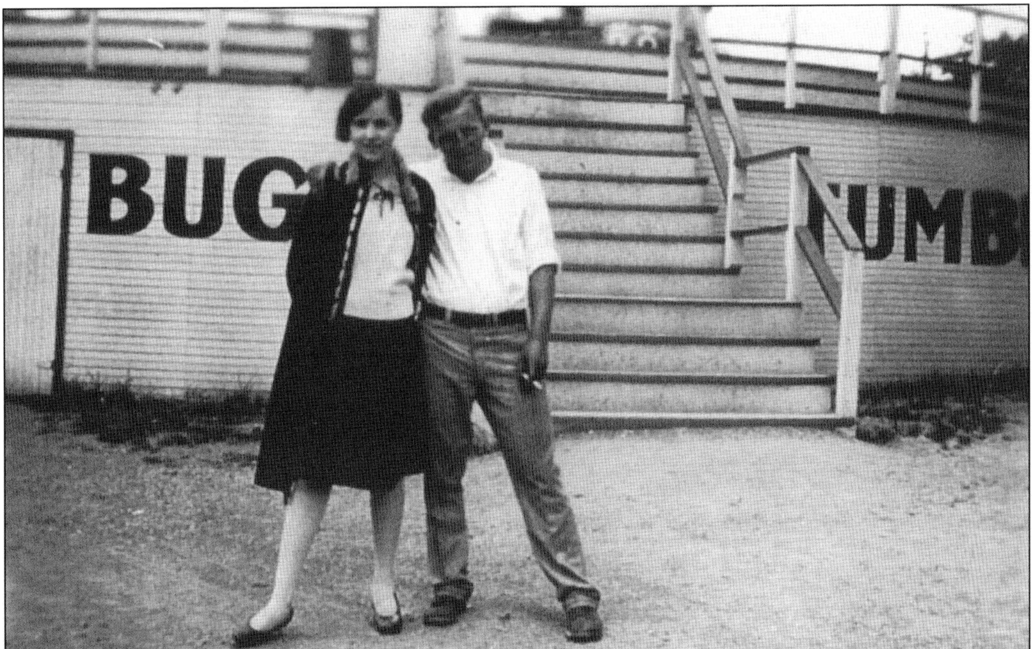

A Couple of Tumble Bug Riders, c. 1920s. Cascade Park was the place to go to meet boys (or girls). A couple could share snacks or cool drinks on the midway or get thrown close together on a Caterpillar curve or sit in the same Tumble Bug car. (Courtesy of Sandra Bumgardner.)

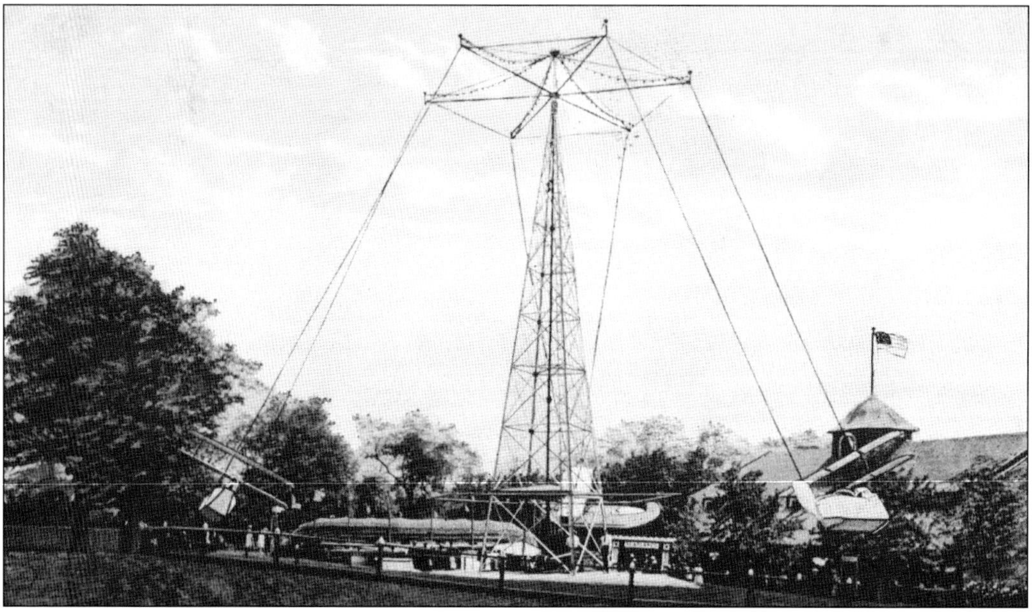

SEAPLANES IN FLIGHT, C. 1920S. Like the Tumble Bug, these seaplanes were made by Harry Traver Engineering of Beaver Falls, Pennsylvania. They were variations of rockets, or circle swings, which were also installed at Cascade Park. The difference among these circular rides was the design of the cabins, or swings. This one, near the dance pavilion, was said to have an 80-foot tower.

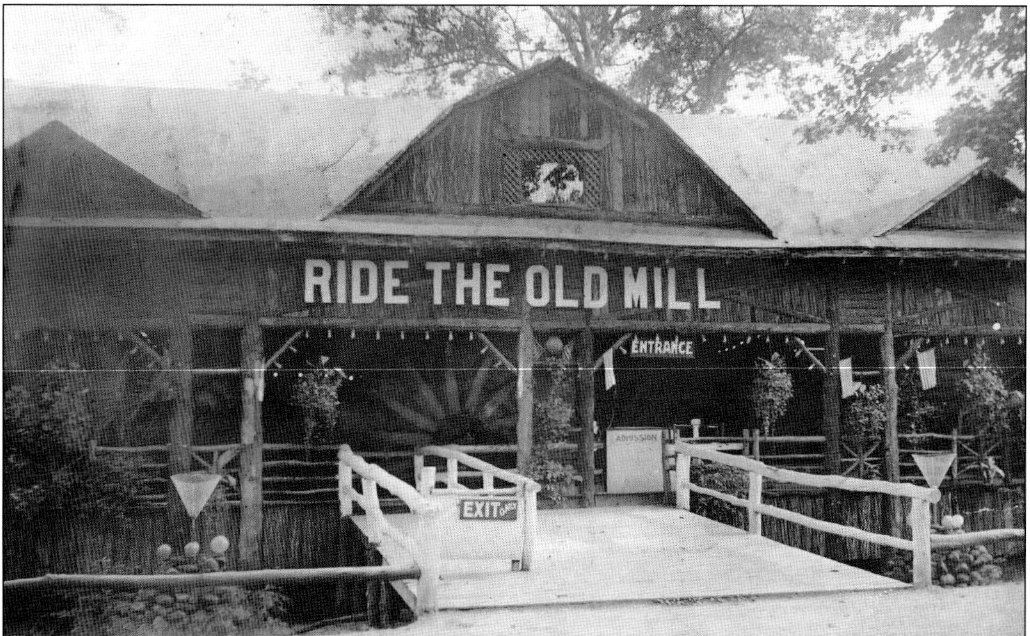

THE OLD MILL, 1924. The Old Mill was a boat ride through a dark tunnel, passing lighted pictures—maybe scary, maybe not. Riders who remember the Old Mill differ on how the ride ended; some say the water suddenly went downhill so the boat would splash the riders. This popular ride on the main walk was called a "dark" ride, that is, amusement parks kept some rides dark for dramatic effect.

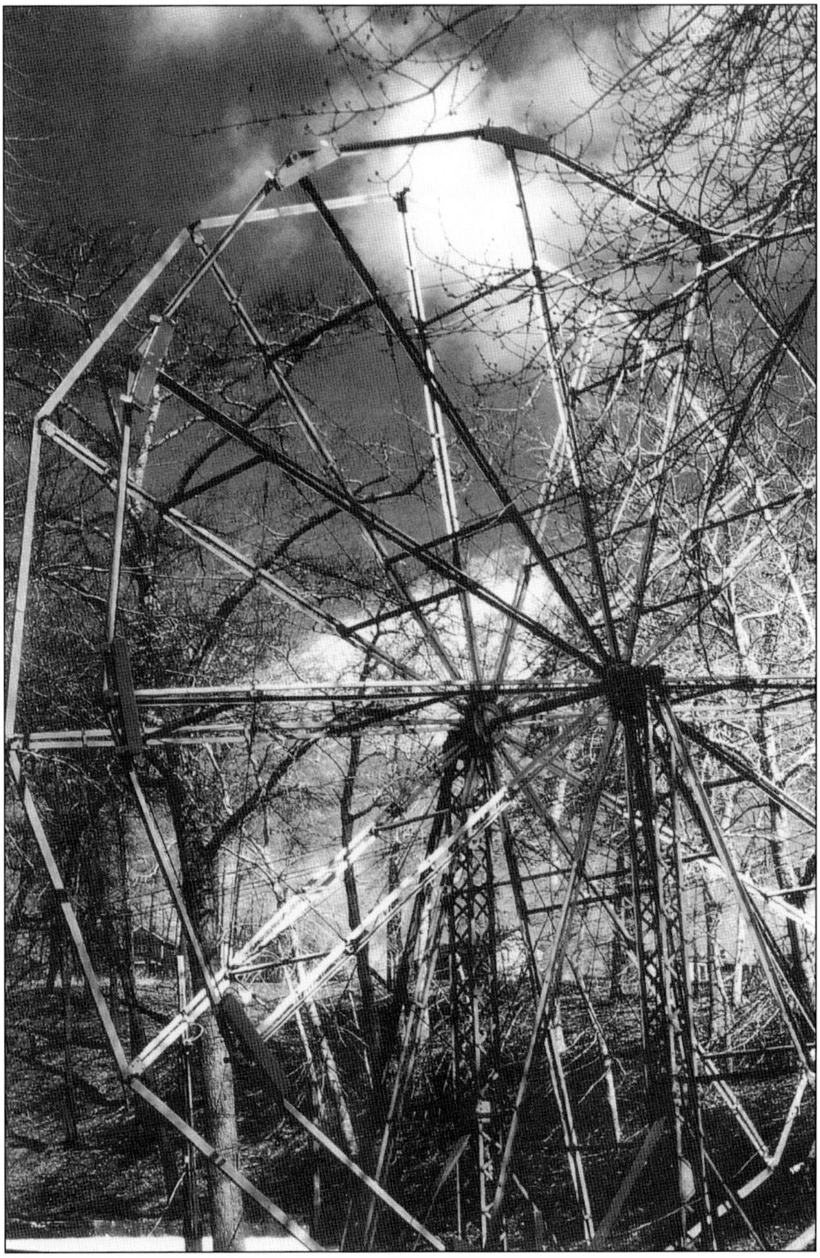

The Ferris Wheel, c. 1950. The Ferris wheel, located to the right of the downhill walk to the grove, offered a unique glimpse of Cascade Park. The Ferris wheel offers a more tranquil ride than most amusement park rides. Also called an observation wheel, it is named for its designer, bridgemaker George W. Ferris, who introduced it at the Columbian Exposition in Chicago in 1893. The most popular attraction there, it was 264 feet high. Today the London Eye wheel, built in 1999, was once the tallest at 443 feet, but it has been exceeded by the Singapore Flyer, 541 feet high, which is almost as tall as the Washington Monument (555 feet). When completed, the Ferris wheel in Beijing will be 680 feet high. The Ferris wheel ride gives an excellent bird's-eye view of the ground. This was illustrated in the famous scene in the classic movie *The Third Man*, where, from the top of the wheel, people on the ground appeared to be insects or moving dots.

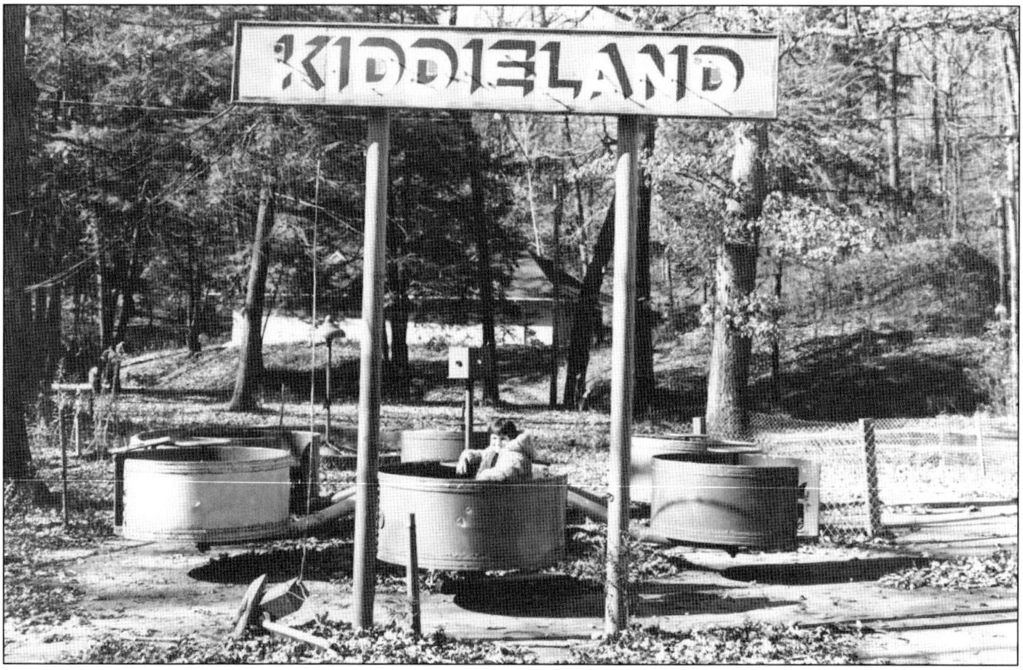

KIDDIELAND. In the 1920s, little children could ride one of six Shetland ponies around a pony track in Cascade Park. Then the miniature train appeared and the little red fire truck. There was also a park playground with swings and slides. In the 1950s, kiddielands could be found around the country, with the most famous, perhaps, in Melrose Park, Illinois, where children could choose among 30 rides. The top photograph, from around the 1970s, shows a popular circular ride. The bottom photograph, from around 1928, shows a kid-sized Ferris wheel. Today mechanical ponies and other rides can be found in front of dollar stores, in shopping malls, and in supermarkets where children now have their very own play areas. Kiddielands evoke precious memories: When Melrose Park's Kiddieland closed with an auction in 2009, one wooden carousel horse was bought for $325,000.

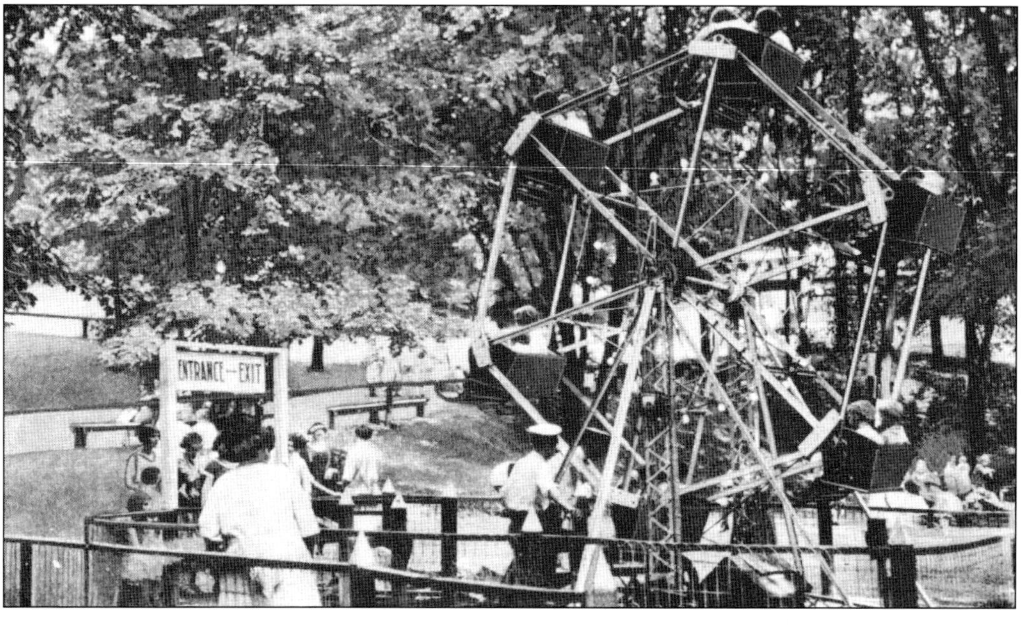

Four

Attractions

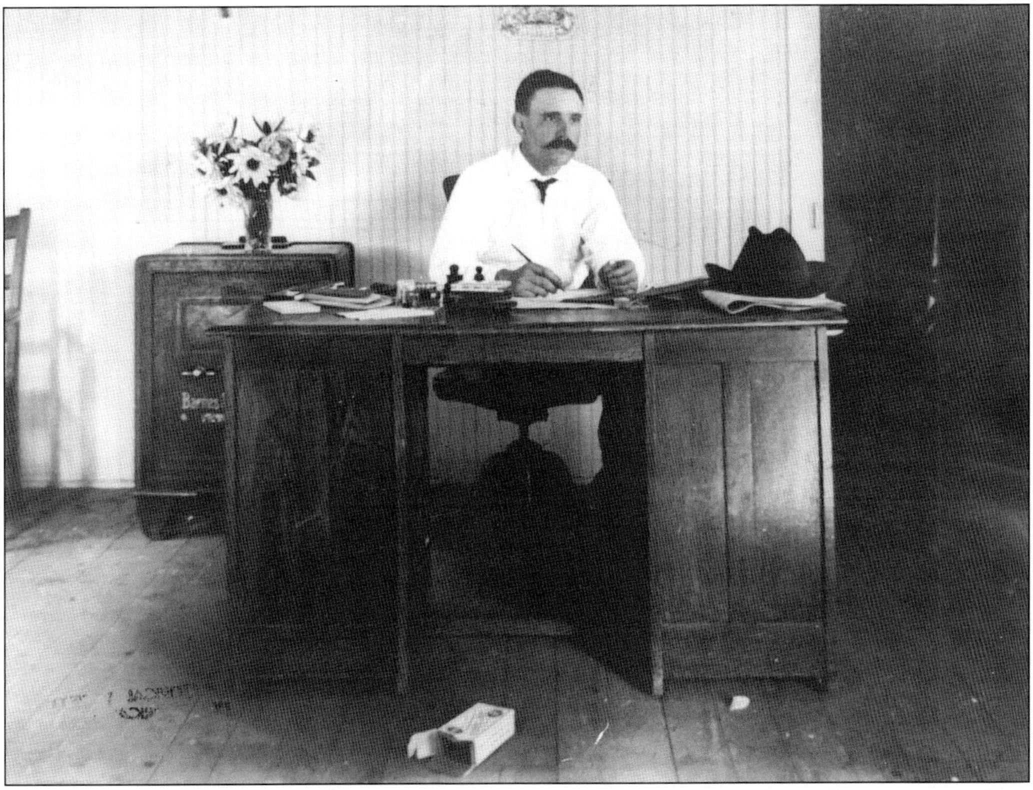

PERRY BARGE, PARK SUPERINTENDENT, 1903. Cascade Park maintained an administrative office located where Brinton's dancing platform used to be. It was the superintendent's job to see that rides were clean and safe and the grounds were neatly kept. Perry Barge was said to have patrolled the park on a white horse, supervising the gardens and the general decorum of visitors.

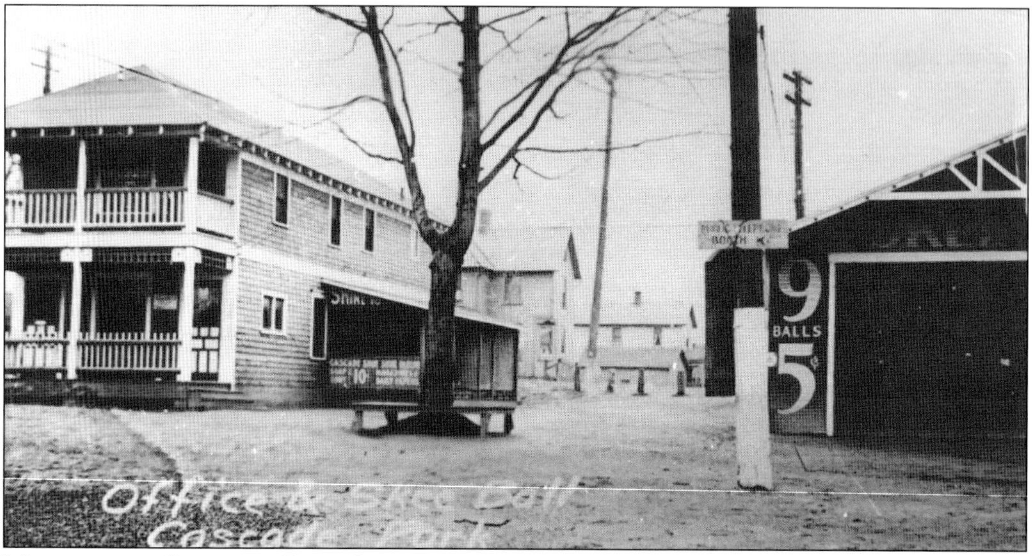

MIDWAY WITH SKEEBALL, PARK OFFICE, AND SHOE-SHINE PARLOR, C. 1920. Skeeball, a game of skill, can still be found in arcades, parks, and even bars. Wooden balls are rolled up a narrow inclined alley. The incline suddenly increases and bumps a ball up into one of the concentric circles at the end of the alley. Large circles have a low number of points, while small circles have a higher number; the points determine prizes.

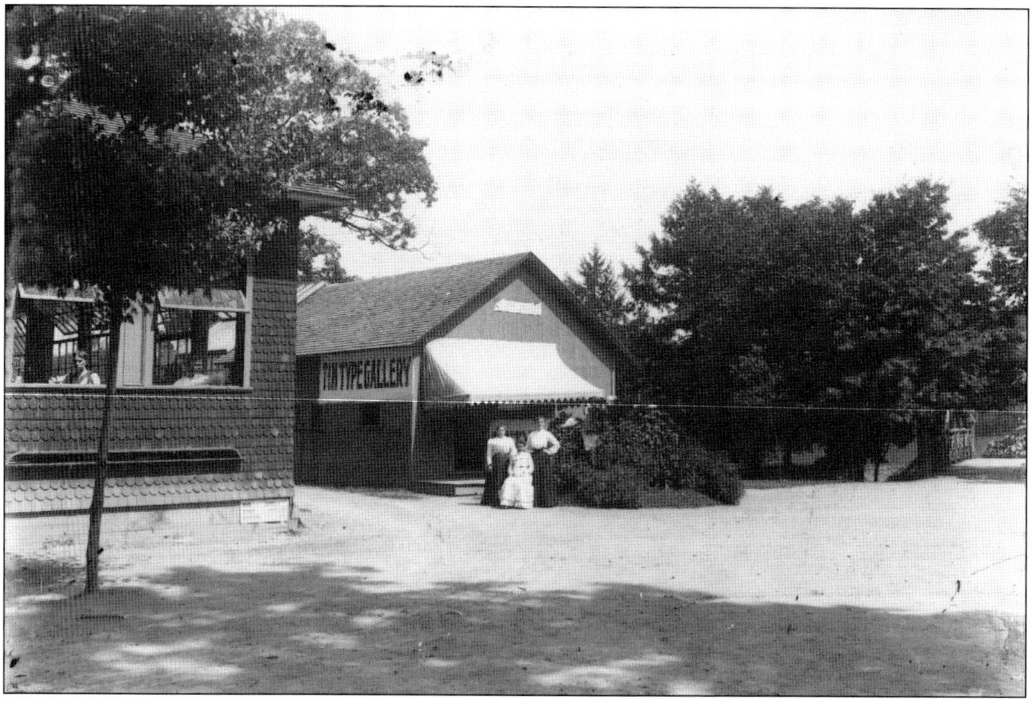

POSING AT THE TINTYPE GALLERY, C. 1900. Excursions to Cascade Park brought in trainloads of visitors from Pittsburgh, Youngstown, and other surrounding towns. Visitors might be church groups, employee groups, or families. Mementos of trips to the park were popular, and tintypes were a good choice. The process was fast. Photographs were taken and then printed on metal. Similar concessions could be found at carnivals and fairs.

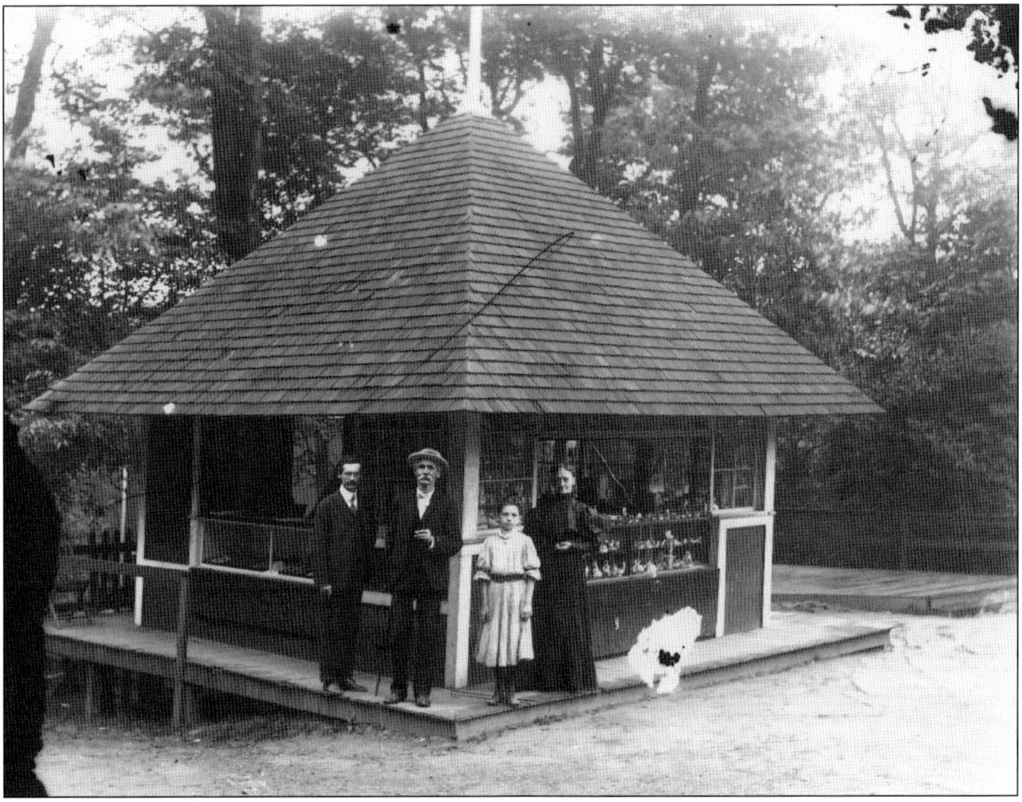

The Souvenir Stand, c. 1900. In addition to tintypes, visitors could buy a variety of souvenirs for themselves, family, or sweethearts. This little shop was on the main walk to the grove, and it probably sold decorative ceramic figurines and other mementos marked "Cascade Park, New Castle, Pa." Today, collectible items carrying the park's name appear on Internet auctions.

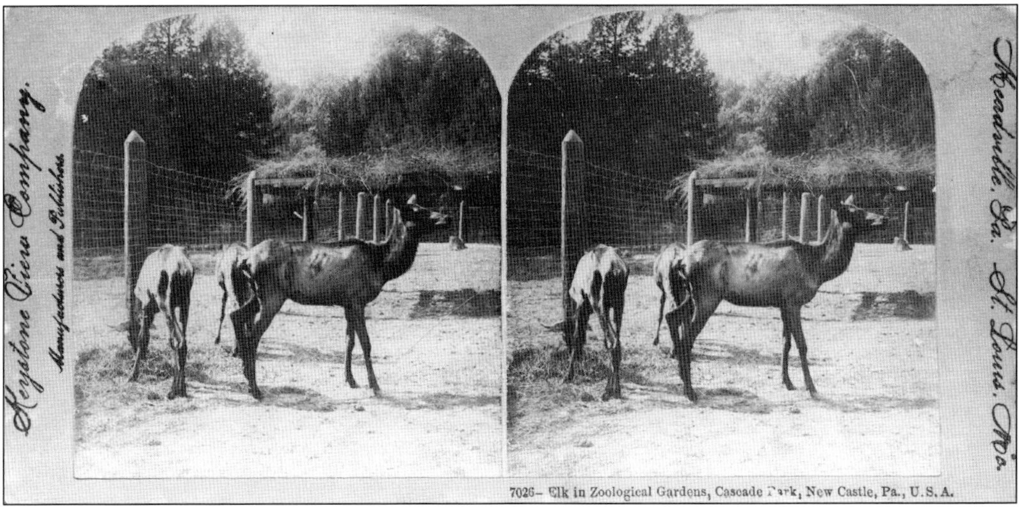

Zoological Garden, 1897. Elk were part of the Cascade Park Zoo installed on the hill above the picnic grove. Here their photograph was duplicated in this special format so that when seen through a stereoscope, the photograph would appear in three dimensions. Until 1963, the Keystone View Company in Meadville was the major manufacturer of stereoscopes and view cards.

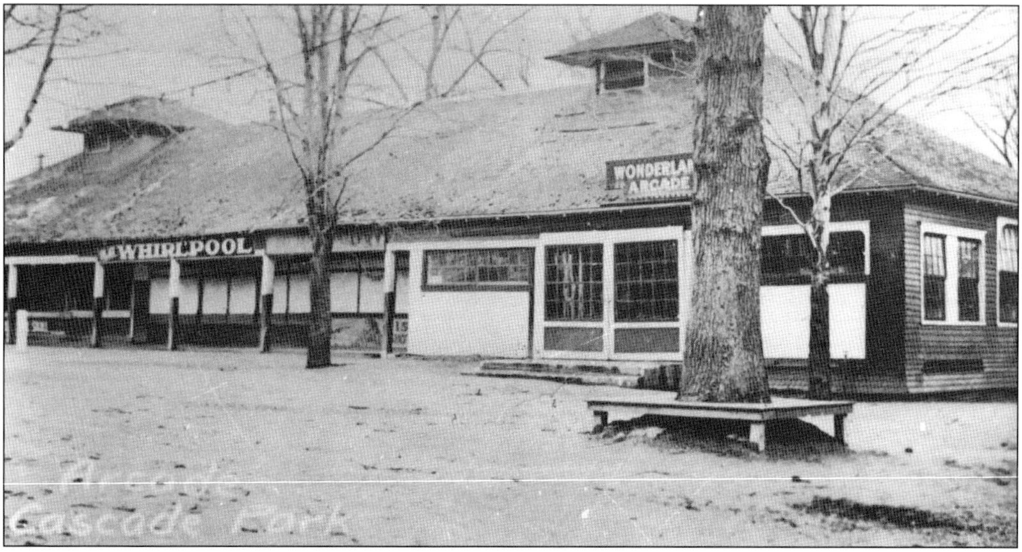

MIDWAY DIVERSIONS, C. 1900. A variety of coin-operated machines lined the walls of Cascade Park's penny arcade. There were fortune-telling machines, tests of strength, silent moving pictures, pinball, peep shows, and animated figures, all activities that today might be electronically driven, but 100 years ago were driven by a penny in a slot.

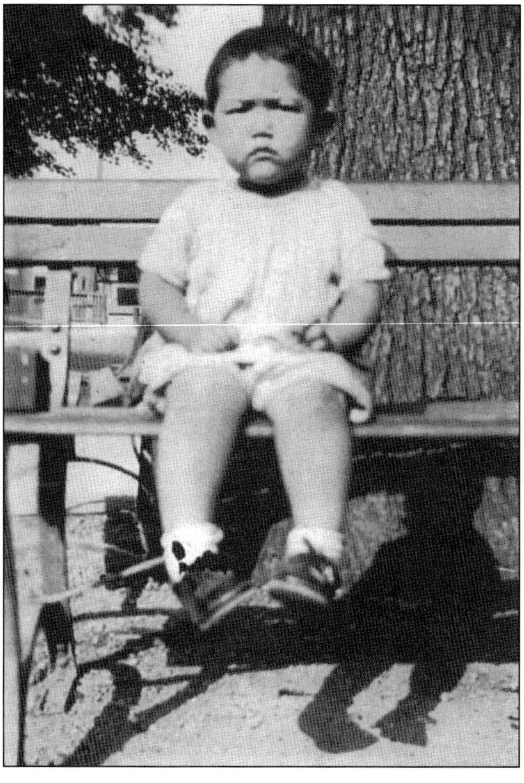

COCO ON THE MIDWAY, LATE 1920S. When the park was in its heyday, children might dream of being at the park every day. This little girl's Chinese parents owned the goldfish concession on the midway, so she was at the park every day. Claude Crill, a park employee, photographed Coco. (Courtesy of Sandra Bumgardner.)

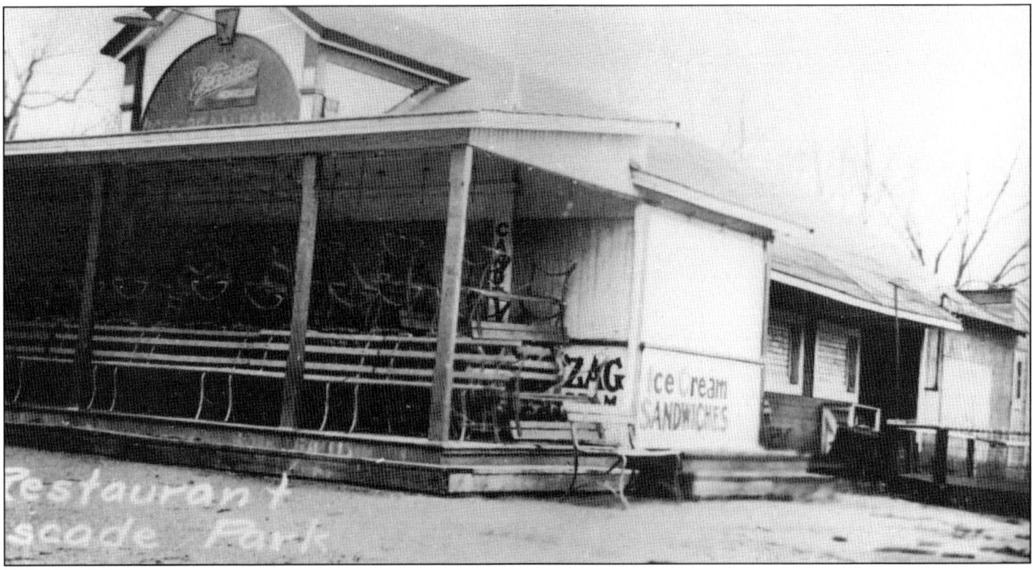

RESTAURANT ON THE MIDWAY, c. 1900. Basket picnics were standard fare at Cascade Park, but refreshments such as candy, cold drinks, and ice-cream sandwiches were available at this restaurant on the midway. The restaurant also offered seats where customers could view the passing parade of park visitors.

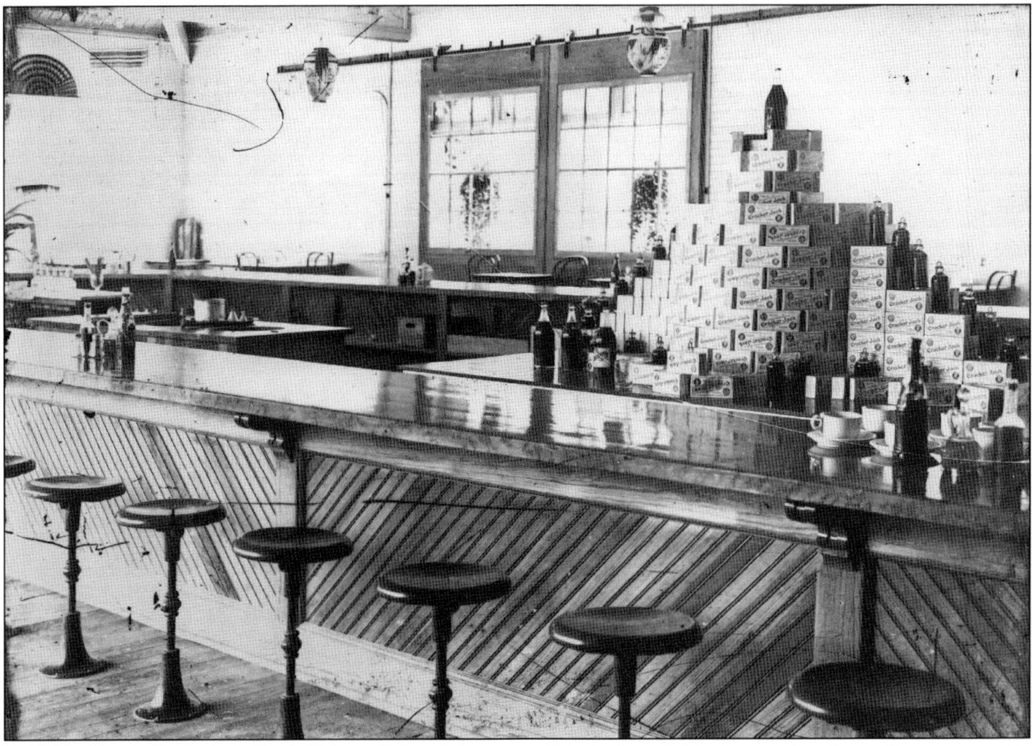

LUNCH COUNTER AND CRACKER JACK BOXES, c. 1900. In 1893, the Columbian Exposition in Chicago introduced, among other things, the Ferris wheel and the snack known as Cracker Jack. They could be enjoyed simultaneously. Starting in 1912, each Cracker Jack box included a small prize. Sailor Jack and his dog, Bingo, appeared on the box in 1918.

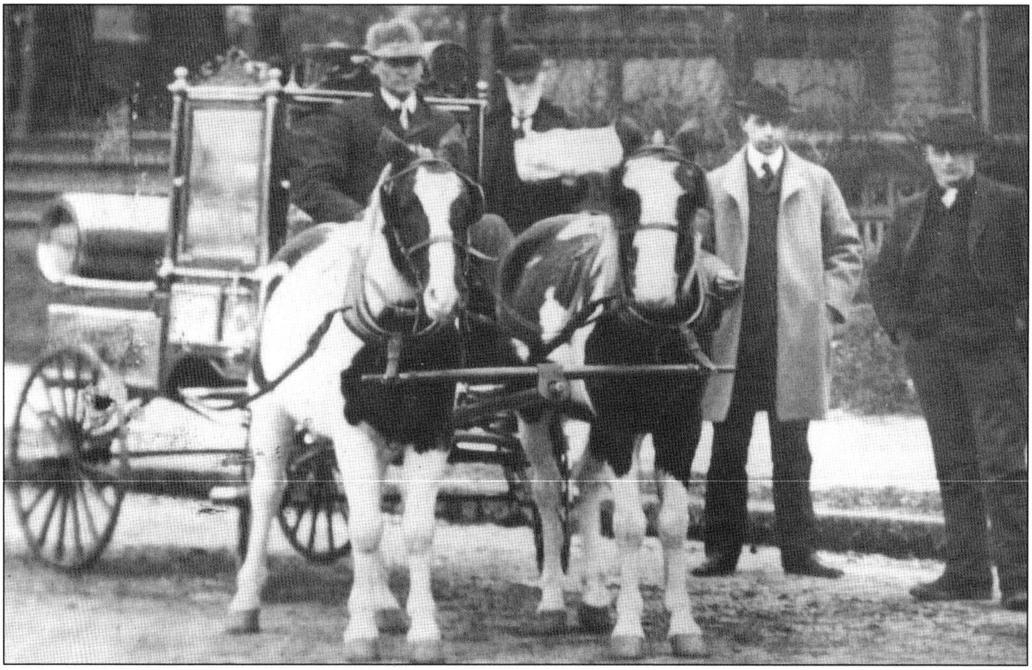

The Legendary Billy Glenn. Generations of Cascade Park visitors remembered Billy Glenn (above right and below) for his peanuts and popcorn wagon on the midway and in downtown New Castle. He ordered his first peanut wagon from a catalog. Glenn worked from a modest stand at the park in the early 1900s, and in 1919, he built a permanent concession. In the 1920s, he leased part of the park for a swimming pool and bathhouse, which replaced the zoo, and for the Fun House and Old Mill attractions to replace the summer theater. His most important undertaking was the unforgettable roller coaster, the Gorge. The Gorge did not harm the park's natural setting, running over the ravine and above the falls. His summer home under the Gorge was a secret for many years. The house's chimney can still be seen.

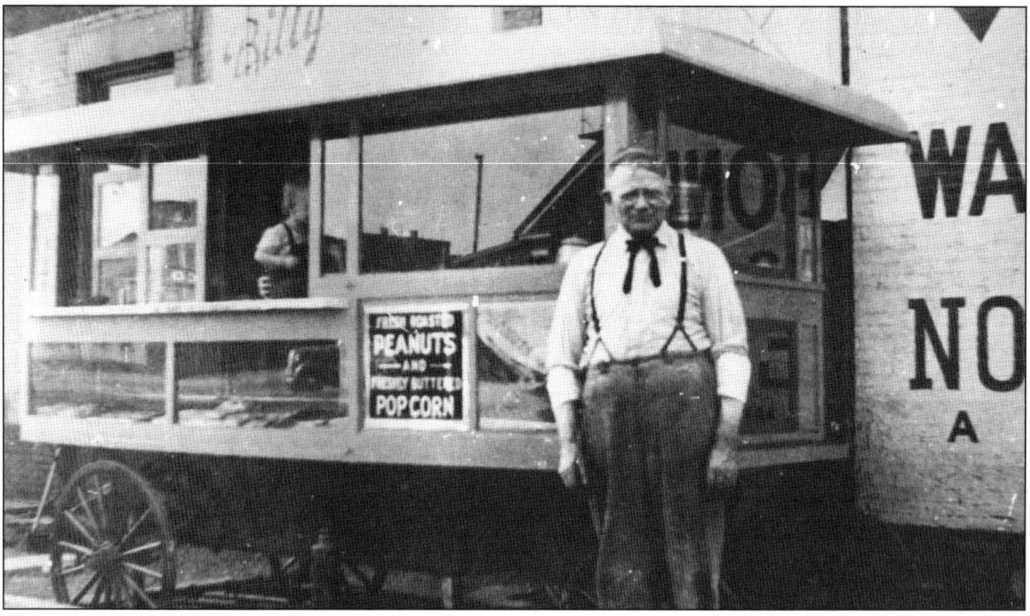

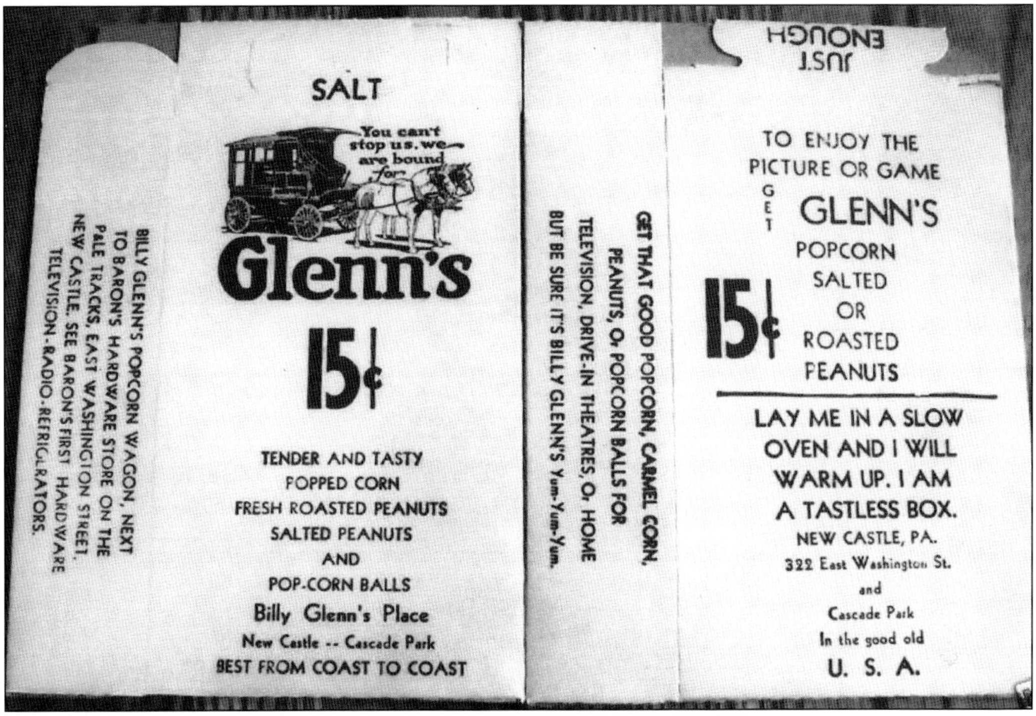

POPCORN BOX, C. 1950S. These nostalgic boxes are prized by collectors of vintage mementos. Billy Glenn's first success was corn-related—as a youth, the first crop of corn he raised brought in more than his father's. Later, he was offered large sums of money for the recipe he used to butter his popcorn, but he never revealed the secret.

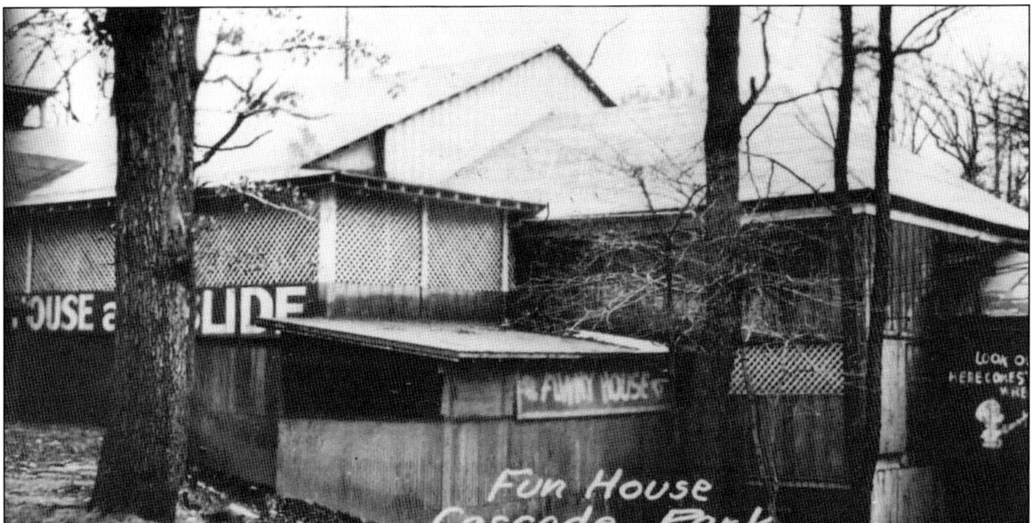

THE FUN HOUSE, C. 1920S. The Fun House was located on the main walk, to the left going downhill. It replaced the summer theater. Visitors to the Fun House walked through a huge rolling barrel, they sat on burlap sacks that carried them down a waxed slide, and they sat on a flat spinning wheel and tried not to be thrown off as the wheel spun faster and faster.

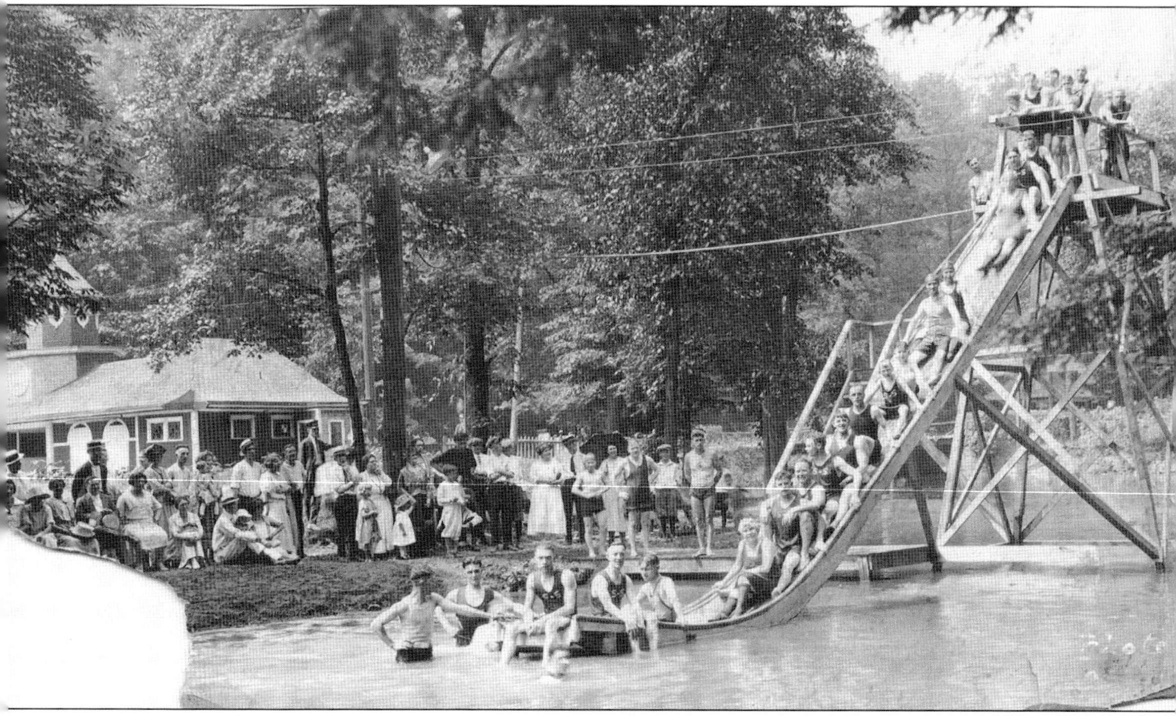

SWIMMING FUN AT THE TERMINAL, C. 1920S. There was no swimming pool at Cascade Park in its early days. The lake, which was built by the traction company when the park first opened in the late 1890s, was intended for swimming. At first, swimmers could jump off the same dock they used for fishing. Eventually a more formal swimming area with a slide was provided at the end of the lake near the streetcar terminal. Onlookers could sit under the trees and enjoy the antics of swimmers who lined up waiting for a turn on the slide. In the mid-1920s, much to the enjoyment of the park's visitors, Billy Glenn had the zoo removed from the area immediately above the grove and installed the first swimming pool and a bathhouse in its place. (Courtesy of the New Castle Public Library.)

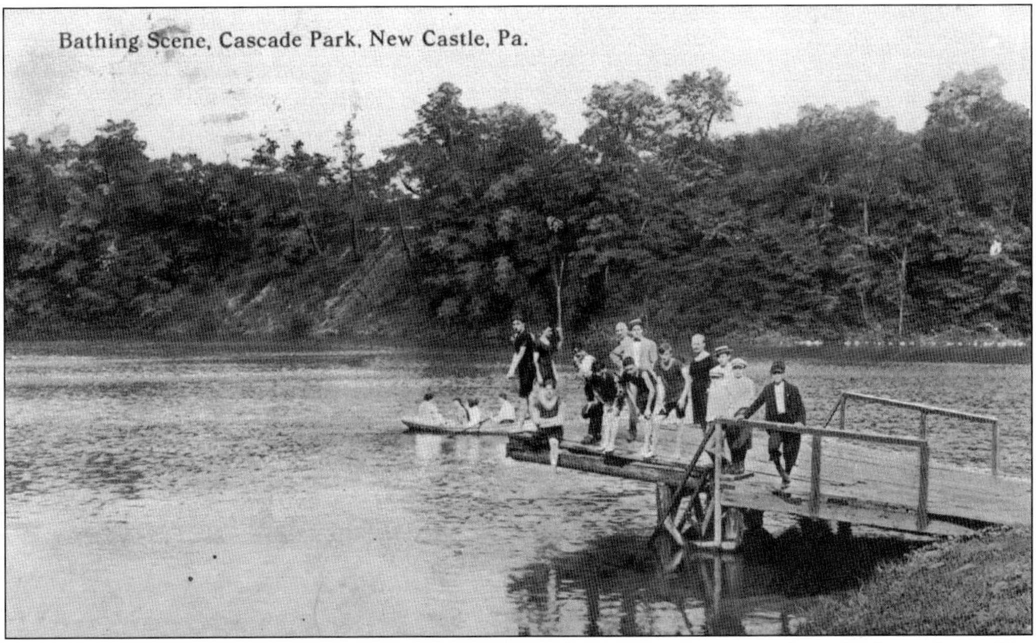

Swimming at the Lake, Early 1900s. Cascade Park visitors who wanted a refreshing dip in Big Run would find the best swimming at the 15-acre lake in the lower park. This swimming area offered few amenities, but the water was cold and the dock was high enough for jumping in.

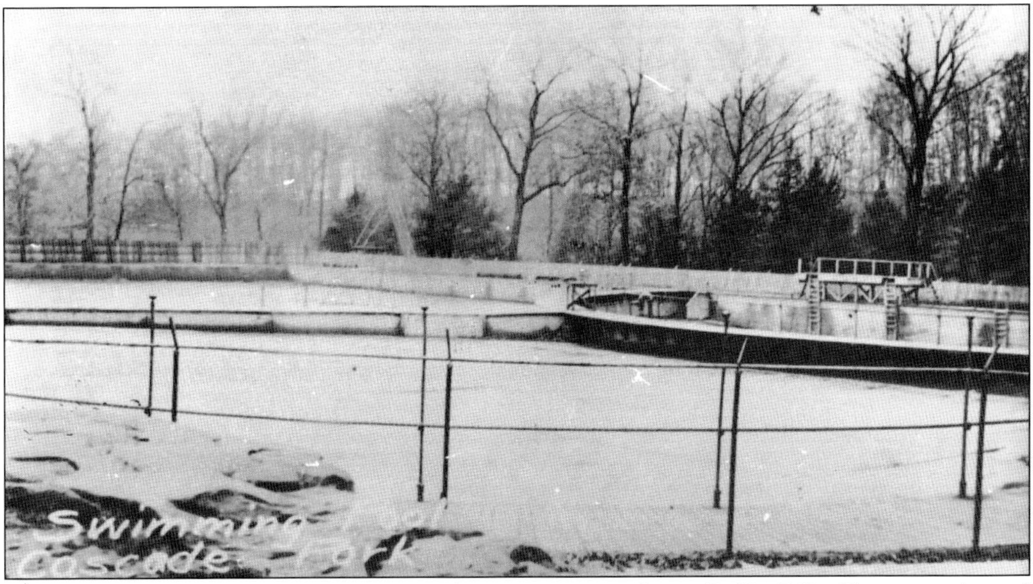

The First Swimming Pool, Mid-1920s. The swimming pool installed by Billy Glenn transformed Cascade Park. At a cost of $60,000, it accommodated 5,000 bathers. The water was filtered, and the area was illuminated at night. Called "the Glenn Pool," one swimmer described it as "the greatest swimming pool arrangement in the country, three pools for all classes of swimmers, the Baby, the Intermediate, and the Deep for the divers."

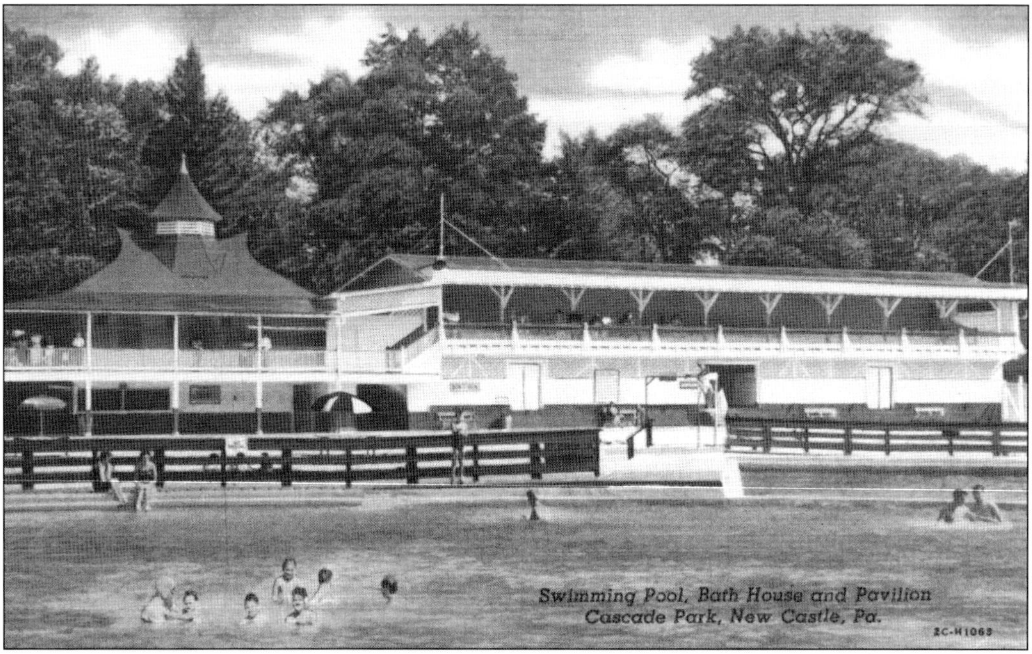

POOL, BATHHOUSE, AND PAVILION, MID-1920S. In the 1920s, there were no public swimming pools in the city except for the YMCA and Cascade Park. The Glenn pool seen in this postcard was replaced in the late 1970s when the city installed a new Olympic-sized swimming pool, two wading pools, and a new bathhouse. The pool was closed in the late 1990s.

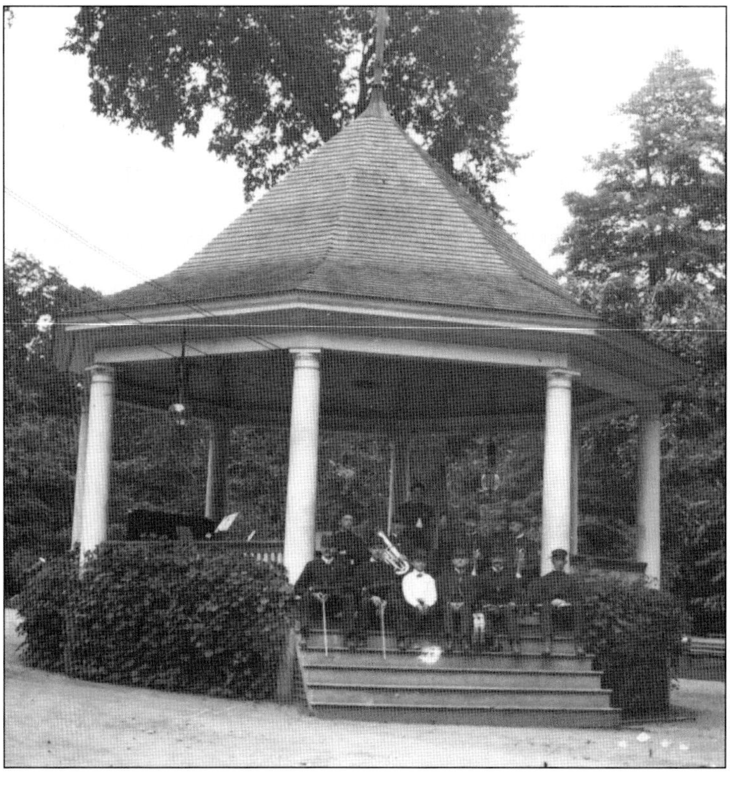

THE BAND AT INTERMISSION, EARLY 1900S. A number of different bands regularly entertained visitors at Cascade Park. Usually they played from this gazebo located on the main walk. The music was light and, unlike most band music today, included violin and piano parts. One of the early violinists was Elsa von Moltke Emery, who taught many New Castle string players.

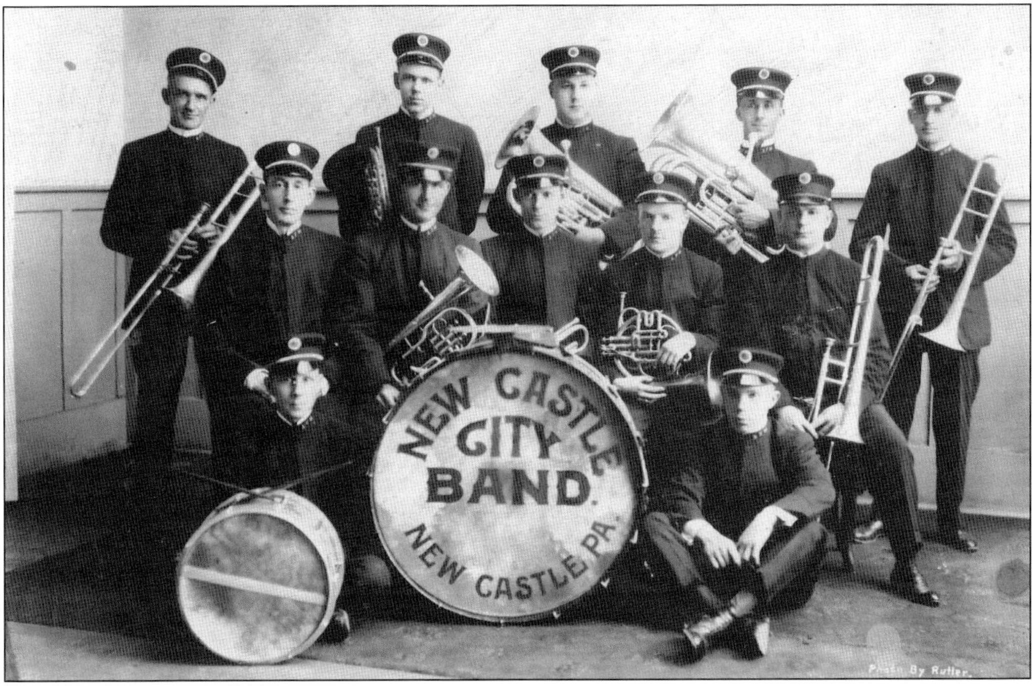

The New Castle City Band, Early 1900s. As Cascade Park's regular band director, William Parsons was in charge of the weekly Sunday afternoon concerts. Little is known about the brass band pictured here, but it was likely one of the many bands engaged to play at special events at the park.

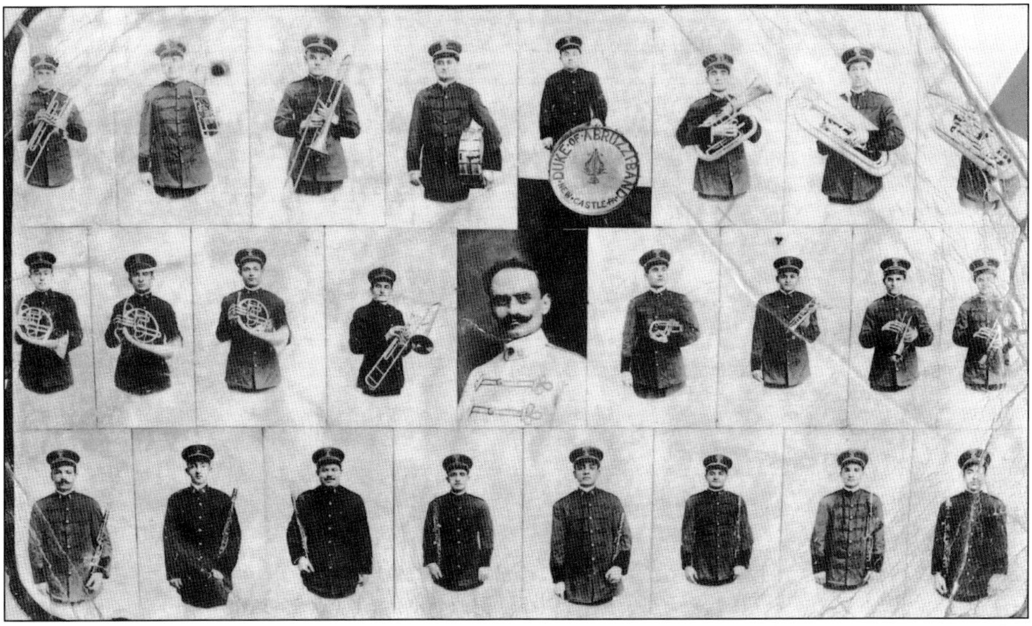

The Duke of Abruzzi Band, c. 1910. Many visitors to Cascade Park were immigrants who worked in mills and for railroads. They came to the park for respite and to hear bands from their fraternal organizations, like this one whose director (center) was Raffaello Gaspare. The second musician to his right is B. J. Biondi, who became manager of the park's dance pavilion in the 1930s. (Courtesy of Emma Rocco.)

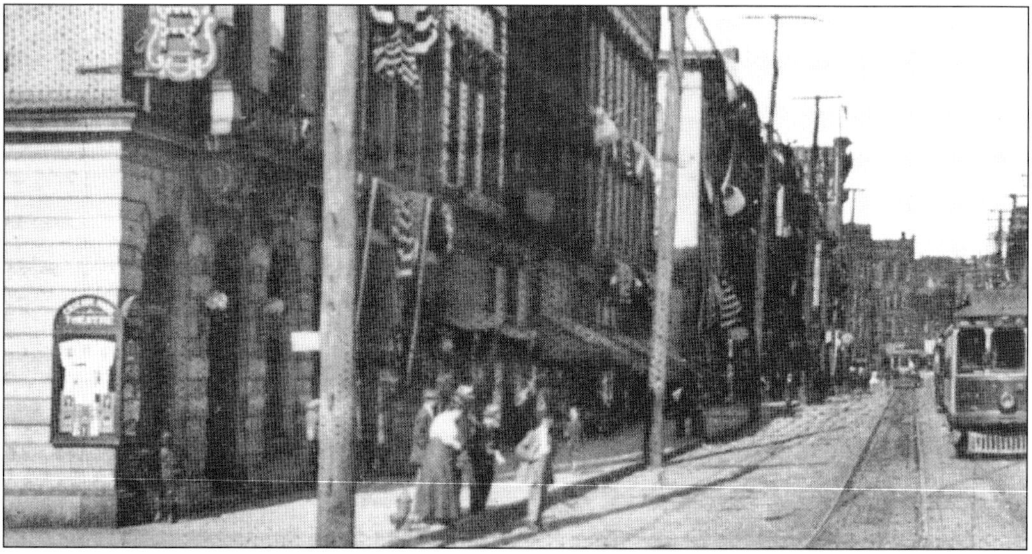

Movies and Theater at the Park, Early 1900s. This postcard shows the corner of a building on East Washington Street advertising a movie performance at Cascade Park Theater. The building, on the Diamond (central square), houses the New Castle Traction Company, which owned Cascade Park. The building eventually became the Penn Power Building.

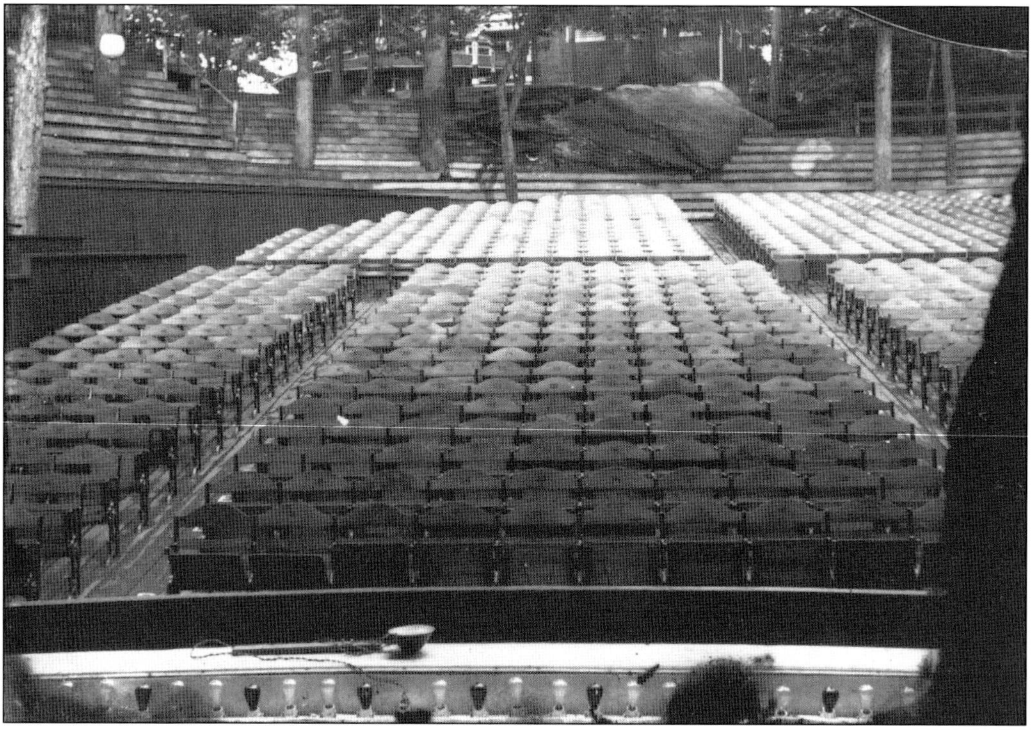

Outdoor Theater from the Stage, Early 1900s. The outdoor theater was just below the carousel along the main walk. Seats were 10¢, but visitors could sit on the huge boulders without paying. The theater presented dramas, films, and vaudeville, which, according to an old report written by journalist Bart Richards, featured song-and-dance men in striped or checkered suits of yellow and purple.

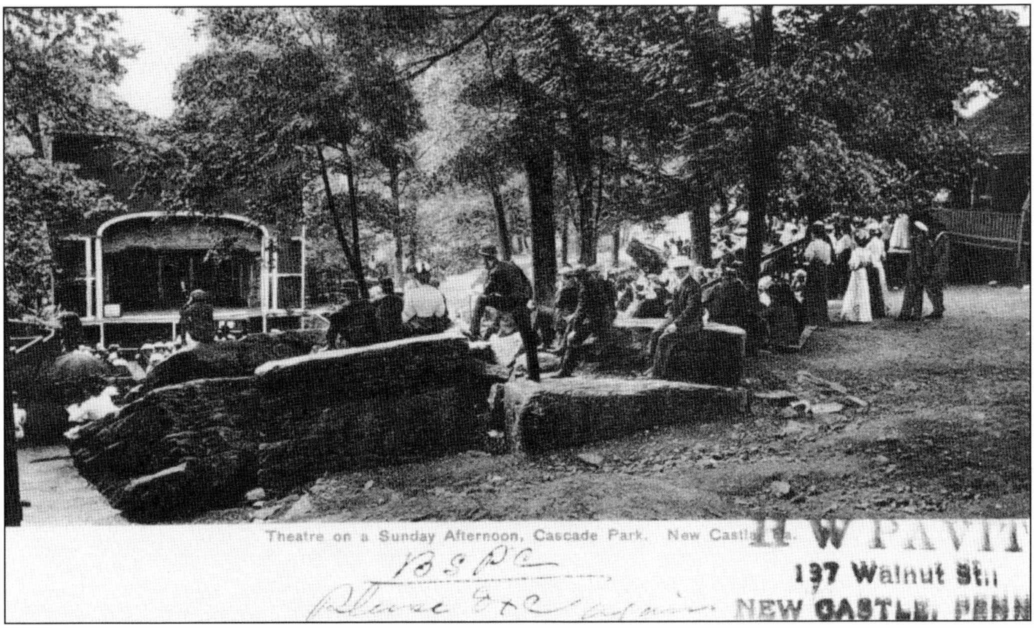

Outdoor Theater Facing the Stage, Early 1900s. The theater was in a natural amphitheater, as shown in this postcard. Boulders were conveniently located on the periphery of the theater area for those who did not reserve seating. Depending on what was playing, two shows were given every day. Occasionally, the stage was used for weddings.

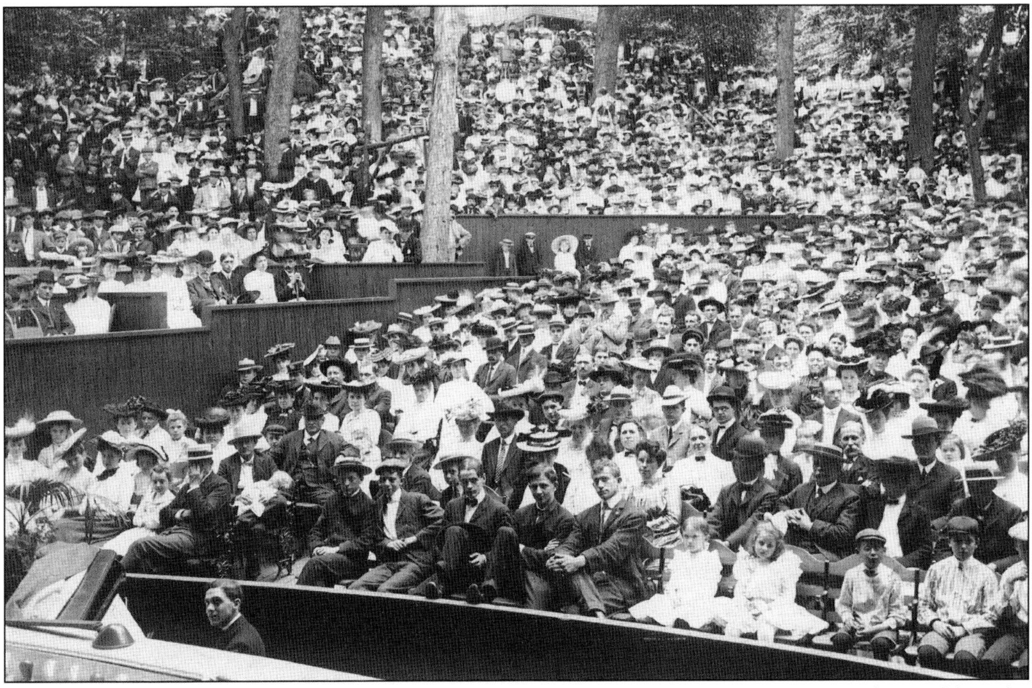

Full House at a Matinee, 1903. The theater had seating for at least 1,000 people. Building for a crowd of this size required the removal of 70,000 cubic yards of dirt for the foundation of the theater. When it was completed, it took in crowds that often spilled over. This photograph shows tiers of seating at a summer matinee, with a musician seated in the orchestra pit.

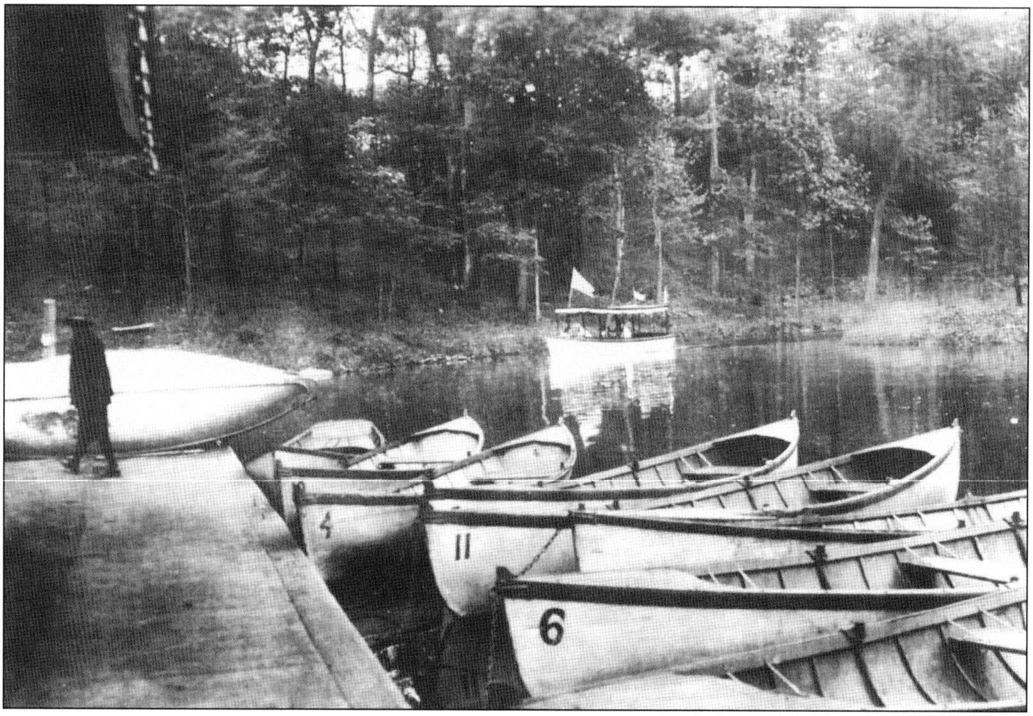

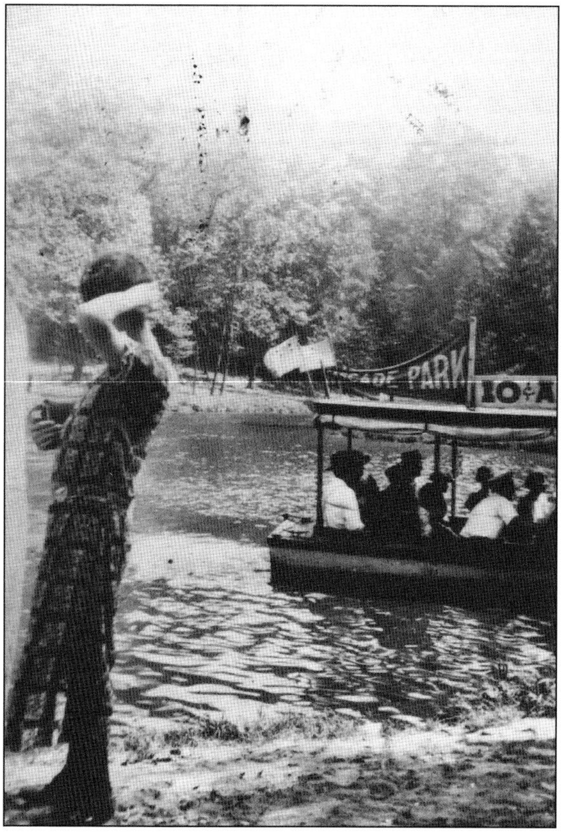

Boats for Rent, Early 1900s. The lake could be seen from the streetcars as riders approached the park. Sometimes called Crystal Lake, the expanse of water was the best destination for many people because it offered swimming, boating, racing, fishing, and, in the winter, ice-skating. The business of renting rowboats provided summer jobs for boys who were boat chasers. When a rowboat's time was up, the chaser would call the boat's number on a loudspeaker and announce, "Your time is up. Please come in." If the boat did not come in, the chaser would row out to bring in the tardy sailors, sometimes deliberately splashing them in the process. Families or other groups who preferred a leisurely ride could rent launches decorated with pennants and fancy canopies. Imagine sailing slowly around the lake at the end of a hot summer day, the setting sun cooling the air, and soft voices floating on the water. This was paradise for 10¢ an hour!

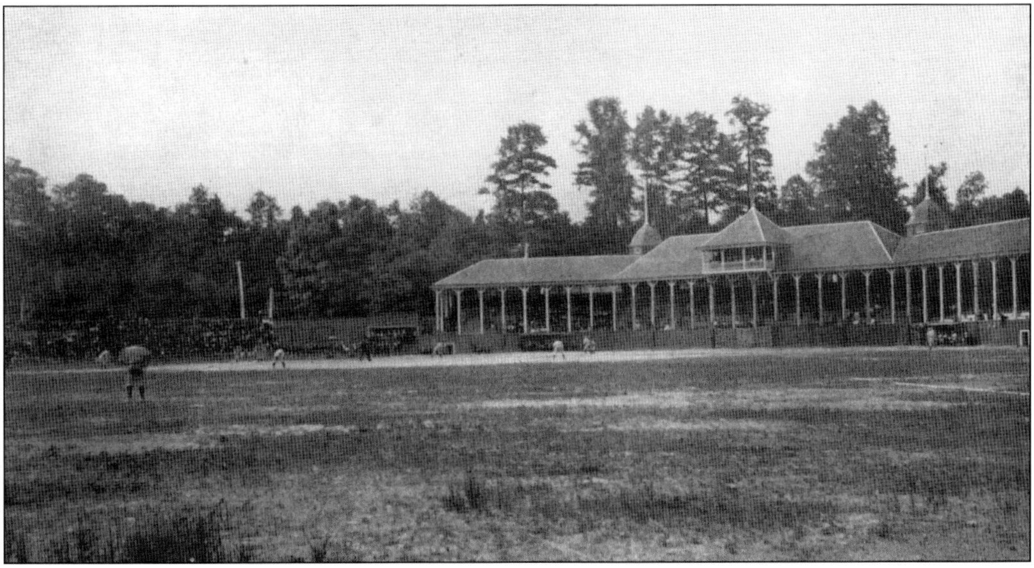

CASCADE PARK BALL FIELD, EARLY 1900S. The ball field was southwest of the field past the lake. The field opened in the summer of 1898 with 140 games scheduled with the Interstate League. Other games were with the Penn-Ohio League. The Quakers and the Knocks were two baseball teams using the field, and between 1918 and 1923, when it closed, the New Castle High School football team played there.

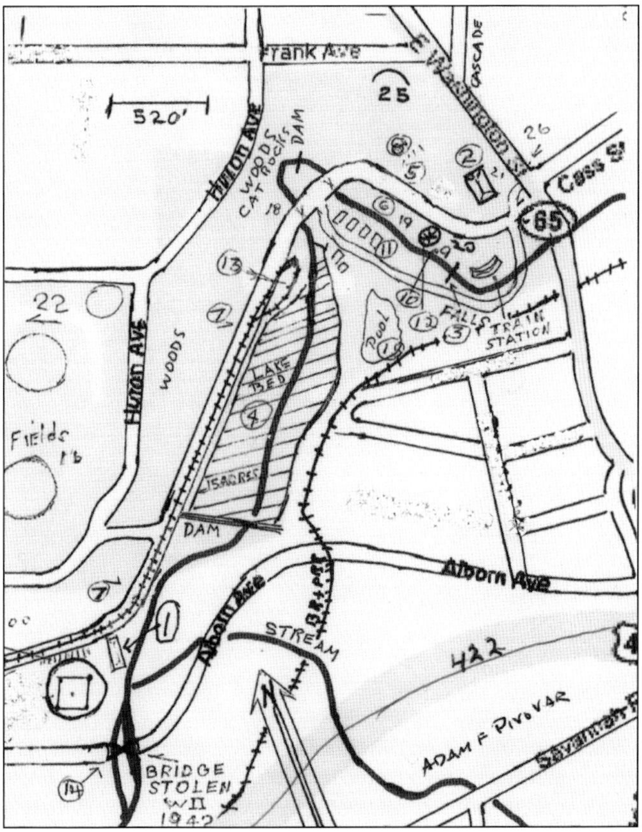

BALL FIELD AND HISTORIC FEATURES. Pictured here are the following: 1) ball field; 2) dance pavilion; 3) falls; 4) lake; 5) Ferris wheel; 6) Kiddieland, bocce; 7) streetcar; 8) first roller coaster; 9) Gorge; 10) Billy Glenn's house; 11) grove; 12) carousel; 13) streetcar turnaround; 14) bridge; 15) pool; 16) Deshon fields; 17) dam; 18) original entrance; 19) Fun House, Old Mill; 20) Dodg'em; 21) Caterpillar; 22) Centennial Field; 23) miniature golf; 24) Cat Rocks; 25) parking; and 26) 1934 entrance.

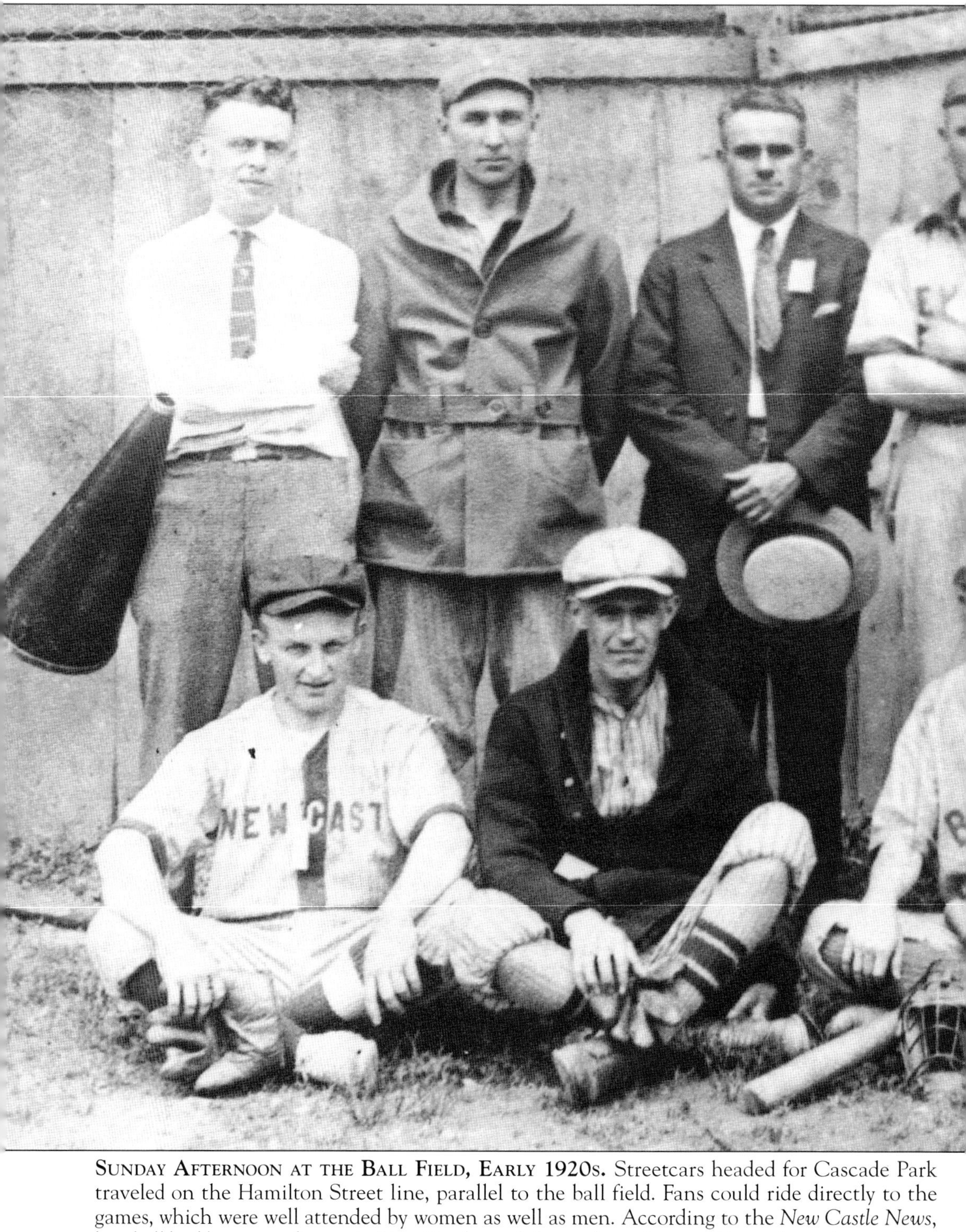

SUNDAY AFTERNOON AT THE BALL FIELD, EARLY 1920S. Streetcars headed for Cascade Park traveled on the Hamilton Street line, parallel to the ball field. Fans could ride directly to the games, which were well attended by women as well as men. According to the *New Castle News*, baseball had become a fixture in New Castle, and those who rode to and from the park were "sure to benefit by the pure air and change of scene." The team pictured here is not named, nor are

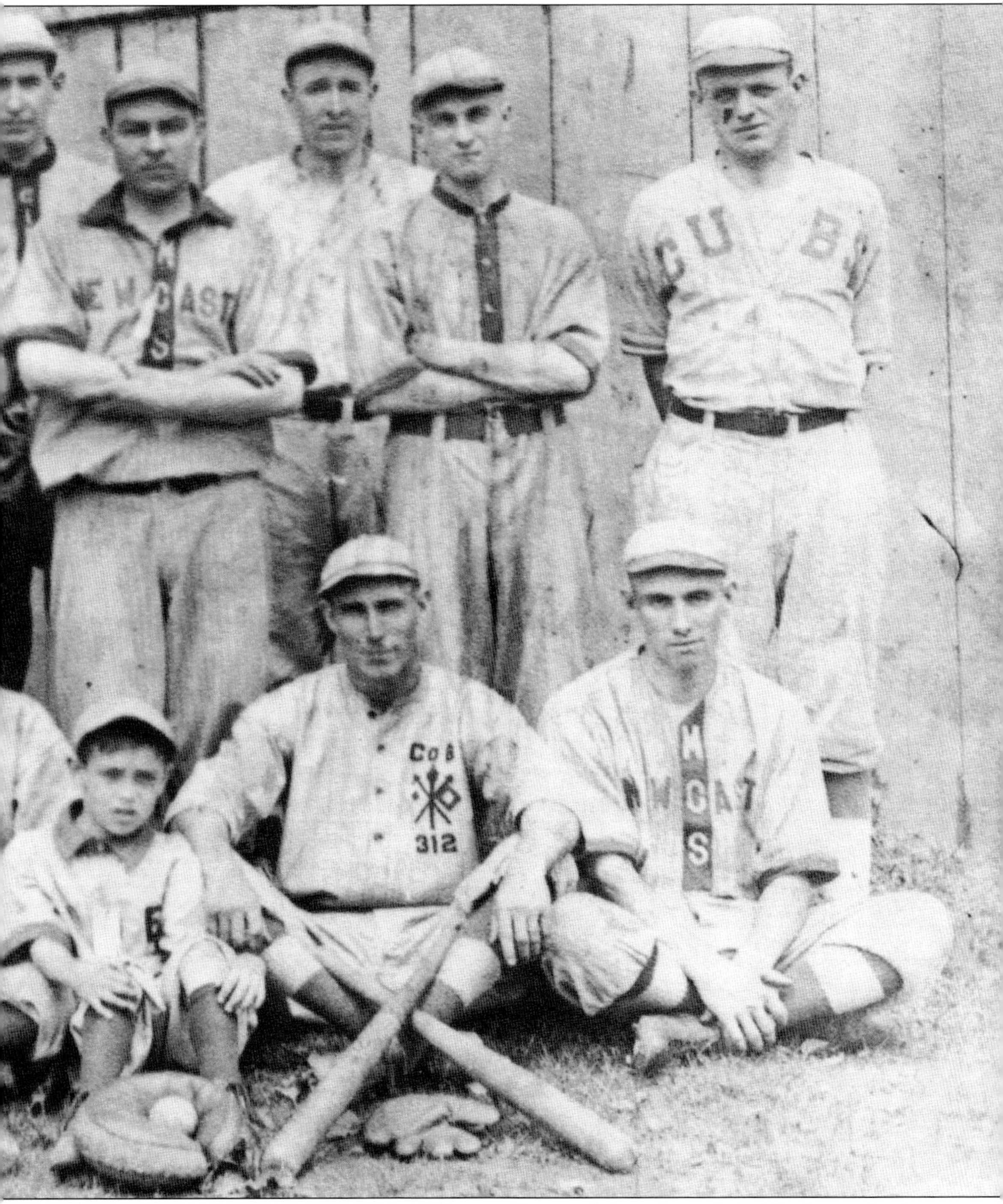

all players identified. Shown, from left to right, are (first row) first player, Jack Matthews; third, Joe Mescal; and fifth, ? Long; (second row) second, Pat Kerns; fourth, Bert Hite; and ninth, John Mariacher. Also shown in the photograph, but not identified, are Roy Davis, Chris Coulthard, Leroy Shoaf, and Ed Bender.

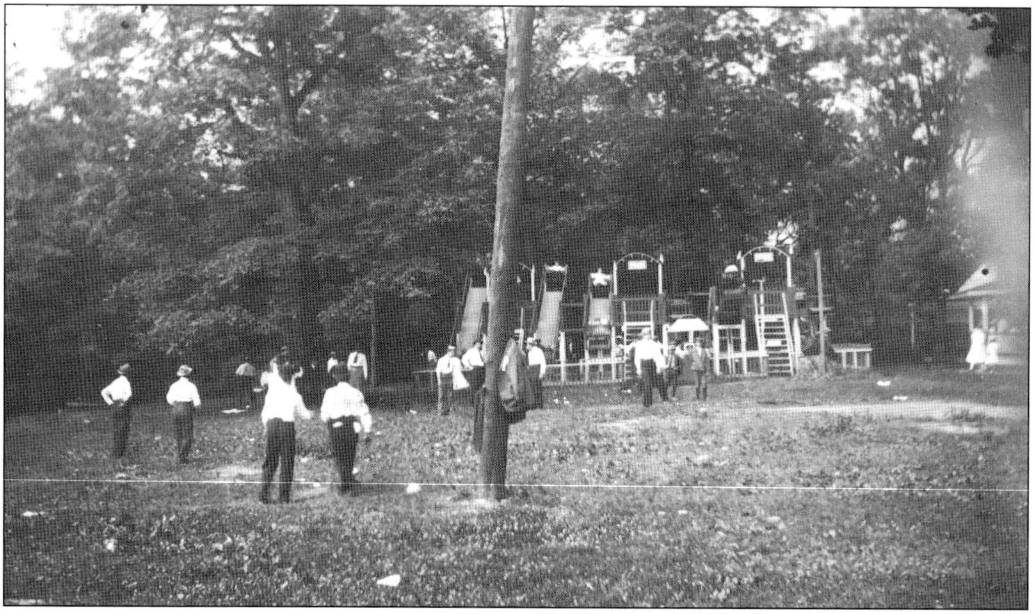

PITCHING HORSESHOES, EARLY 1900S. Pitching horseshoes was a traditional sport requiring very little equipment and a lot of grass. The park grounds were ideal for horseshoe tournaments. There was plenty of shade and plenty of space. In the background of this photograph is a children's play area, safely out of reach of the horseshoes. Historically, pitching horseshoes is related to quoits and the children's game of ringtoss.

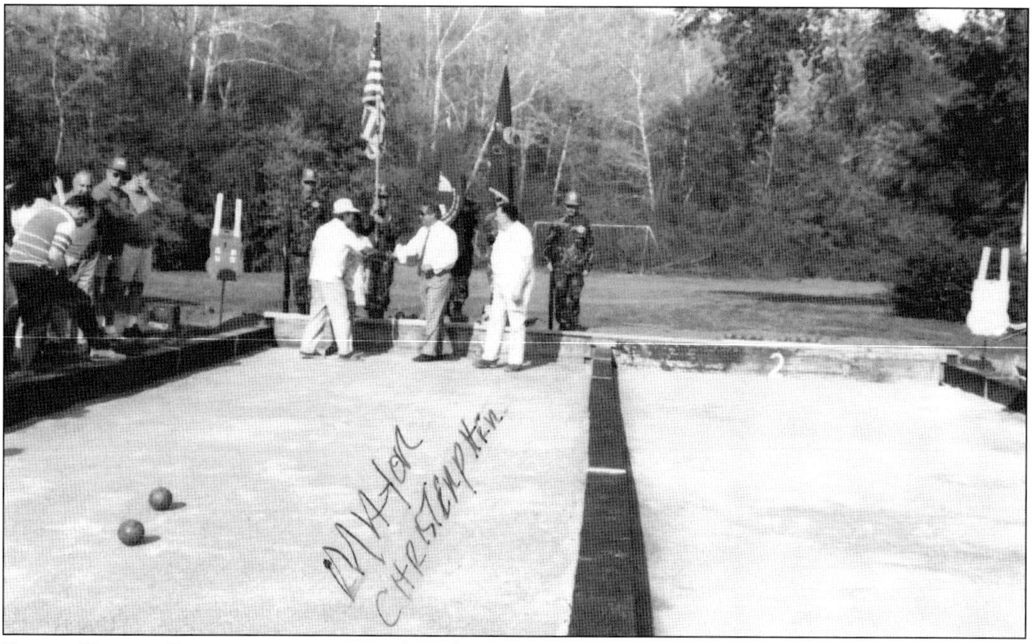

BOCCE COURTS INSTALLED, 1993. In this photograph taken at El Rio Beach, then-mayor Richard Christofer congratulates the Vincent Scungio Memorial Bocce League and promises that the city will provide new bocce courts at Cascade Park. Several courts are now in Cascade Park near the grove. Bocce, next to soccer and golf, has the third highest participation of world sports. (Courtesy of Frank Cavelli.)

Five

The Dance Pavilion

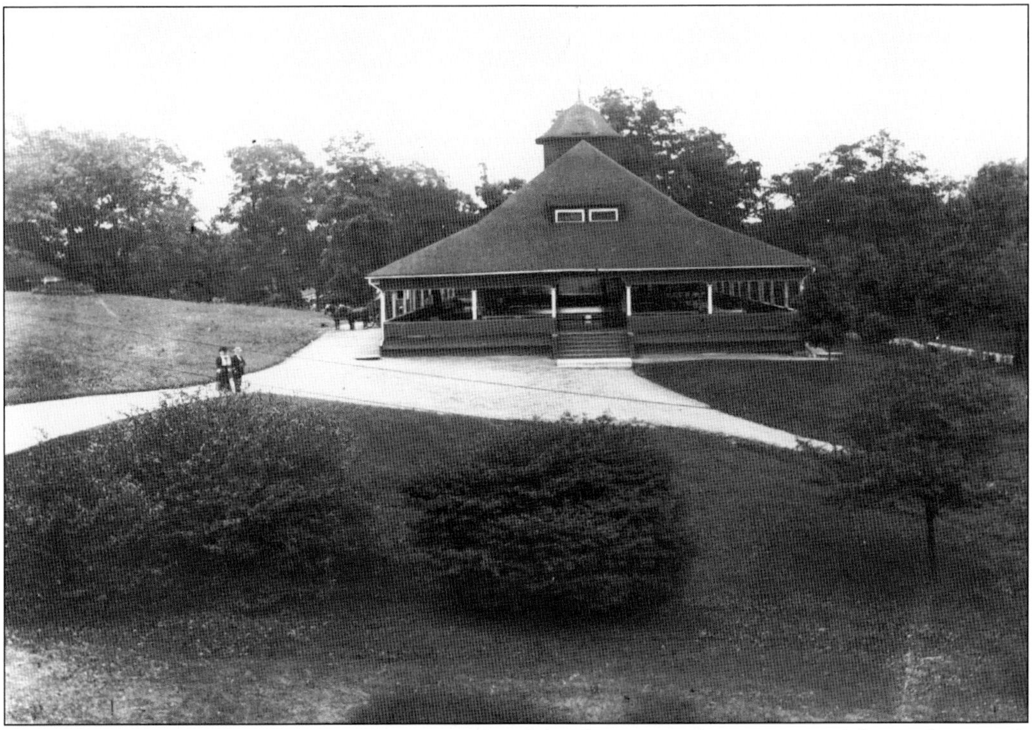

Dance Pavilion, early 1900s. From one side of the dance pavilion, a view of the midway with the rides, games, refreshment stands, and people milling about can be seen. The dance pavilion is a busy place, too. After more than 100 years, this gathering place still accommodates crowds for a variety of events.

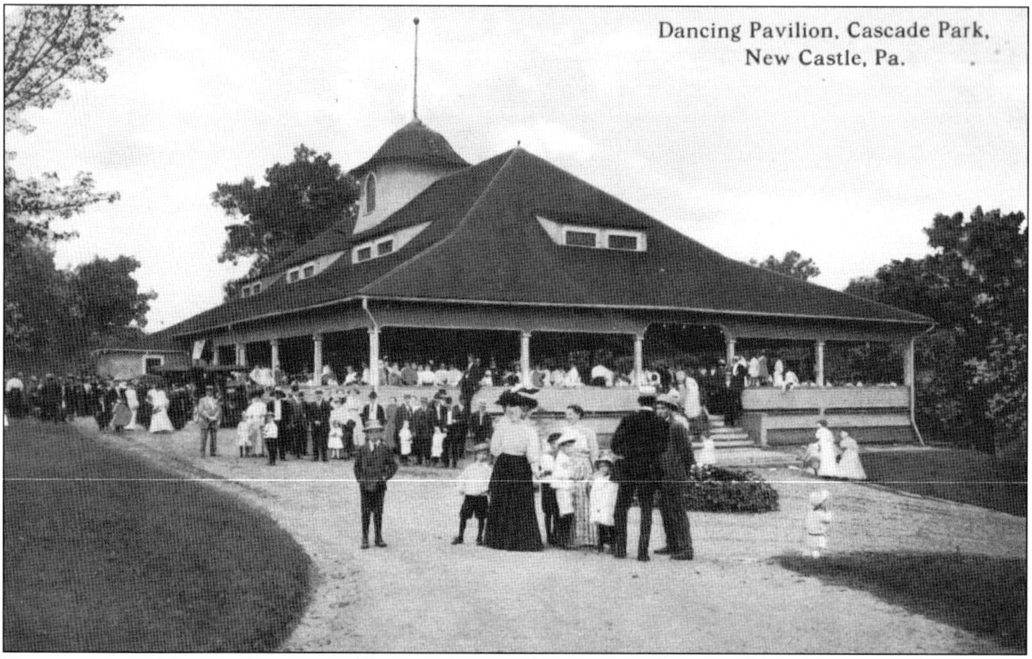

Event at the Dance Pavilion, Early 1900s. This postcard view of the dance pavilion shows visitors to the pavilion dressed in finery for an occasion. The building is inviting with its open-air windows, shingled sides, cupola, and dormers. The design conveys spaciousness, echoing the outdoor spaces of the park designed by landscape architect Frank Blaisdell.

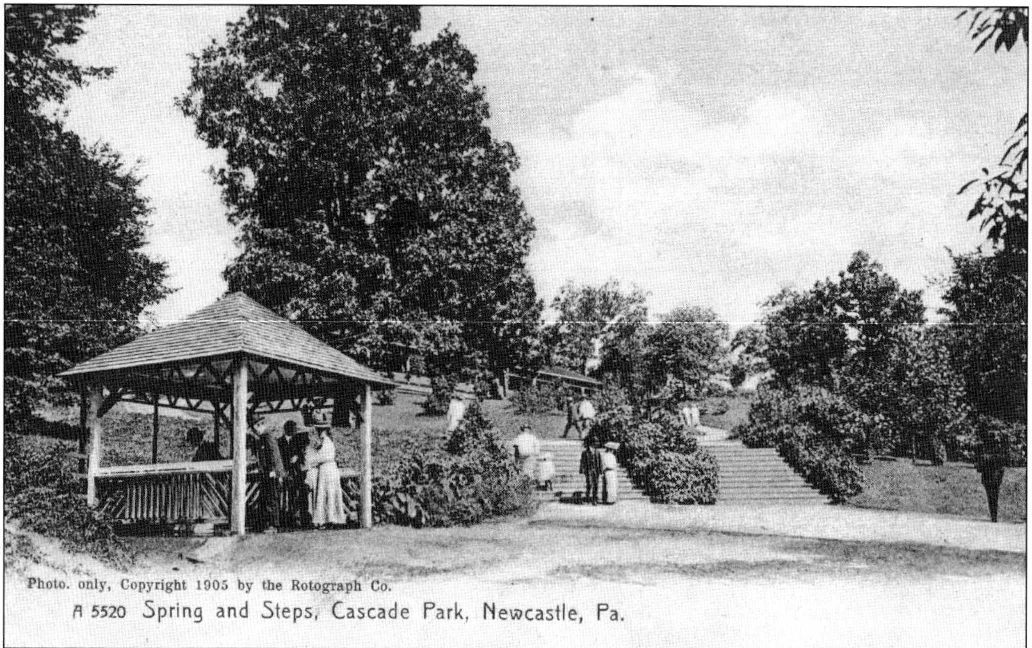

Spring and Steps at the Dance Pavilion, 1905. This postcard shows the dance pavilion sitting above the general traffic of Cascade Park. The steps were called "floral steps" because of their opulent plant borders. Under the gazebo is one of Cascade Park's many springs that offer refreshing cold water to thirsty visitors.

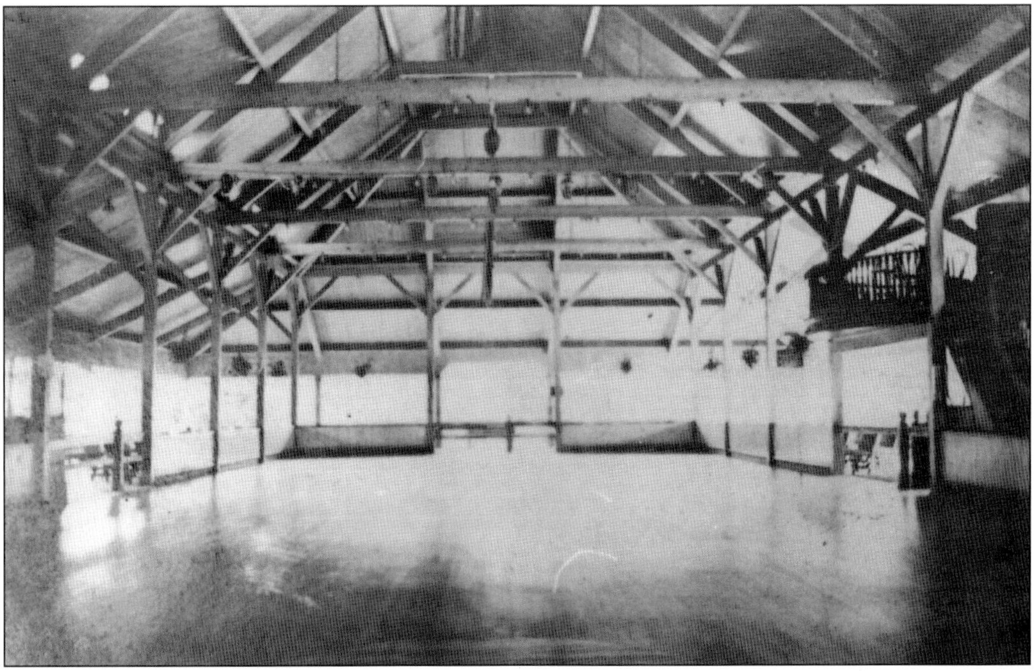

INTERIOR OF THE DANCE PAVILION, EARLY 1900S. This dance floor was designed to hold a crowd of dancers. It measured 156 feet long and 80 feet wide, one of the largest dance floors in western Pennsylvania. It was lit by 45 arc lights, and the open sides provided natural air-conditioning.

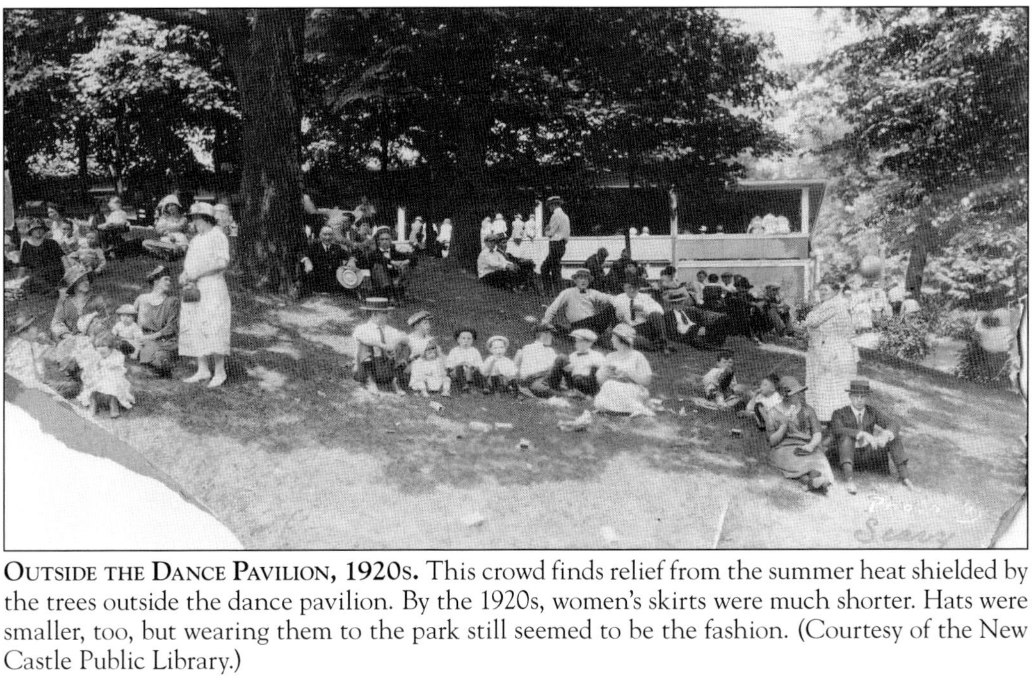

OUTSIDE THE DANCE PAVILION, 1920S. This crowd finds relief from the summer heat shielded by the trees outside the dance pavilion. By the 1920s, women's skirts were much shorter. Hats were smaller, too, but wearing them to the park still seemed to be the fashion. (Courtesy of the New Castle Public Library.)

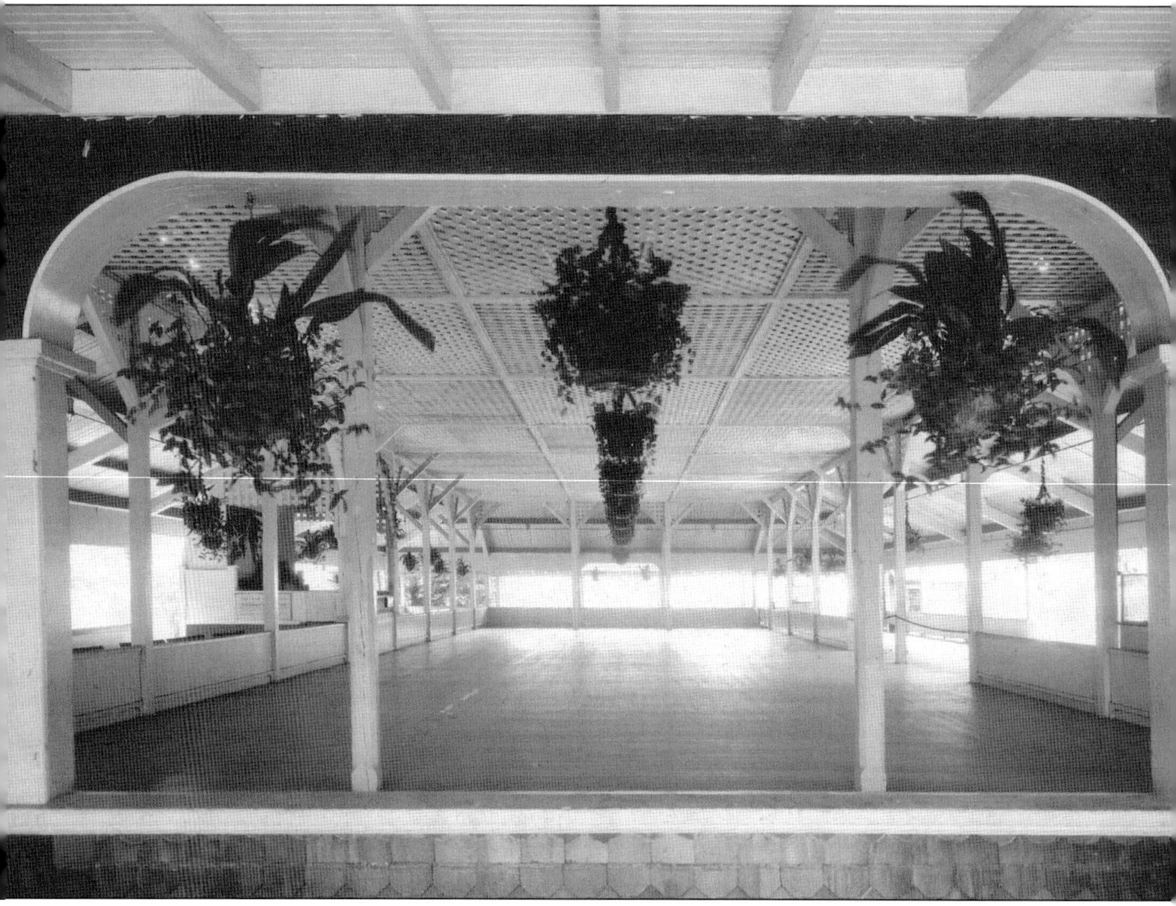

DECORATED DANCE PAVILION, EARLY 1930s. In this photograph, a bower of hanging greenery enhances the elegance of the Cascade Park dance pavilion. By the 1930s, the popular pavilion had reached maturity. Although park attendance had fallen off with the Depression, it was known as one of the largest dance floors in western Pennsylvania, and it had an active schedule of dances. Under the new management of the city, the pavilion was renamed Rainbow Terrace with local orchestras engaged for regular dances, and name bands such as Guy Lombardo, Red Nichols, and Vaughn Monroe were brought in for special occasions. Holidays, company picnics, and club gatherings brought in dancers, and more frequent newspaper ads reminded readers of weekly polka nights, Scotch nights, and ladies' nights. (Courtesy of the Mahoning Valley Historical Society, Mahoning Valley Regional Mass Transit Authority Collection.)

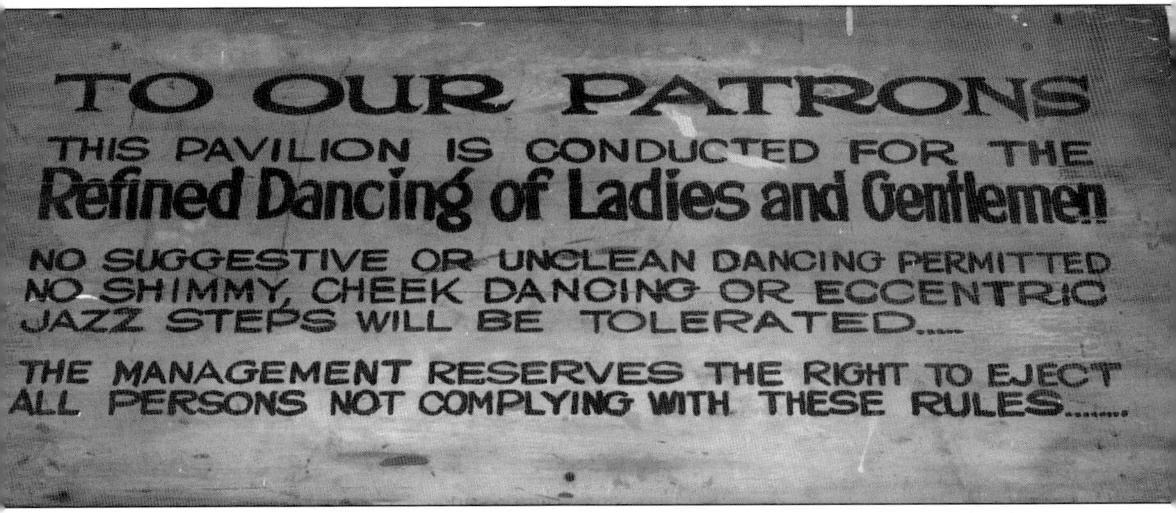

Sign in the Dance Pavilion, 2007. This sign was originally placed at the entrance to the dance pavilion (see previous photograph, left center). It was buried for many years, but in the 1970s, it was discovered under the floor when the pavilion was being improved. The sign was restored and now hangs high on a wall to the left of the pavilion's entrance. This kind of guidance became unnecessary in the 1930s and 1940s. With the exception of the Lindy and the jitterbug, the big band dances of that era were more sedate affairs. When a big name band was playing, couples danced close to the stage to catch a glimpse of the band leader and his musicians or to watch special events like a singing contest. Noted band leader Paul Whiteman was asked to judge one such singing contest. Admission was $1.10 per person for the event, and the band played from 9:00 p.m. to 2:00 a.m. The newspaper report did not reveal the winning song, but the winning singer was Florence Berry. (Courtesy of Adam Pivovar.)

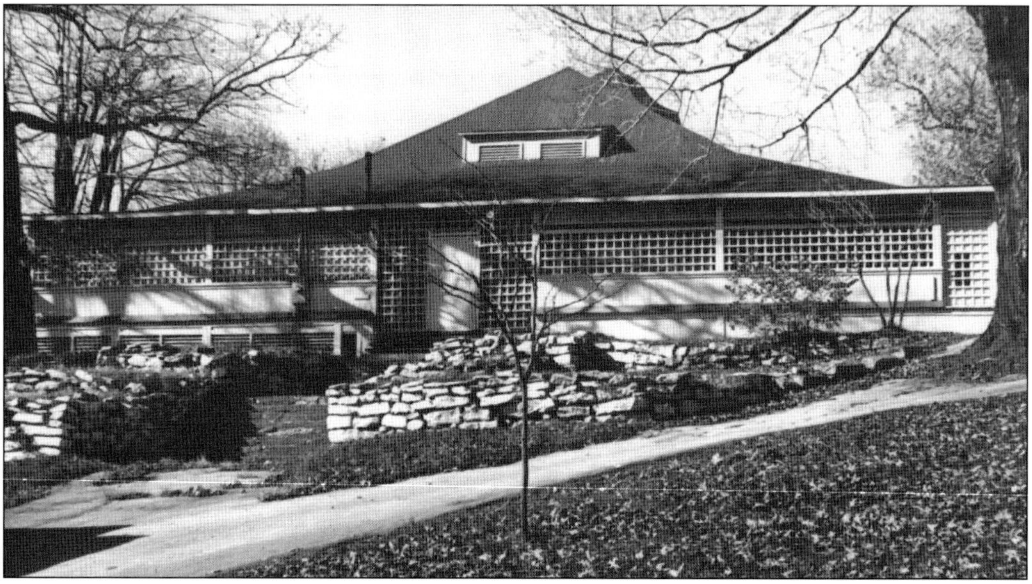

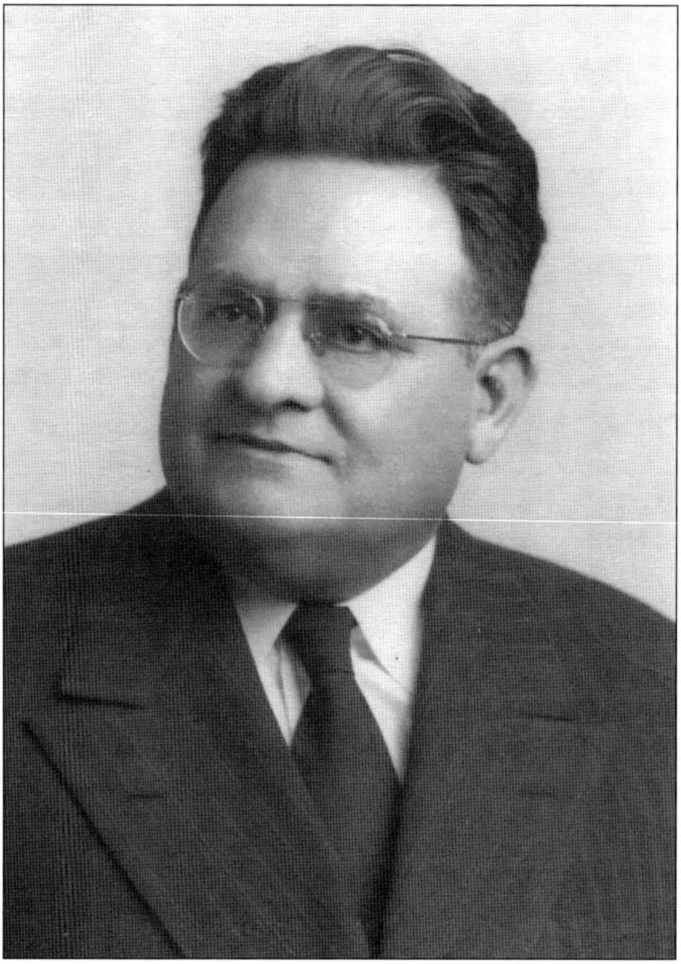

Dance Pavilion from the Midway, c. 1960s. This scene, empty of people, is a reminder that places as popular as the dance pavilion are occasionally deserted. For example, in 1905, on the evening of Labor Day, the orchestra played to an empty floor. The park had doubled its 25¢ admission charge to the pavilion and not one couple appeared.

B. J. Biondi, Manager, Rainbow Terrace, c. 1950. B. J. Biondi, often called "Be-Be," was a civic leader, businessman, and distinguished musician. An elected alderman, he was president of the Local 27 musicians' union for many years and was the longtime director of New Castle's Red Coat Band. Be-Be brought local and nationally known bands to the renamed dance pavilion. (Courtesy of Ray Micaletti.)

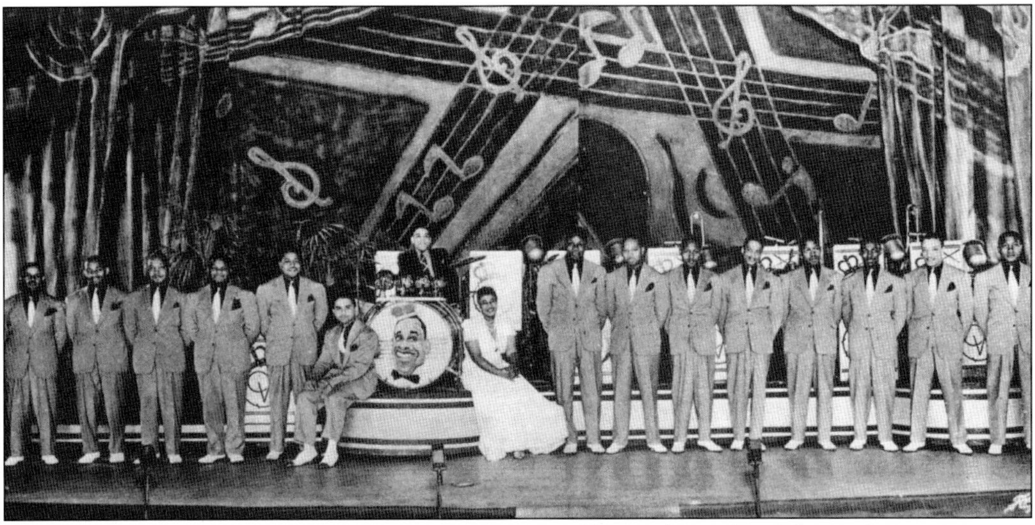

Chick Webb and Ella Fitzgerald, Late 1930s. Well into the 1950s, African Americans were restricted from Cascade Park except on special days called "colored days." In July 1938, black people would have to go to Idora Park to hear drummer and band leader Chick Webb and singer Ella Fitzgerald. Tickets for that show could be bought in advance at Fleming's Music Store in downtown New Castle for 85¢.

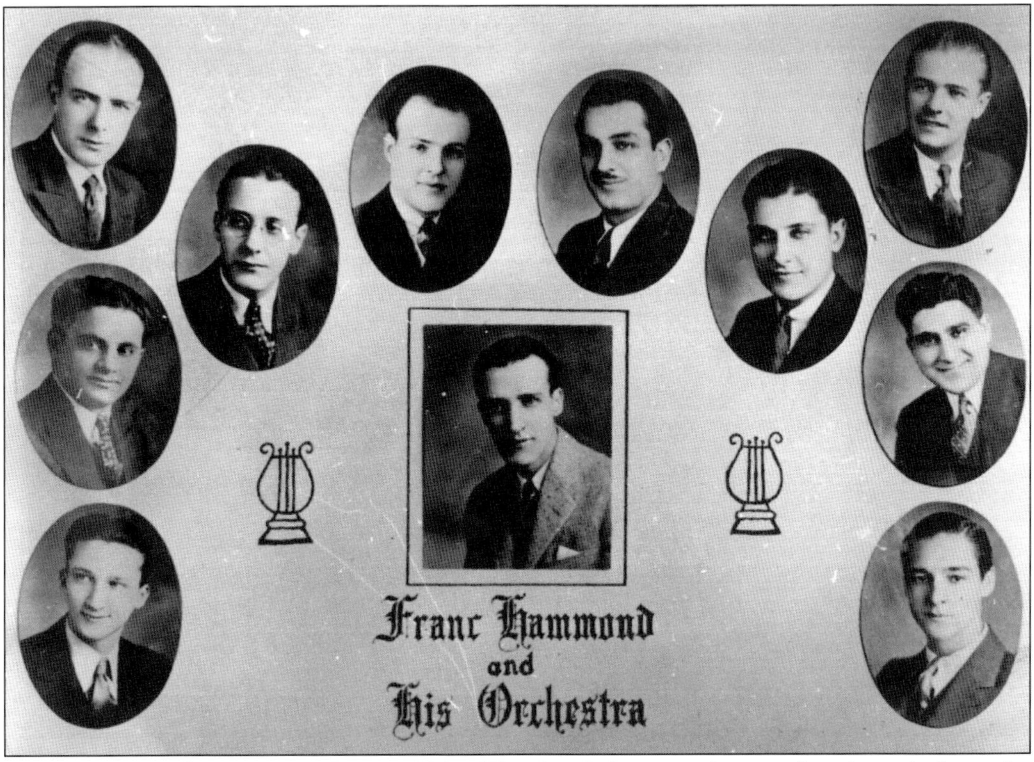

The Keystone Serenaders, Late 1930s. This local dance orchestra played regularly at the dance pavilion. "Franc" or Francis Hammond (center) and his brother Harry (left, with glasses) were both accomplished musicians. Others identified in this photograph are Jack Treser (lower left), John Bonfield (center left), and Hugo Caiazza (center right).

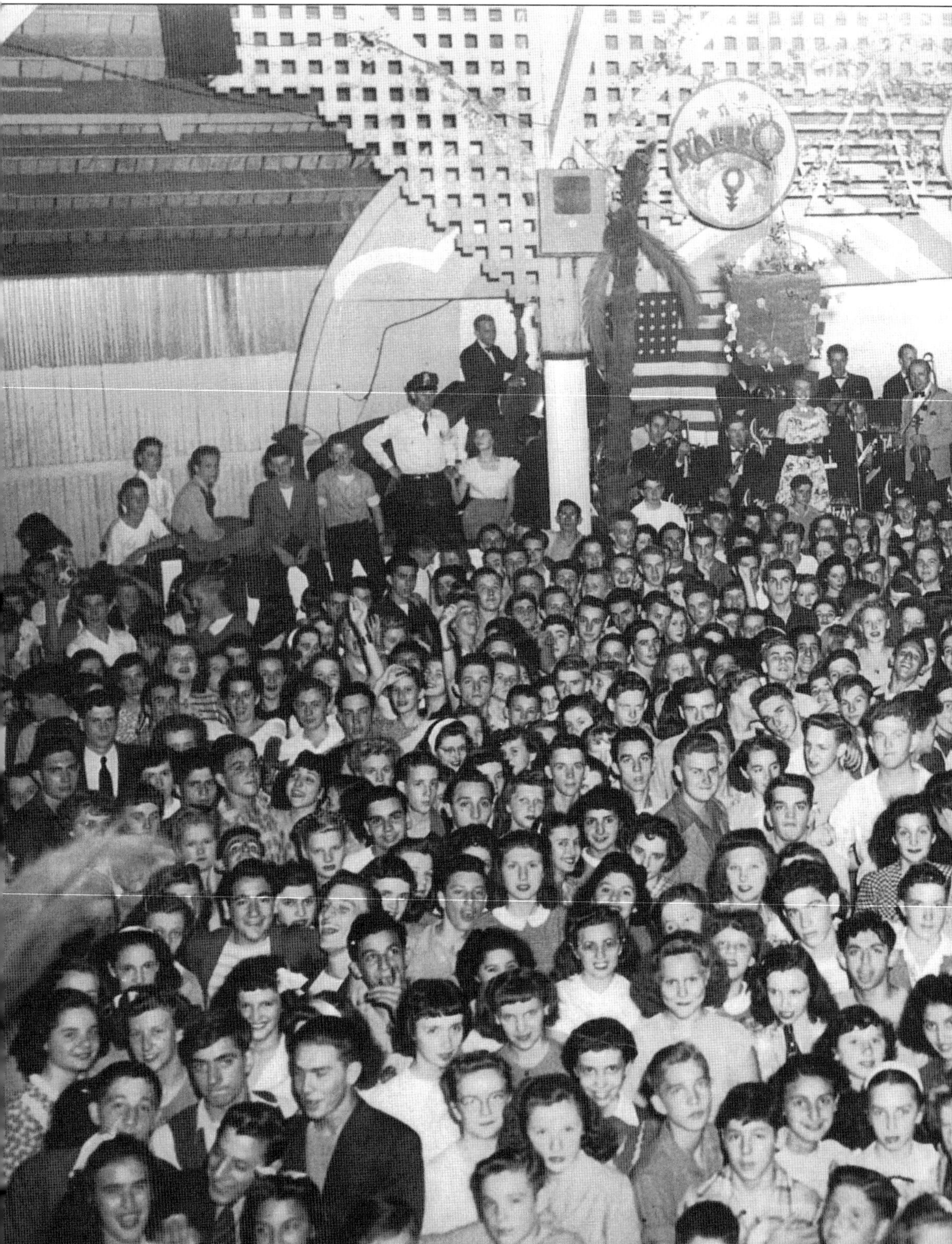

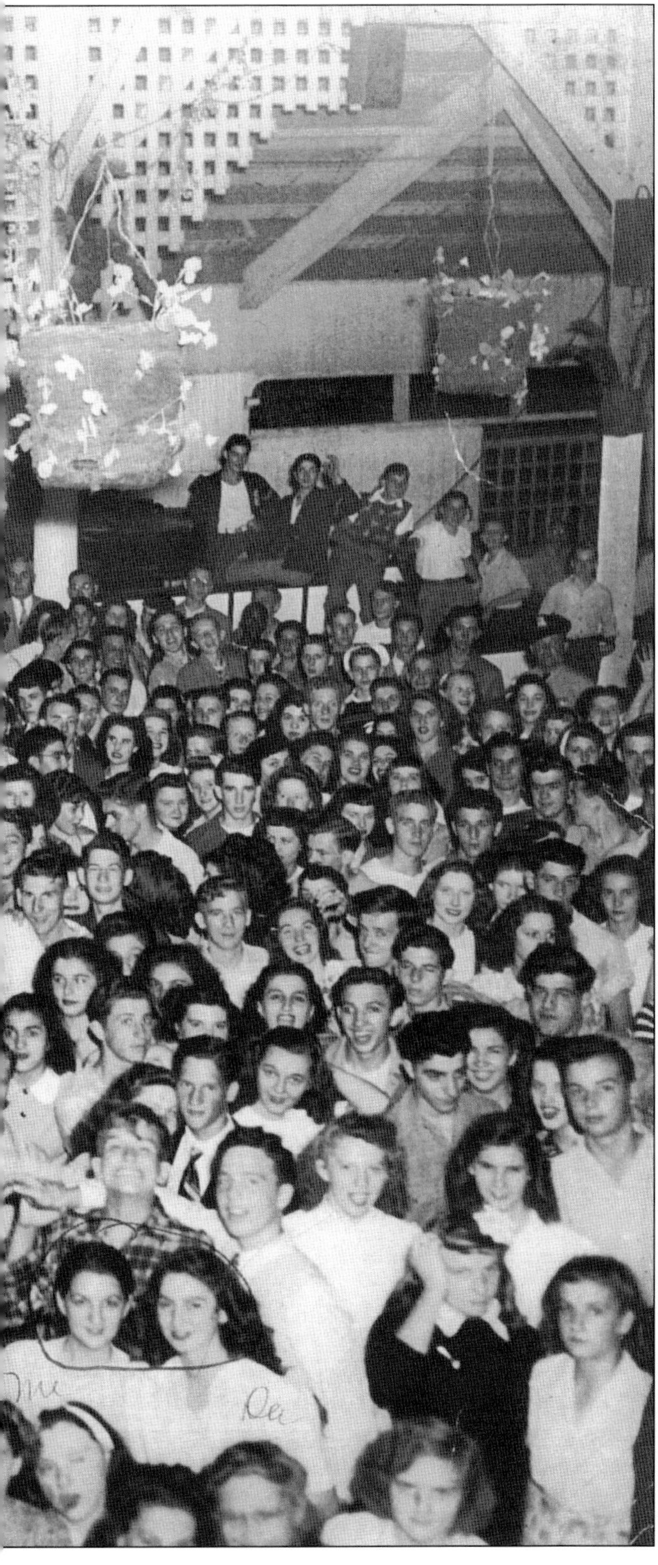

Swing Lobby, c. 1948. Swing Lobby started back in the 1940s when piano tuner Victor Wagner played records for dancing on the second floor of downtown's city hall. Then-mayor John Haven asked police lieutenant Cecil Suber to organize the event as part of a city recreation project. In the summer, the dances moved to Cascade Park's dance pavilion, where capacity crowds from New Castle and surrounding communities turned out on Mondays and Fridays. From time to time, the format of the dances changed; square dance lessons were introduced, and local musicians offered free dances with live music. In 1949, city government moved to its new building on North Jefferson Street, and for the following school months, Swing Lobby continued at the American Legion hall and the New Castle High School gymnasium. The popularity of these dances continues today in the form of annual reunions arranged by volunteer supporters. (Courtesy of Kathryn Francazio.)

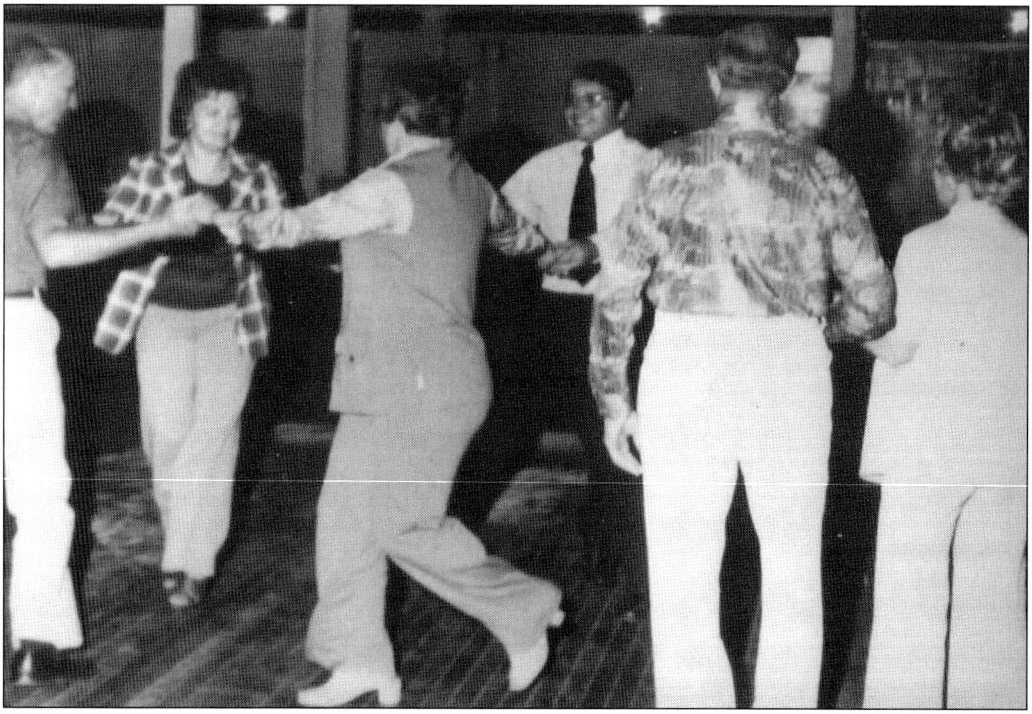

The Castle Paws and Taws. The Castle Paws and Taws is a square dance group that was organized in the early 1970s. When, on a rainy evening in 1976, they moved from the local business college to Cascade Park's dance pavilion, they found a water-soaked dance floor. When they heard that the deteriorated pavilion might be demolished, member Jim Riggans enlisted the Rotary Club and committees to help with fundraising. They collected $50,000; equipment, paint, and supplies from local businesses; and labor from local schools. The top photograph, dated 1976, shows dancing on the pavilion floor before restoration. The bottom photograph shows the interior of the pavilion several years after the restoration. In addition to square and ballroom dancing, the pavilion can be reserved for events such as the annual dinner of the Lawrence County Historical Society. (Both, courtesy of Bobbie Gibson.)

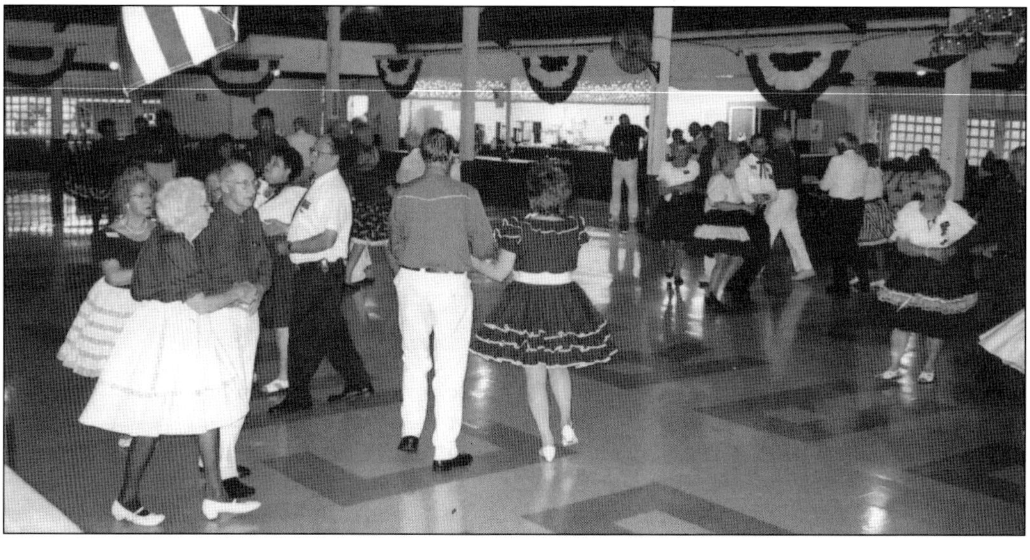

Six

Events

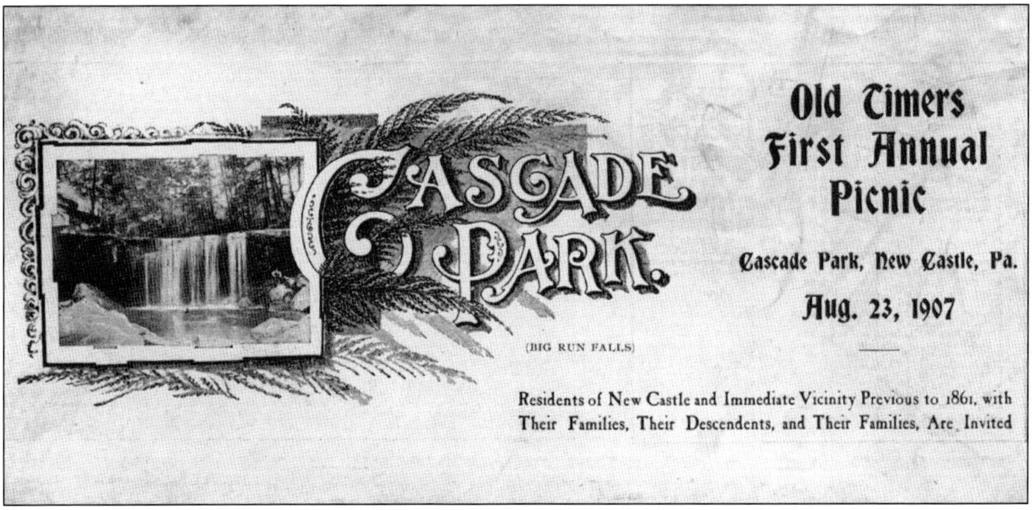

Old Timers First Annual Picnic. Cascade Park had been operating for 10 years by the time the first Old Timers Picnic took place. A number of committees were formed for the event. Perry Barge, park superintendent, chaired the men's refreshment committee, and Mrs. George Greer (Alice), wife of the owner of the tin mill, chaired the women's refreshment committee. The largest committee was the Reminiscence Committee with 90 members, all of whom were men.

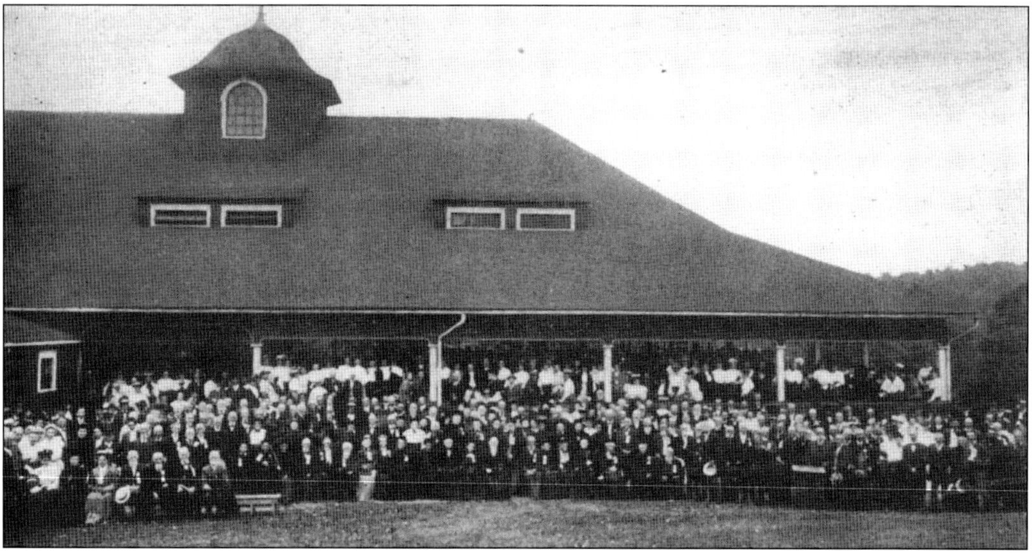

OLD TIMERS FIRST ANNUAL PICNIC, 1907. The first Old Timers day drew 7,000 people, many pictured here at the dance pavilion. The second year drew 11,000 people, and by 1909, the third year, the number was 17,000. Numbers are smaller now, but the picnic is still held each August, with 2010 marking its 104th year. The Grand March and the Waltz Contest remain on the program, but reminiscing is still the main activity.

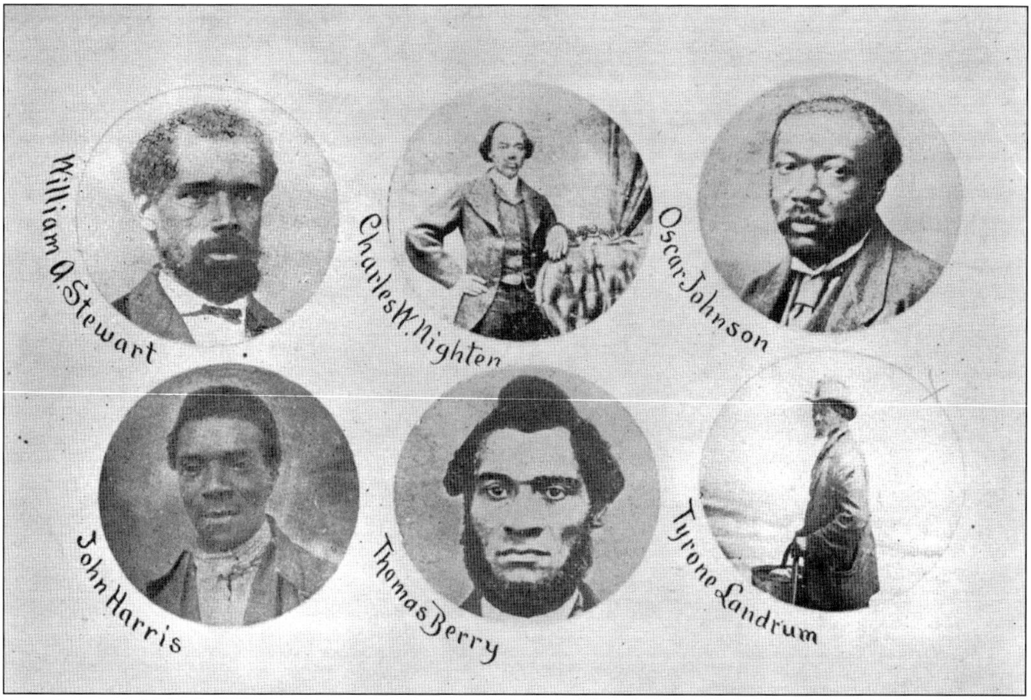

OLD TIMERS FIFTH ANNUAL PICNIC, 1911. These pictures of distinguished African American men appeared in the program for the fifth Old Timers Picnic. They are, clockwise from top left, William Stewart, Charles W. Nighten, Oscar Johnson, Tyrone Landrum, Thomas Berry, and John Harris. They were among the 300 citizens the program described as "people who laid the foundations of New Castle, and who were prominent and influential in their day."

THE 36th ANNUAL REUNION

You are cordially invited to attend the 36th Annual Picnic of the **Old Timer's Association, at Cascade Park, New Castle, Pa.,** on **Wednesday, August 19th, 1942.**

Program Starts Promptly at 1:30 P. M.

Grand March will take place in the Pavilion at 2 P. M.

Executive Committee:—Richard F. Dana, President; Fred L. Rentz, O. H. P. Green, Fred B. Sankey, Vice-Presidents; Fred Paul Butz, Treasurer; Herbert S. Kirk, Secretary; R. H. Whaley, Frank H. Robinson, Guy J. Wadlinger, James K. Love, Samuel DeGraff Pearson, Alex Crawford Hoyt, George S. Long, S. Reed Megown, Sam H. McGoun, Robert H. Cunningham, Thomas H. Hartman, Harry G. Preston, Louis G. Genkinger, James Mayberry, J. Cam Liebendorfer, Louis P. Dean, Leo G. Griffiths.

P. S.—The Reynoldstown Annual Reunion will be held Tuesday, Aug. 18th, 1942, in Epworth Church.
Reception 5:00 P. M., Supper 6:00 P. M.

OLD TIMERS DAY, 1942. Old Timers picnics started in 1907. The original idea was to bring together people who had lived in and around New Castle before 1861. Guests were expected to bring their families. By 1942, the invitation, seen here, called the picnic a reunion, and it did not limit attendance by age. The invitation went out on a penny postcard.

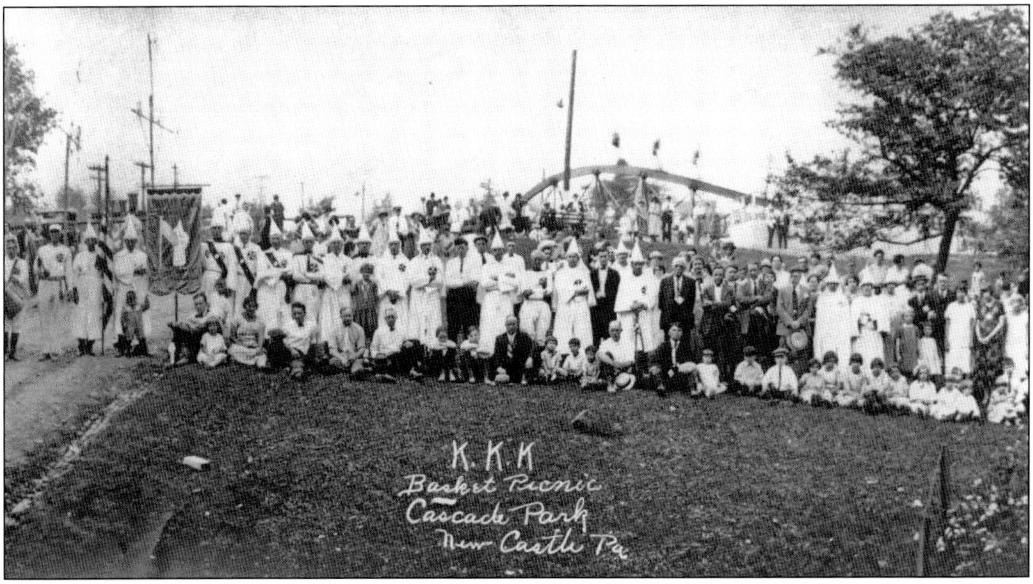

KU KLUX KLAN BASKET PICNIC, EARLY 1920S. The Ku Klux Klan held a major parade in downtown New Castle in the 1920s, when many citizens were becoming aware of what the Klan represented. The photograph shows a gathering of Klan members and their families at a picnic at Cascade Park.

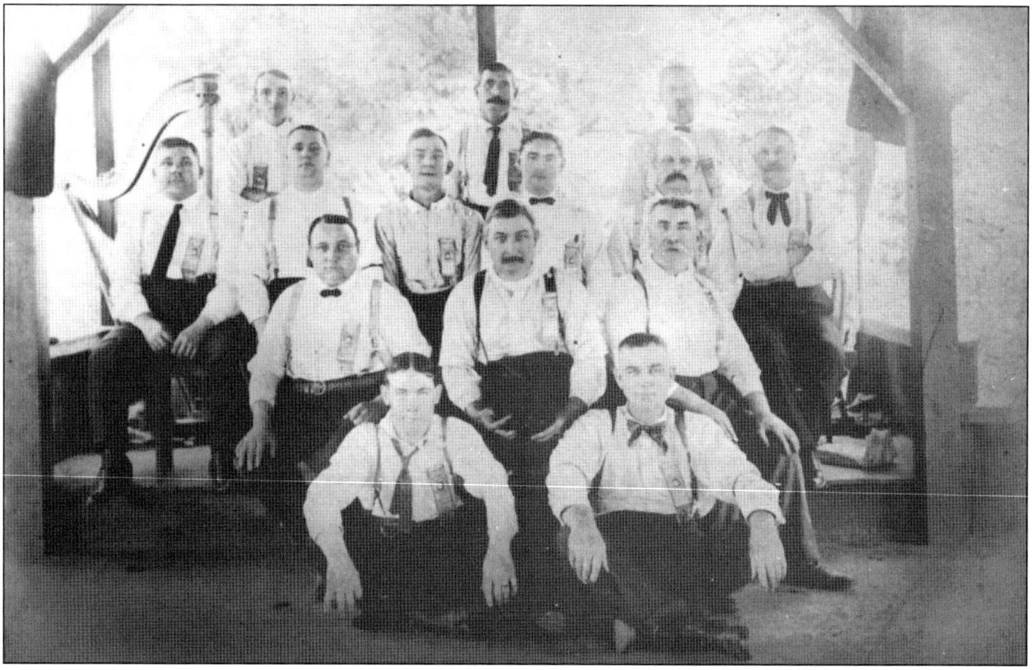

BARTENDERS PICNIC, 1908. Given the prosperity and level of employment in New Castle in 1908, trade unions and other occupational groups were numerous. Such groups often chose Cascade Park for picnics and other events. The group in this photograph shows white-shirted bartenders who, though usually hardworking, appear relaxed for the day.

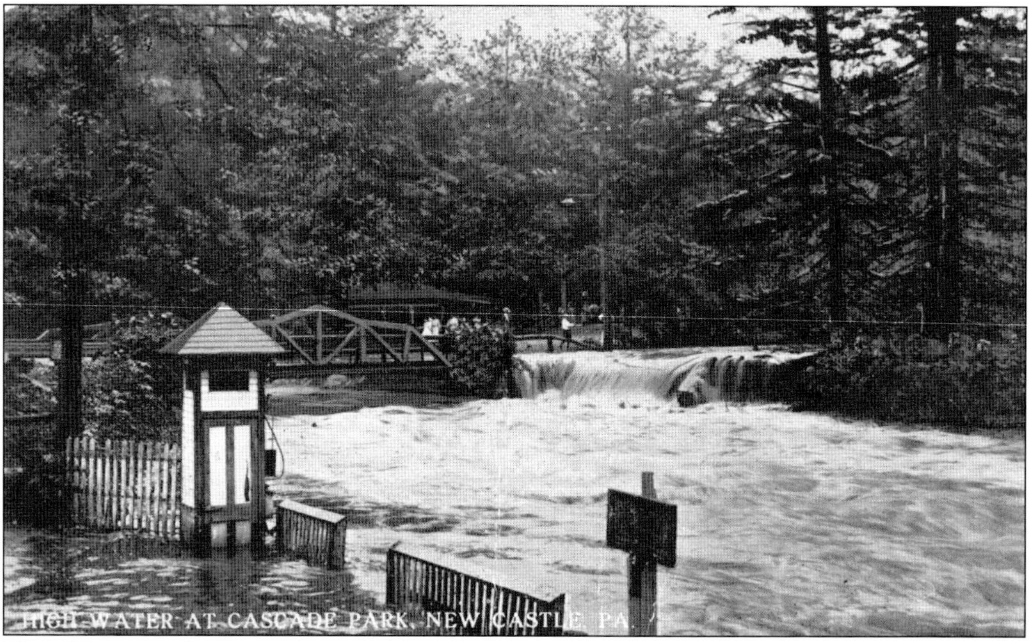

HIGH WATER AT CASCADE PARK, C. 1913. This event was unforgettable. The Shenango River and the Neshannock Creek in downtown New Castle had flooded the city in late March 1913. Like the downtown streams, Big Run also had high water, and scenes like this one could be observed throughout the park. This postcard is postmarked May 13, 1913.

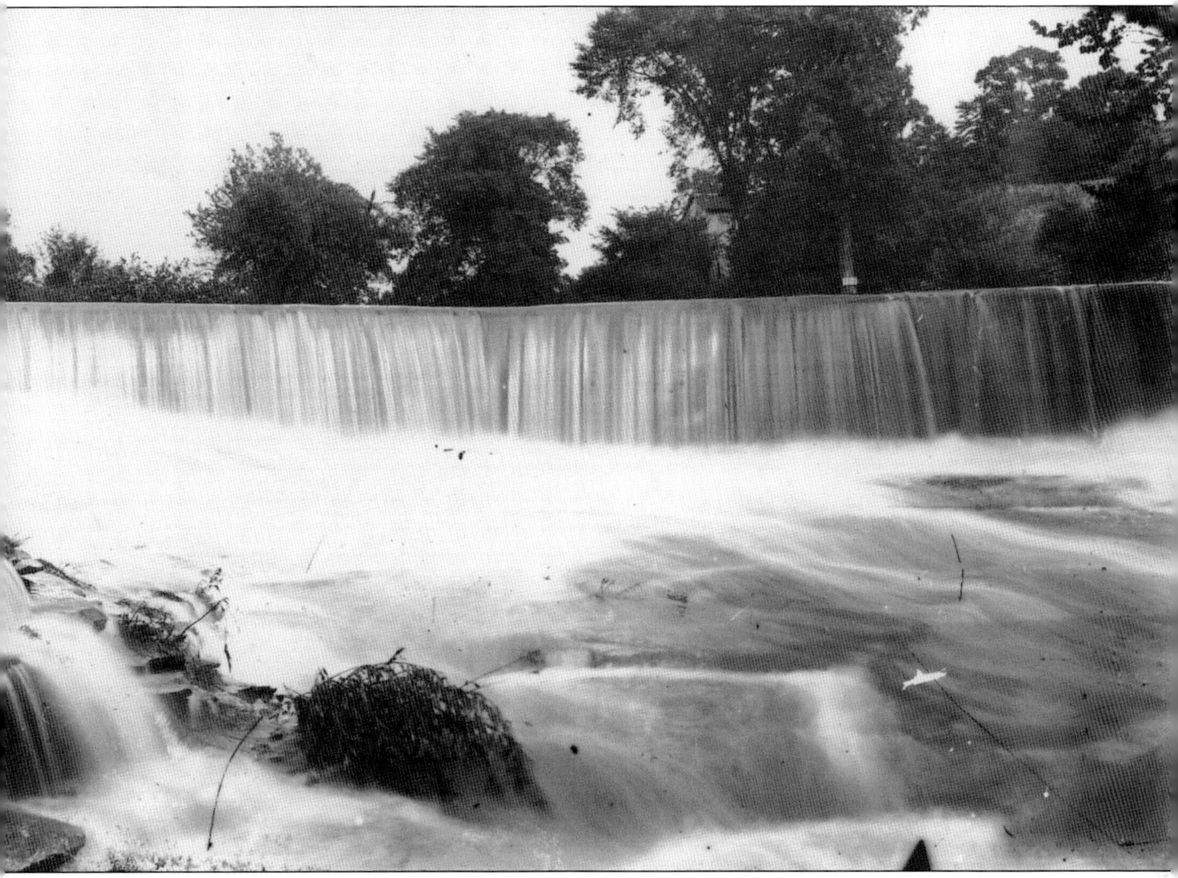

CASCADING FALLS, C. 1913. The deluge that afflicted the downtown streets of New Castle fell on Big Run. And when Big Run got high, its rushing water became a torrent. This would be the time to see and hear the falls and, if one owned a camera, to take a picture of the racing waters.

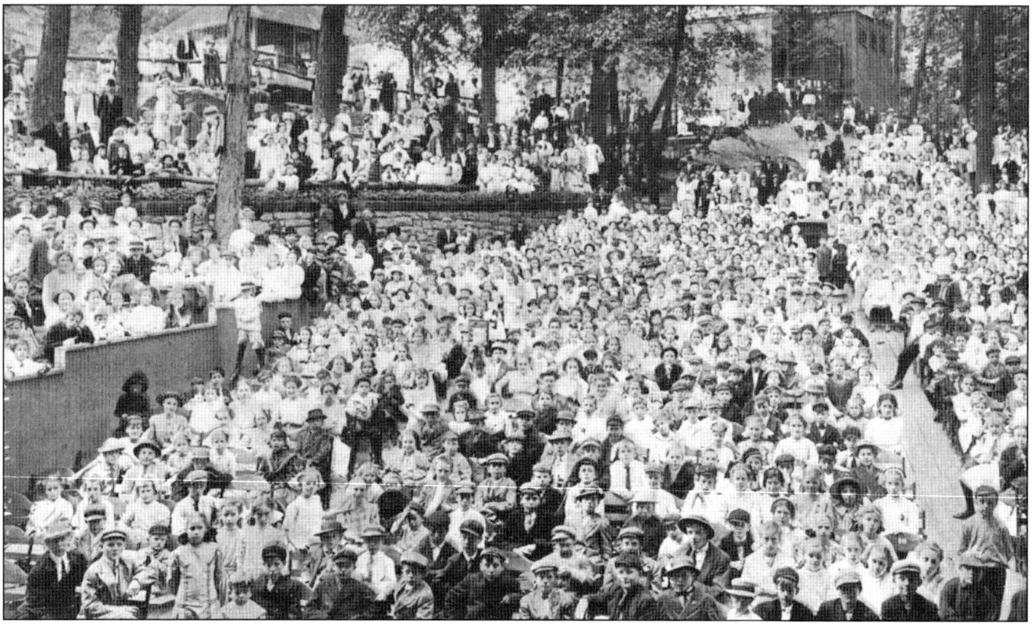

Public School Picnic, c. 1909. This postcard shows schoolchildren sitting in the open-air theater on the main walk of Cascade Park. Admission to this annual school picnic was free. All children were given tickets entitling them to free rides and amusements. Teachers were encouraged to be on hand for the event.

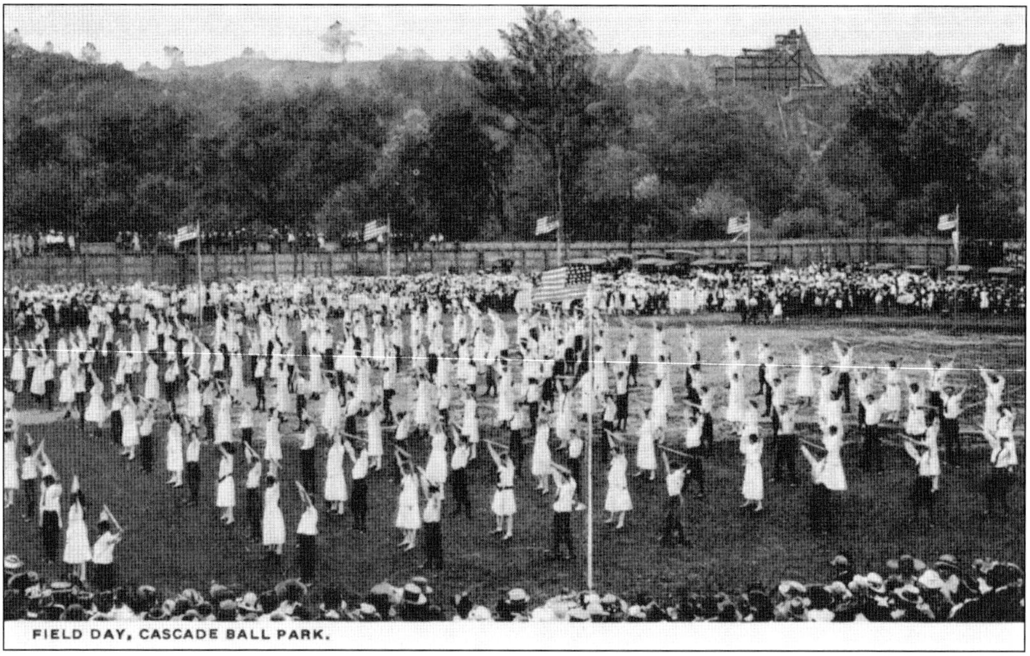

Field Day at the Cascade Ball Park, 1915. This postcard shows the public schools' first field day, an event in which 2,000 schoolchildren performed for 7,000 parents. All the seats in the grandstand and bleachers were filled. While the Duke of Abruzzi band played, the children performed with flags, dumbbells, intricate formations, and marching drills. Grades were identified by the color of their hair ribbons and ties.

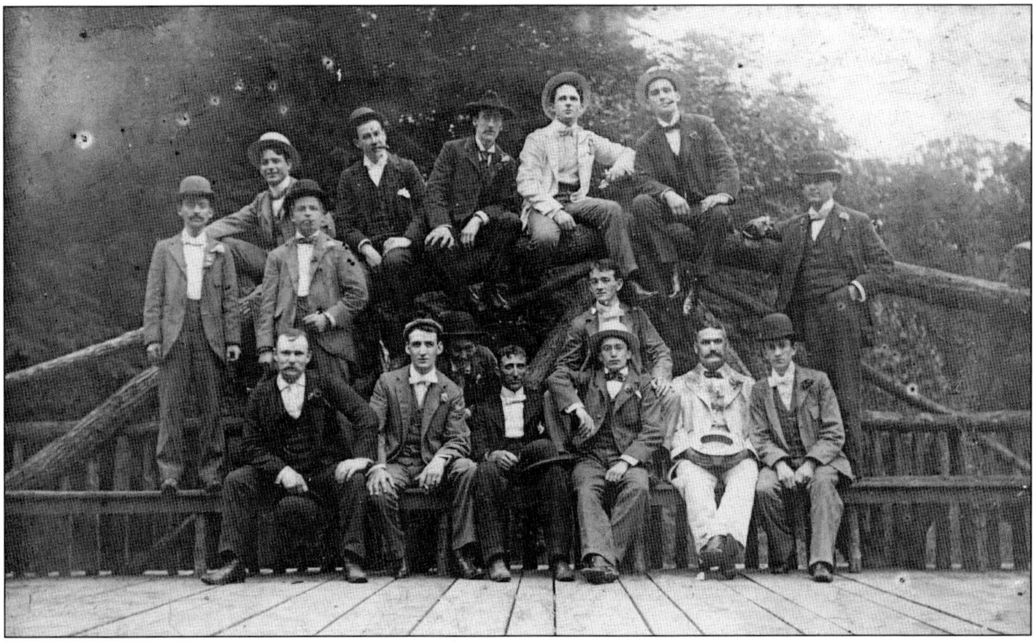

Men's Picnic, 1919. This photograph of a group of men enjoying a summer day at Cascade Park shows a good close-up of one of the park's rustic bridges. The logs are sturdy, and the fencing is supportive. Note the men's cigars. They are good indicators that the men are relaxed and having a good time at this special event.

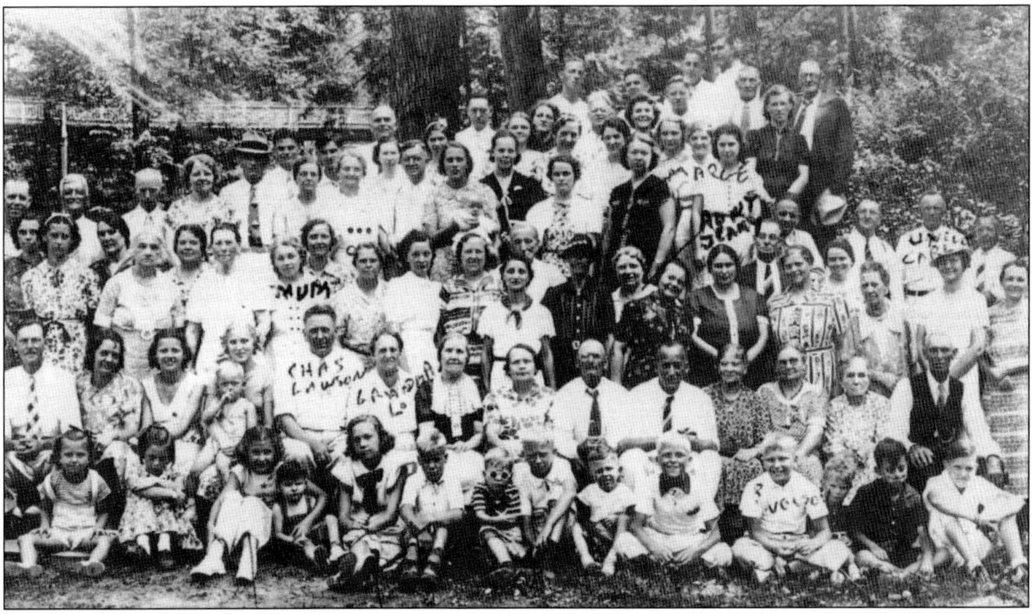

Lawson-Strahl Family Reunion, 1938. Charles Lawson of Erie (first row of adults, sixth from the left) was the host of the annual Lawson-Strahl reunions. In 1938, the reunion moved to Cascade Park (above) from the previous year's event at the downtown police station. The colorful family included railroad workers, furniture manufacturers, and the owner of Grandpa's Soap Company, who employed Tim Hennessey, a well-known citizen of downtown New Castle. (Courtesy of Don Lawson.)

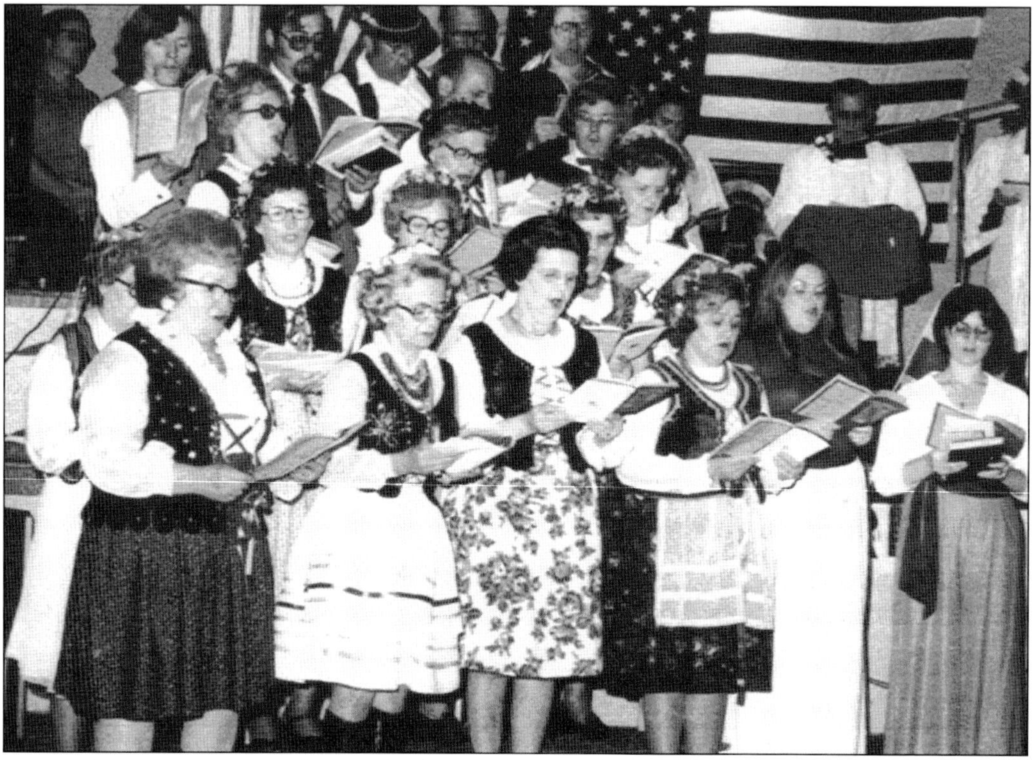

Polish Day at Cascade Park, 1976. In 1976, hundreds of Polish Americans gathered at Cascade Park to celebrate the American Bicentennial with cultural and religious programs. The Polish Day celebration became a yearly event, which continues to take place in September of each year under the sponsorship of the American Polish Central Committee. (Courtesy of Bernadette Przybylski.)

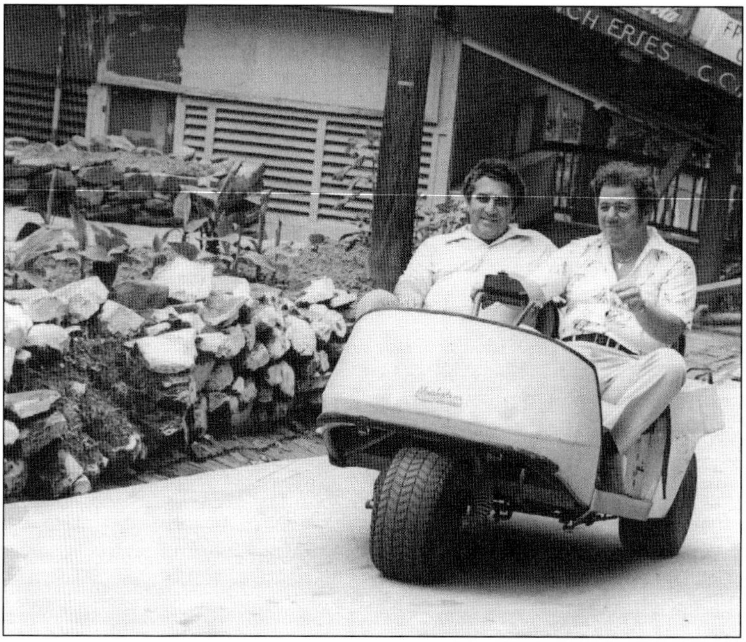

Italian Day at Cascade Park, 1979. Three men served as cochairmen of the Fourth Annual Italian Day, Pete "Figo" Carvella, Joe DeLillo, and Sam Marino. In this photograph, DeLillo (left) and Marino ride past the French fries stand ahead of visitors coming from the grove. The day's activities included children's races, mandolin music, a concert by the Red Coat Band, fireworks, and the crowd favorite, the Gong Show.

CIVILIAN CONSERVATION CORPS, 2009. In 1933, congress established the Civilian Conservation Corps (CCC) to provide work and vocational training to unemployed single men during the Depression. Membership was voluntary, and the men were paid $30 a month. Three million men joined the corps. They were trained to perform many services: building roads, repairing dams, planting trees, and conserving and developing natural resources in general. The program ended in 1942. The statue in this photograph is the result of a fundraising effort by former CCC members, New Castle Chapter 125. They went door to door for donations and secured city and state grants. The bronze statue by sculptor Derek McEvers was dedicated in the year 2000. In 2007, it was moved from an area close to the dance pavilion and placed near the carousel building. (Both, courtesy of Adam Pivovar.)

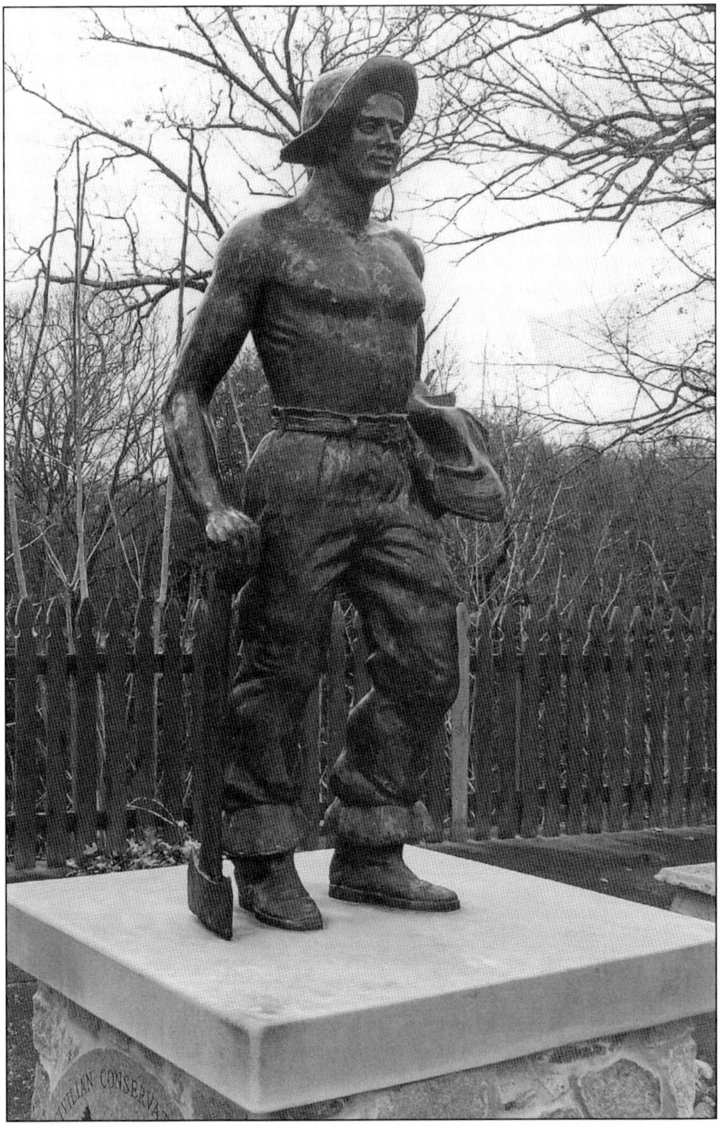

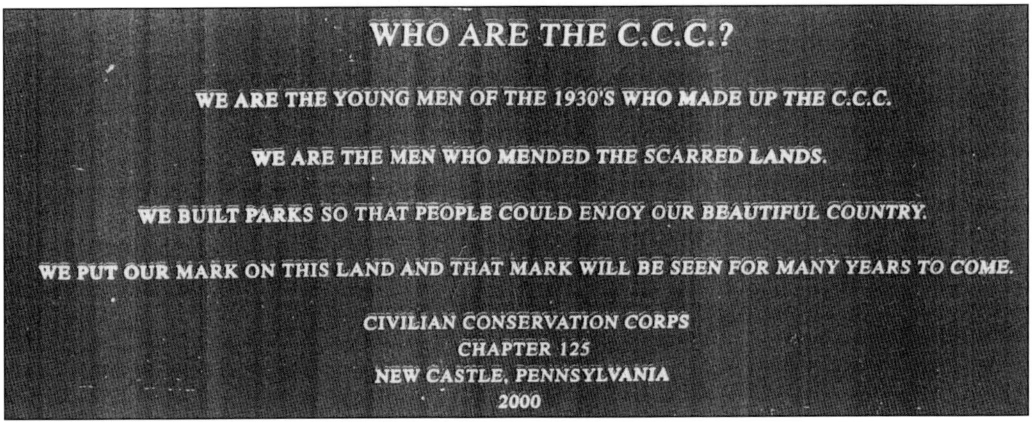

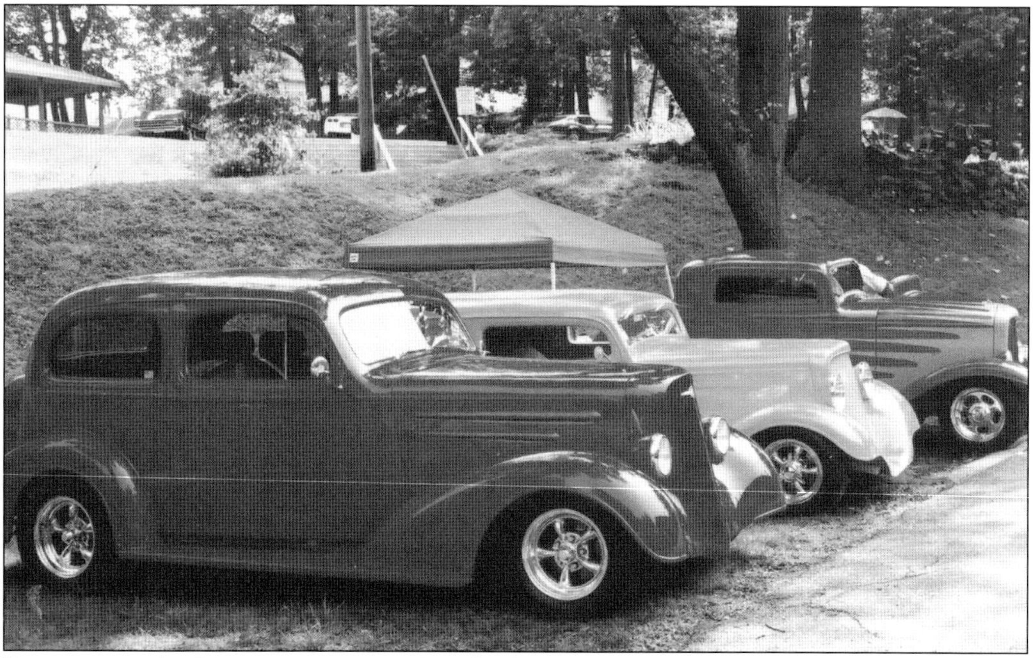

Back to the 50s Weekend, c. 2000. Fourth of July weekend at Cascade Park has been a major classic car weekend for 24 years. Drivers bring their families and vintage cars for car talk, car cruises, golden oldies music, and other nostalgic entertainment. The colorful cars are exhibited throughout the park. (Courtesy of LeeAnn Fulena.)

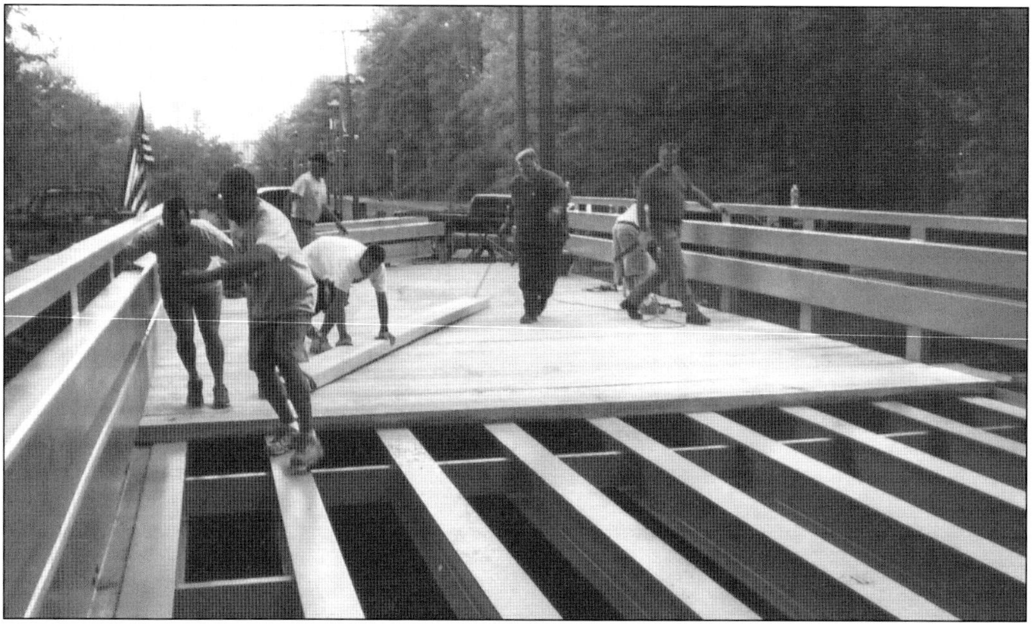

A New Bridge, 2009. When the 50-year-old bridge at the lower entrance to Cascade Park deteriorated, safe parking for the Back to the 50s Weekend was reduced. In 2009, regular attendees Jim Lombardo and Bob Smith organized the Cascade Park Bridge Committee. These volunteers donated all labor and materials for rebuilding the bridge using steel beams and oak planks. Parking at the lower entrance is safe again. (Courtesy of James Lombardo.)

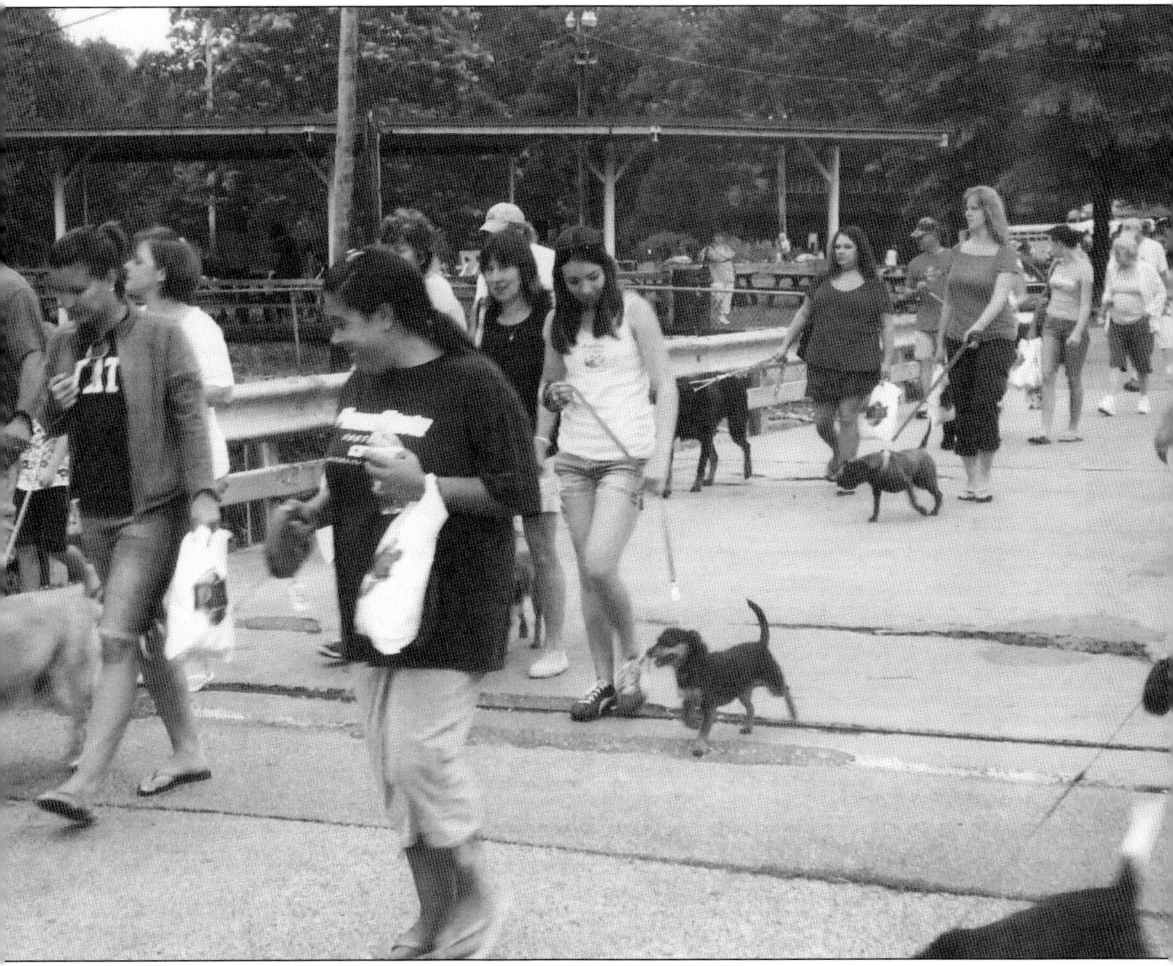

Canines in the Cascades, 2008. This photograph shows a procession of enthusiastic dogs during the annual dog walk and pet festival known as Canines in the Cascades. This gathering of pets and their owners at Cascade Park has been held in September since 2001. At this event, dogs participate in games, agility trials, contests, and dog walks. It is a colorful event, free to the public, with vendors offering a variety of pet products. The organization that sponsors Canines in the Cascades is called Promises for Pets. As a nonprofit organization, it is dedicated to serving the community on matters of pets' health and welfare. Their concern is homeless, unwanted, neglected, and abused dogs and cats, and they work to eliminate unwarranted euthanasia. Cascade Park is an ideal setting for walking dogs, and on any given day, dog owners can be seen walking the paths along Big Run. (Courtesy of Promises for Pets.)

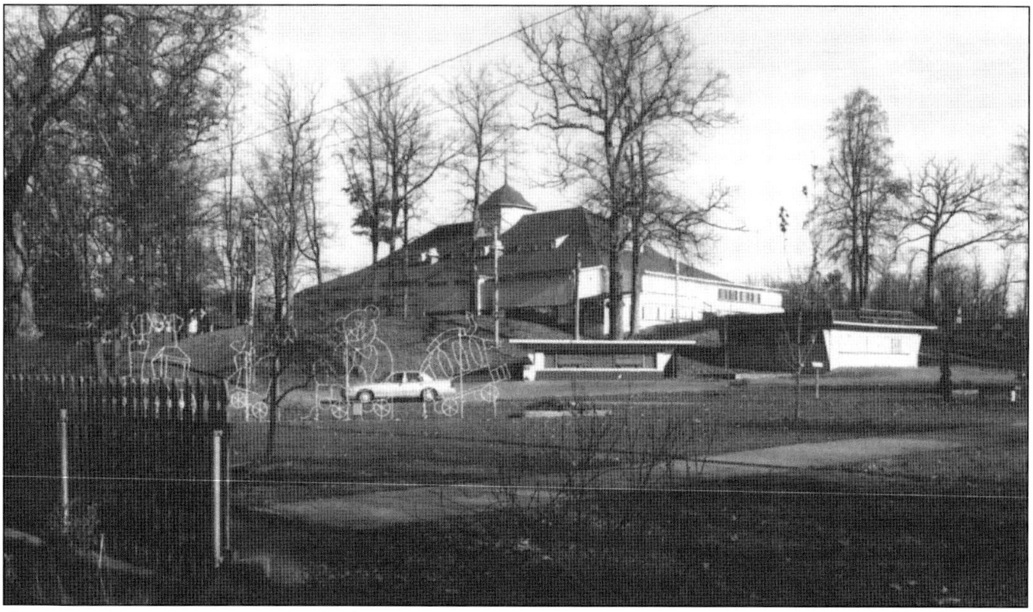

CASCADE OF LIGHTS, 2009. One of Cascade Park's regular events is a holiday light show sponsored by the City of New Castle. Visitors drive through the park at night to see holiday scenes silhouetted by lights. This photograph shows white outlines of holiday figures around the car. They will be lit after dark. In the distance are the dance pavilion and refreshment stands. (Courtesy of Adam Pivovar.)

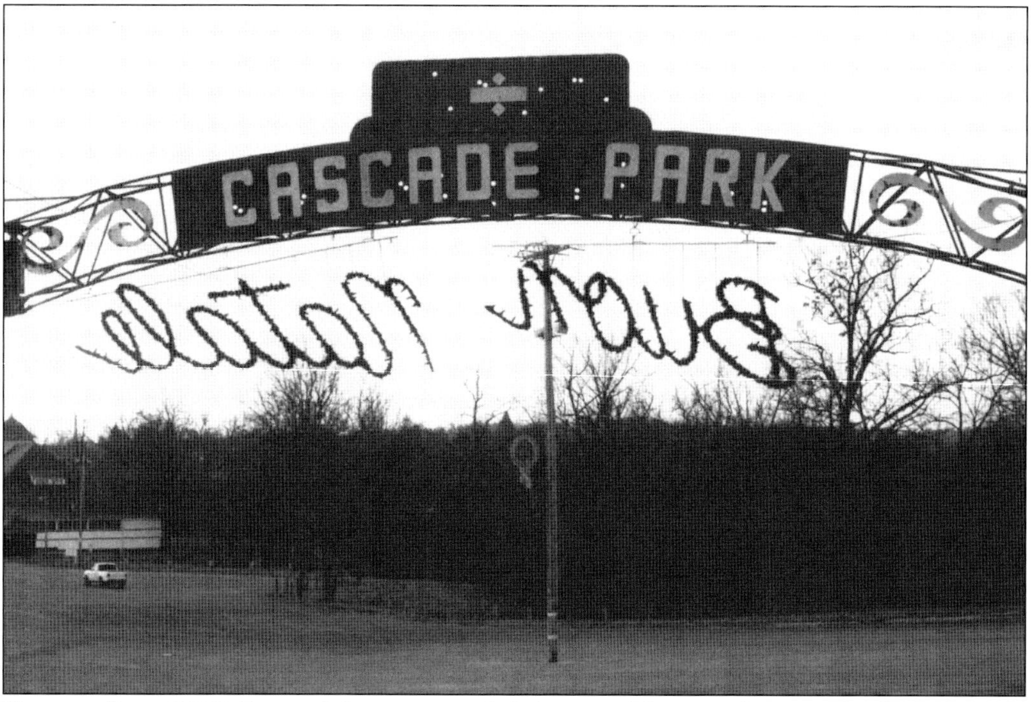

VINTAGE SIGN, 2009. Research has not revealed the age of this sign, but it is clearly many years old. Visitors to Cascade Park entering the parking lot from East Washington Street pass under the sign shown in the photograph. In December, visitors leaving the park see "Buon Natale," a holiday greeting in Italian (literally "Good Christmas"). (Courtesy of Adam Pivovar.)

Seven

CHANGES

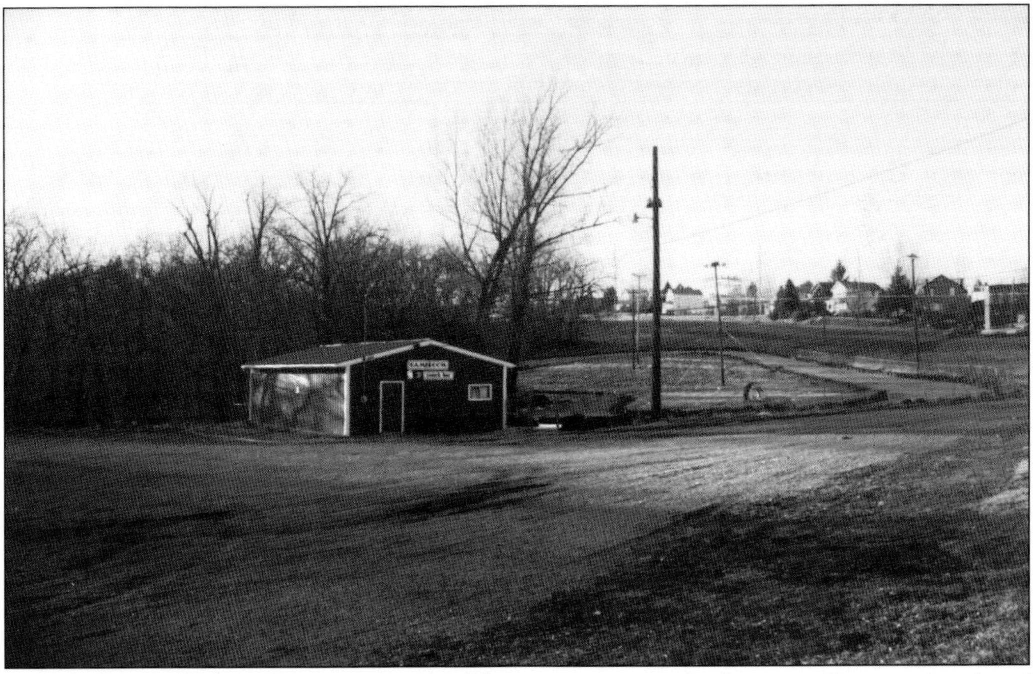

FORMER SITE OF ROLLER COASTER, C. 1990. This is an area near the dance pavilion, on the edge of the main parking lot and looking away from Washington Street, where the original roller coaster stood. Called the Toboggan Roller Coaster, it operated from 1897 to 1922. It was dismantled when Billy Glenn built the Gorge roller coaster in 1922.

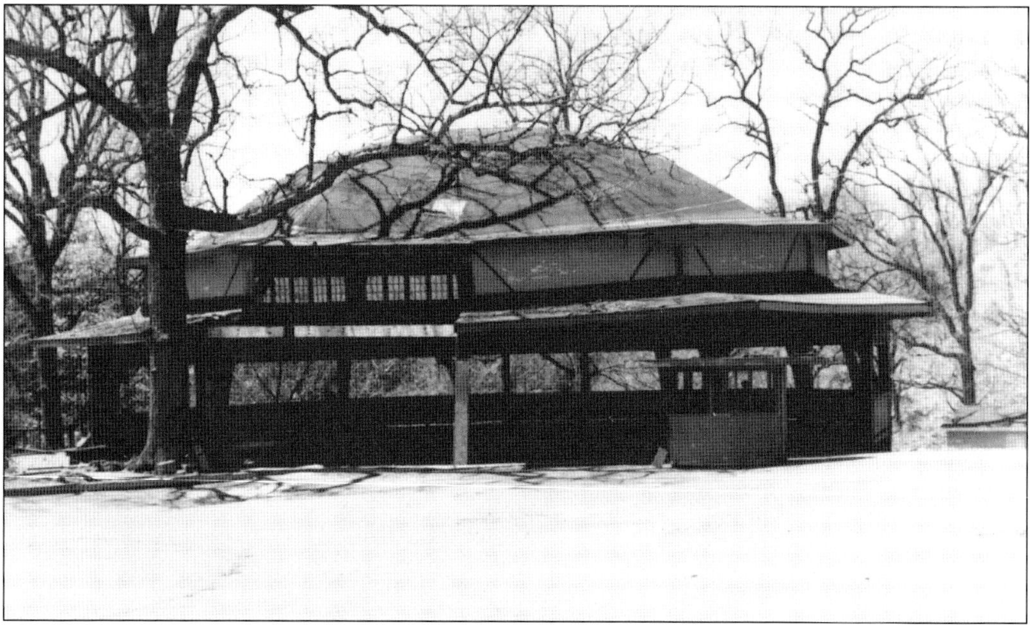

CAROUSEL BUILDING, BEFORE (1980S) AND AFTER (1990S). In the early 1920s, the traction company considered replacing the original carousel with a billiard parlor, but instead they acquired a new merry-go-round and enclosed it in the building pictured above. Eventually the building began to deteriorate and suggestions for an open air dance hall or a roller rink were heard. When that second merry-go-round was replaced, the building remained. Demolition seemed to be the fate of the building after vandals ravaged it and the carousel itself in the 1980s. In the early 1990s, the Rotary Club stepped in to assist the city with restoring the carousel building. The lower photograph shows the results of the restoration. Today, the building serves as a site for weddings and other social occasions and for vendors who set up their booths for various special events.

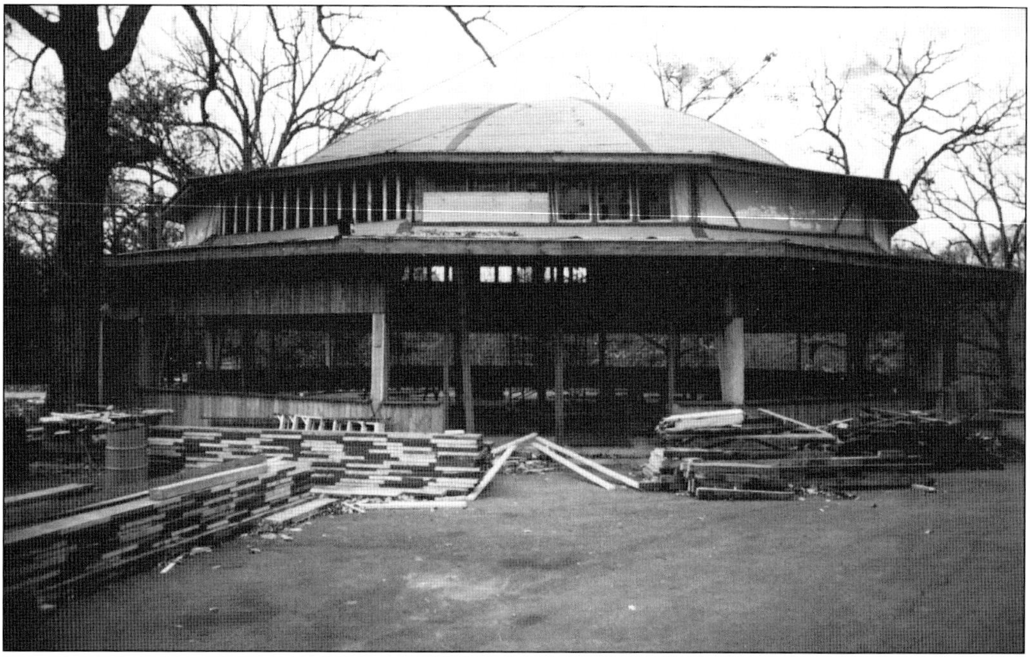

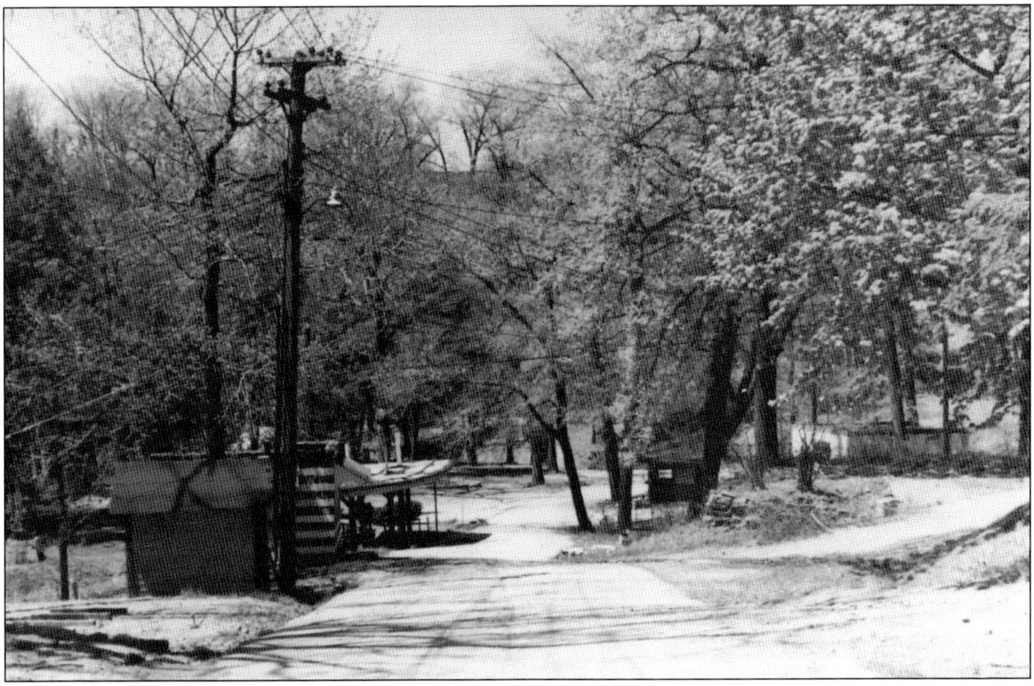

TOWARD THE GROVE, 1986. Gone are the open-air theater of the early 1900s, the Ferris wheel of the 1950s, and the stand where the beloved French fries with vinegar were sold. Today the bocce courts can be seen on the walk to the picnic grove. At the bottom of the hill is the old mineral spring. A century ago, when previous park owner Levi Brinton was followed home by a sickly dog, he took the dog in and fed him. The dog did not get well. Suddenly one day, the dog started eating and gaining weight. Brinton noticed that the dog disappeared for a short time each day, so he followed him. He found that the dog was drinking from a spring in Cascade Park. The *New Castle News* described it as "the one with the high wall around it," the park's mineral spring.

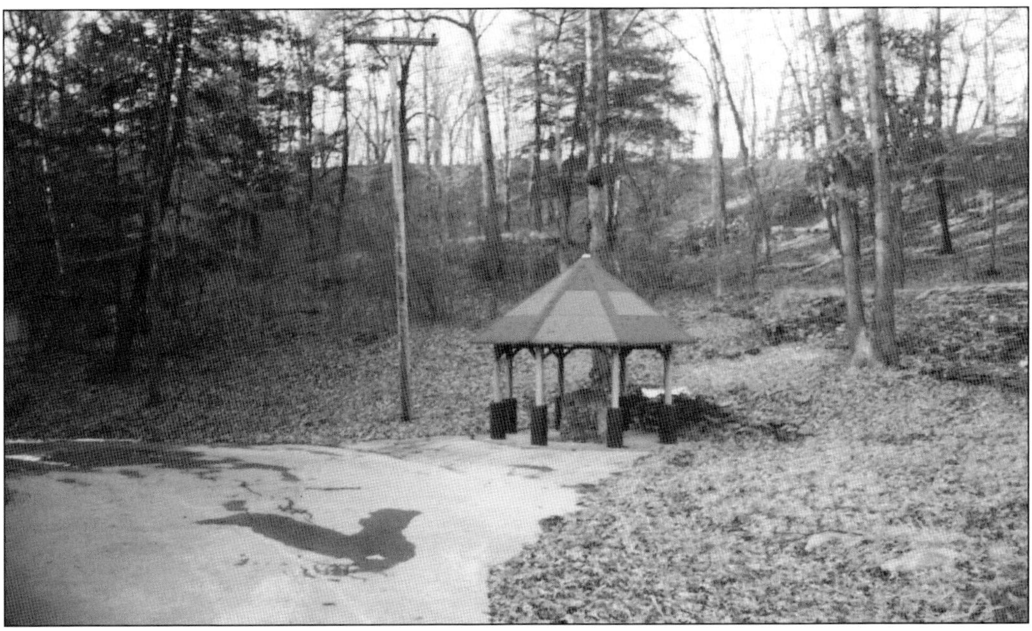

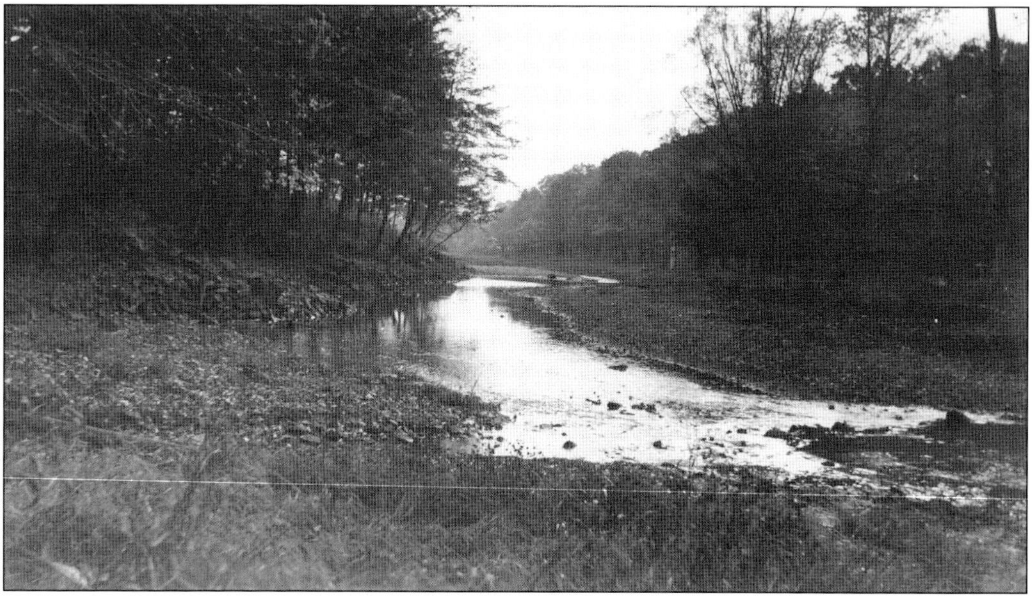

THE DISAPPEARING LAKE, 1950S. First the lake ran dry in 1946, when there were problems with the dam. Then in the 1950s, silt began to destroy the lake, 40,000 square feet of it. One of the most inviting spots at Cascade Park began to disappear. Gone were the boat rides, the boathouse, the boat chasers, and the many fishermen who used to visit regularly. It took several years to raise funds to restore the lake. Local businessman Jack Gerson took the lead, enlisting Harry Mack of the Optimist Club, then-congressman Frank Clark, and ultimately, the Marines. An ad in the *New Castle News*, donated by Jack Gerson, listed more than 200 contributors to the dredging project. Among them were local industries, small businesses, merchants, unions, church groups, and individuals.

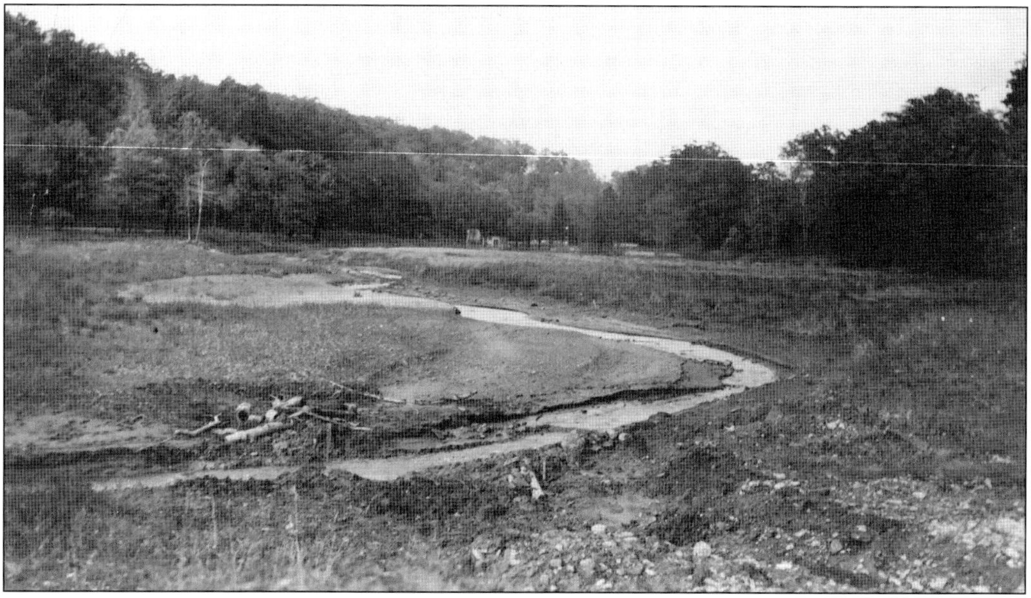

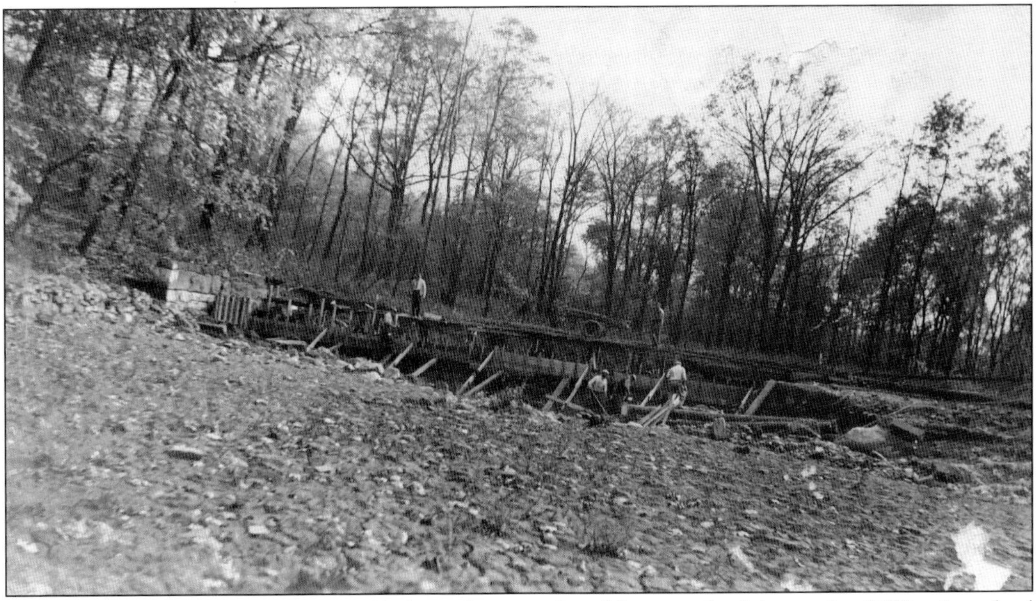

A NEW DAM AT THE LAKE, 1946. Before silt created problems at the lake in the 1950s, there had been earlier trouble. In 1946, the force of high water broke the dam and the lake ran dry. The loss of boating and other water recreation was particularly debilitating to the operation of the park, which was having one of its best seasons since the city took over in 1934, so reconstruction began.

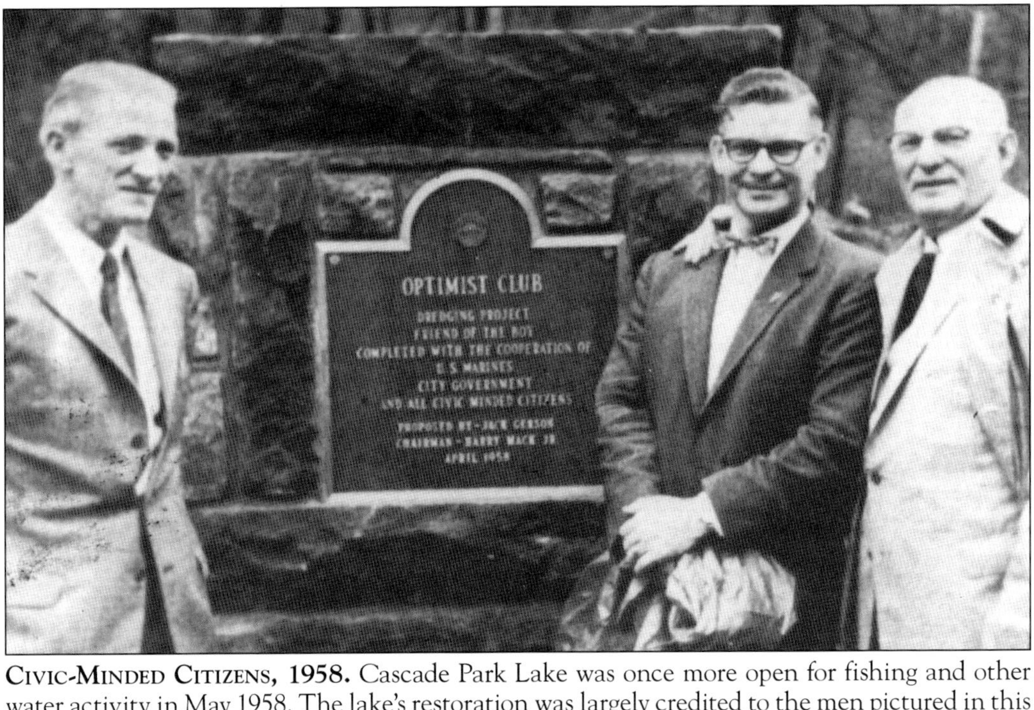

CIVIC-MINDED CITIZENS, 1958. Cascade Park Lake was once more open for fishing and other water activity in May 1958. The lake's restoration was largely credited to the men pictured in this photograph: Harry Mack of the Optimist Club (left), then-congressman Frank Clark (center), and Jack Gerson, who was the initiator of the effort.

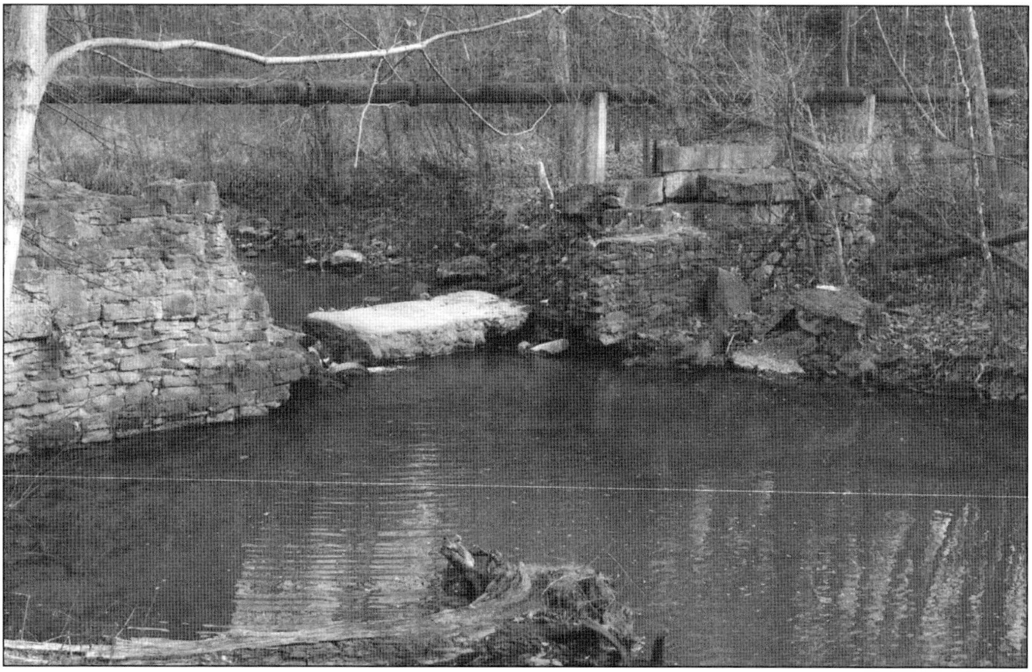

Lake in Trouble Again. In 1972, a section of the lake's spillway collapsed and the lake began to drain. It was fully drained by the city in 1974, when repairs were estimated to cost $100,000. In 1981, the dam gave way. The photograph, taken in 2009, shows the break in the dam. The dam was never rebuilt. (Courtesy of Adam Pivovar.)

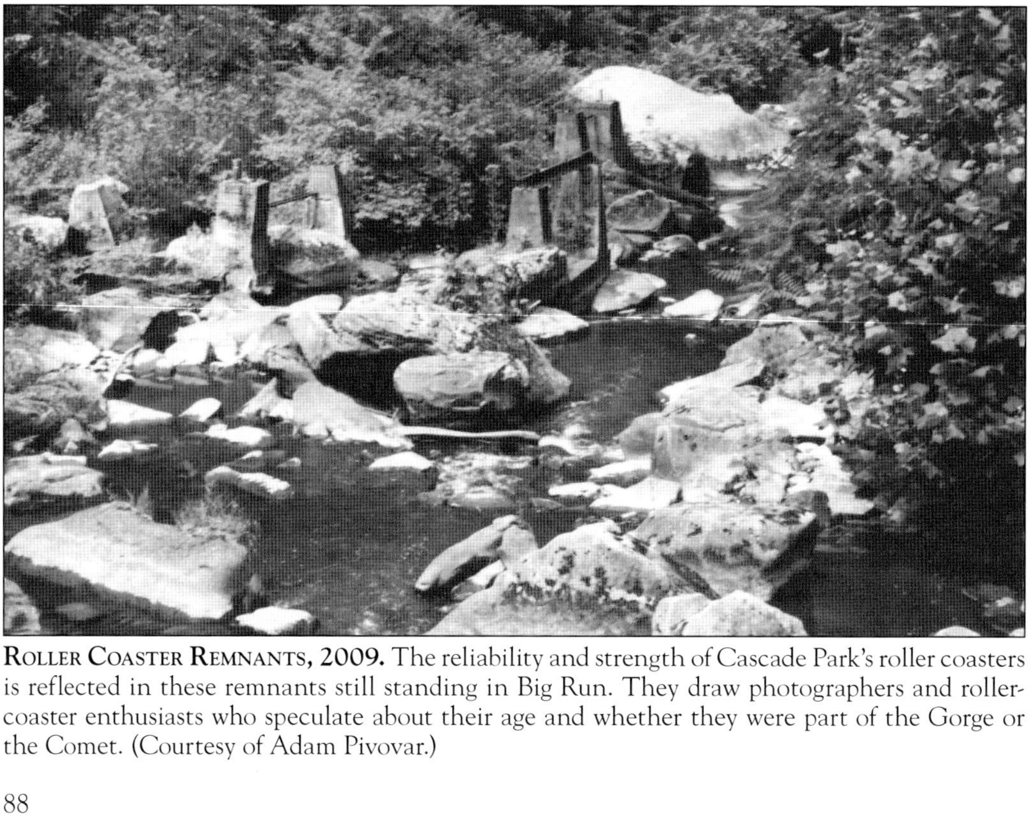

Roller Coaster Remnants, 2009. The reliability and strength of Cascade Park's roller coasters is reflected in these remnants still standing in Big Run. They draw photographers and roller-coaster enthusiasts who speculate about their age and whether they were part of the Gorge or the Comet. (Courtesy of Adam Pivovar.)

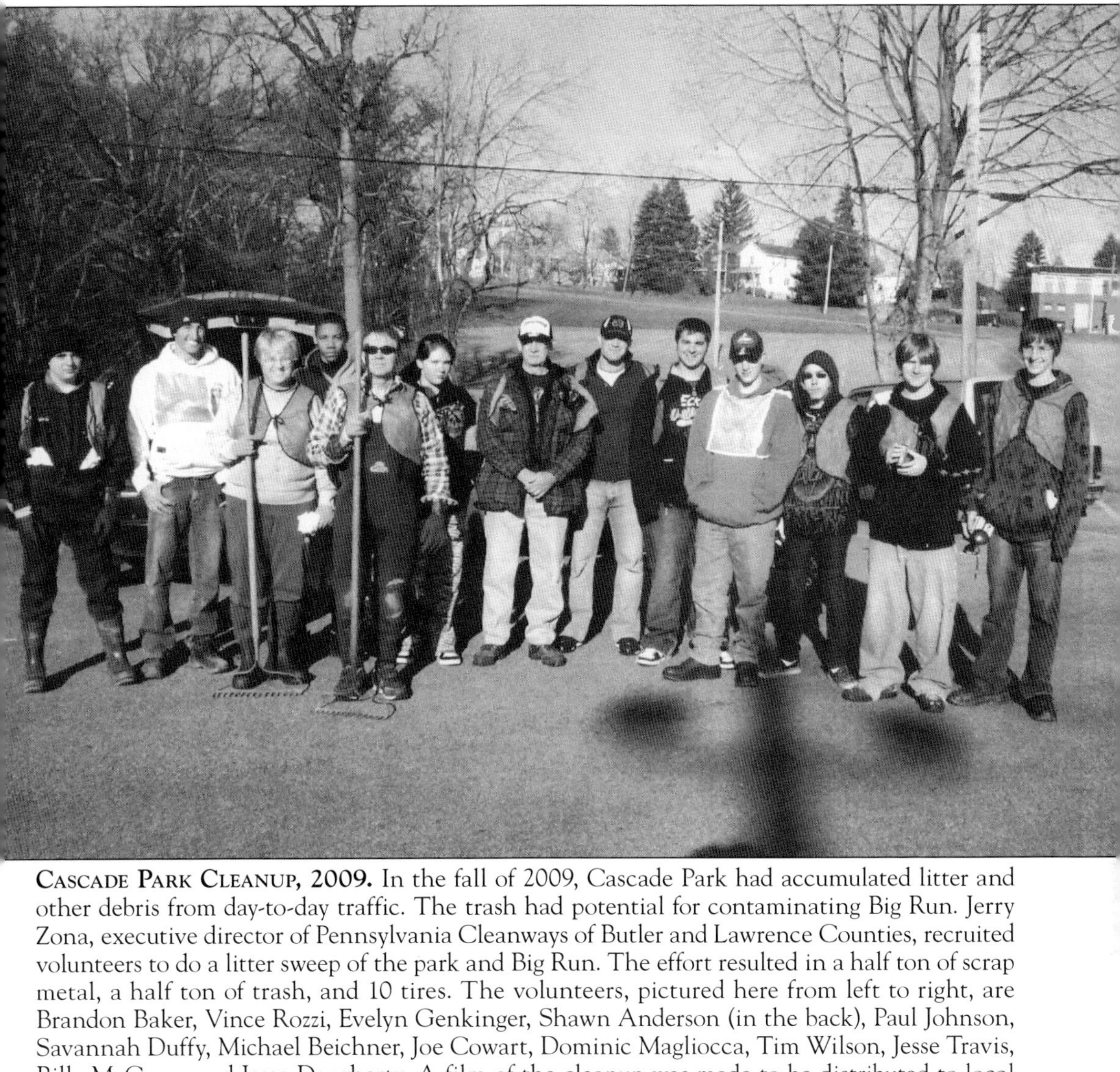

Cascade Park Cleanup, 2009. In the fall of 2009, Cascade Park had accumulated litter and other debris from day-to-day traffic. The trash had potential for contaminating Big Run. Jerry Zona, executive director of Pennsylvania Cleanways of Butler and Lawrence Counties, recruited volunteers to do a litter sweep of the park and Big Run. The effort resulted in a half ton of scrap metal, a half ton of trash, and 10 tires. The volunteers, pictured here from left to right, are Brandon Baker, Vince Rozzi, Evelyn Genkinger, Shawn Anderson (in the back), Paul Johnson, Savannah Duffy, Michael Beichner, Joe Cowart, Dominic Magliocca, Tim Wilson, Jesse Travis, Billy McCune, and Jesse Daugherty. A film of the cleanup was made to be distributed to local schools as part of an effort to stem illegal dumping. (Courtesy of Jerry Zona.)

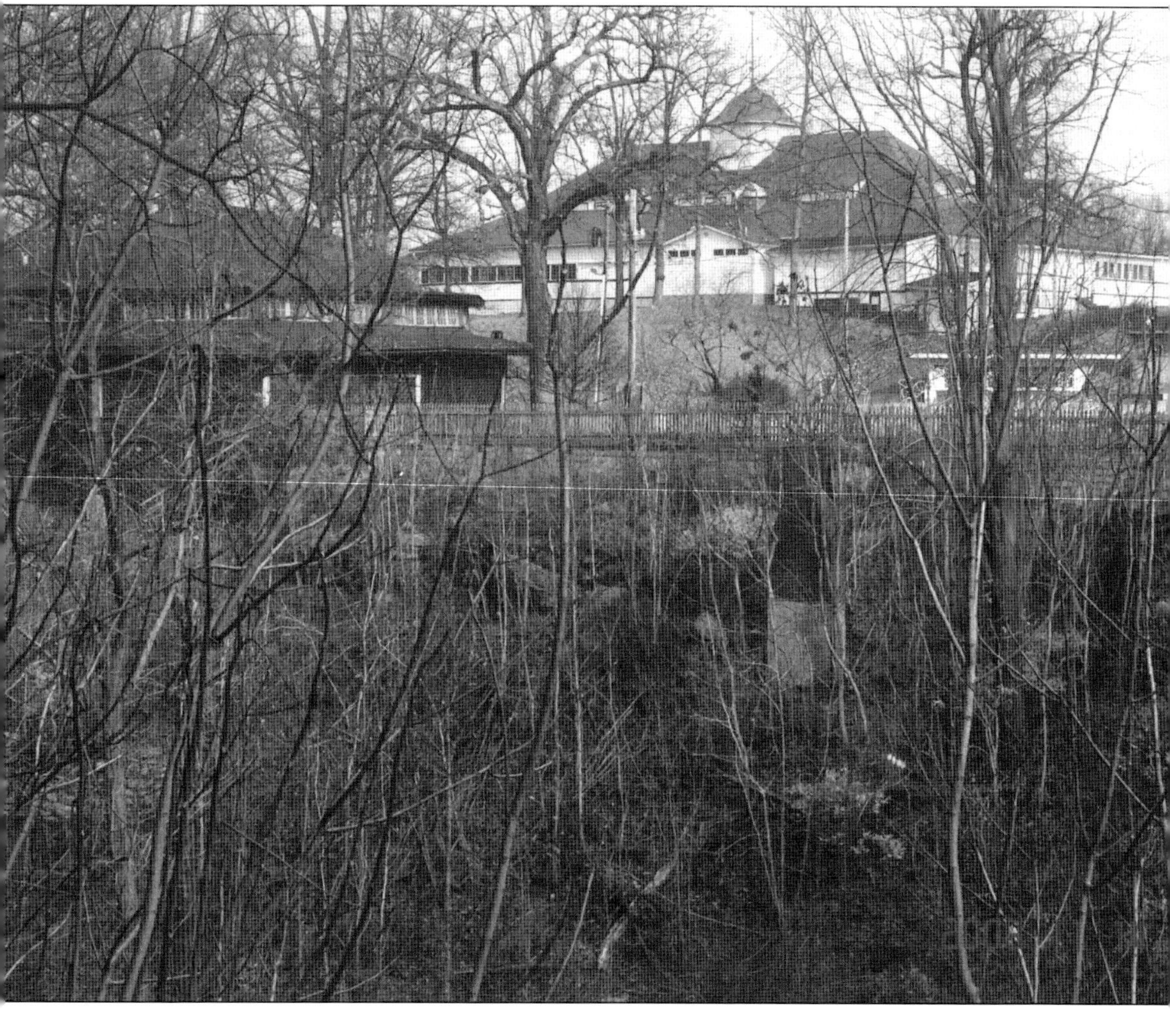

Echoes of Billy Glenn. In the 1920s, after Billy Glenn installed the Gorge, the swimming pool, and the Fun House, he got permission to build a summerhouse under the Gorge. Billy's children were working the concessions and the hours were often late. A house under the Gorge was a convenience, even though the roller coaster overhead was noisy. One daughter, Maxine, recalled that the day they moved in, three men were waiting; they thought the house was a restaurant. Her mother, Mary, was kind enough to fix breakfast for them. The house's brick chimney is still standing. The chimney is hard to see when the trees are full, but it can be seen through the trees in this 2009 photograph, under the person standing on the bridge. The carousel building is at the upper left. (Courtesy of Adam Pivovar.)

Eight

Winter in the Park

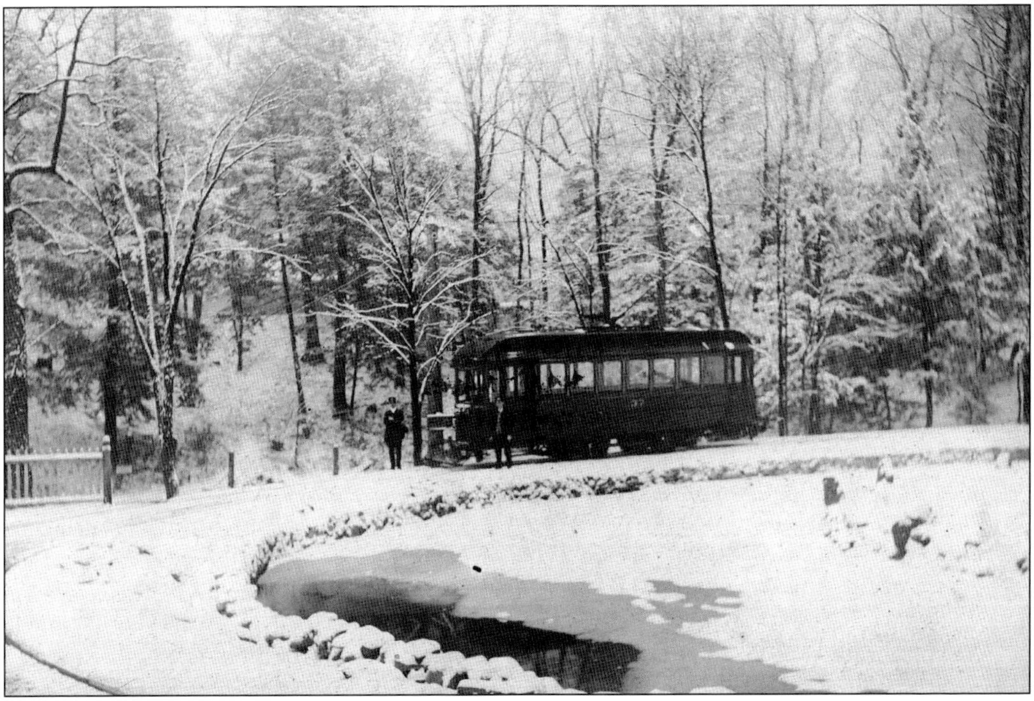

Streetcar Service in Winter, Early 1900s. At the park entrance, the lagoon plantings are almost completely frozen. The thick shrubbery and water lilies are gone for the season. In spite of the snow, the streetcar conductors appear to be warm enough to start the return trip to town.

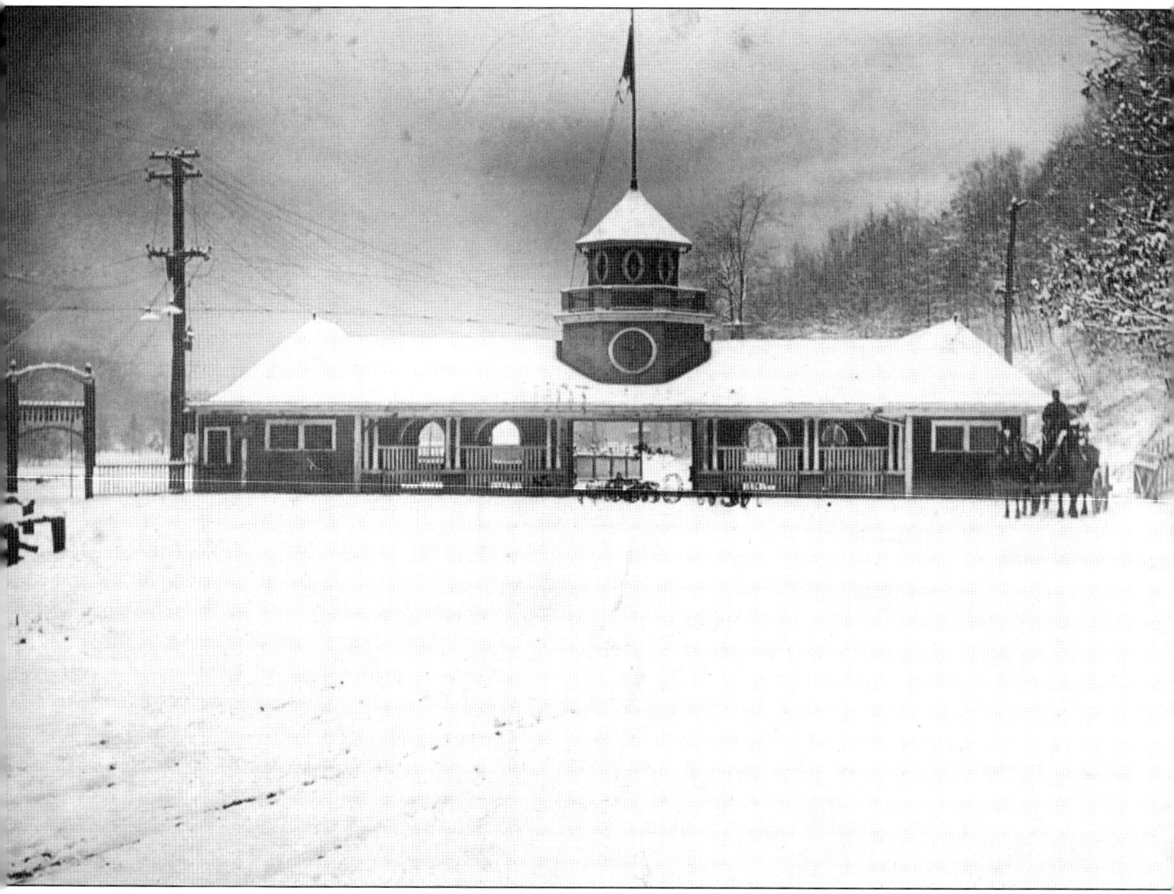

THE STREETCAR TERMINAL, EARLY 1900S. In 1897, when Cascade Park was new, The streetcar terminal was the first building visitors to the park would see as they left the streetcar. Surrounded by the lake and the lagoon on one side and the Cat Rocks on the other, it was situated for convenience. Both the lake and the grove were a short walk away. The terminal was the only building in the lake area , and visitors would have to continue to the main walk to see this view. The terminal's design was distinctive. The cupola rose like a funnel on a steamship, and the flagstaff rose like a mast. The widow's walk around the cupola was also nautical: New England's sailors' wives were said to look out from the wooden perches waiting for their husbands to return from sea. In this photograph, the terminal is dramatically silhouetted against the snow. The team of horses (right) is ready for work. (Courtesy of Dan Martwinski.)

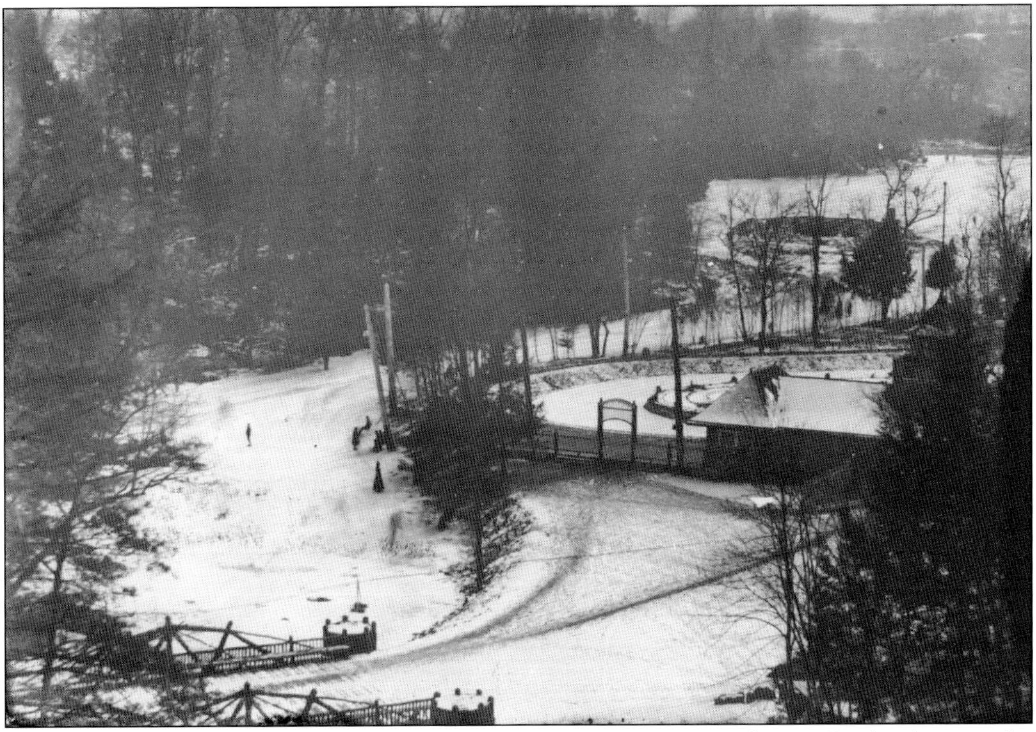

SNOWFALL ON THE LAKE, EARLY 1900S. This is the winter view from the Cat Rocks, showing the lagoon, the terminal, and the lake covered with snow. The arched lines of the rustic bridge (lower left) contrast with the snow and, at a distance, look like spans of much larger bridges.

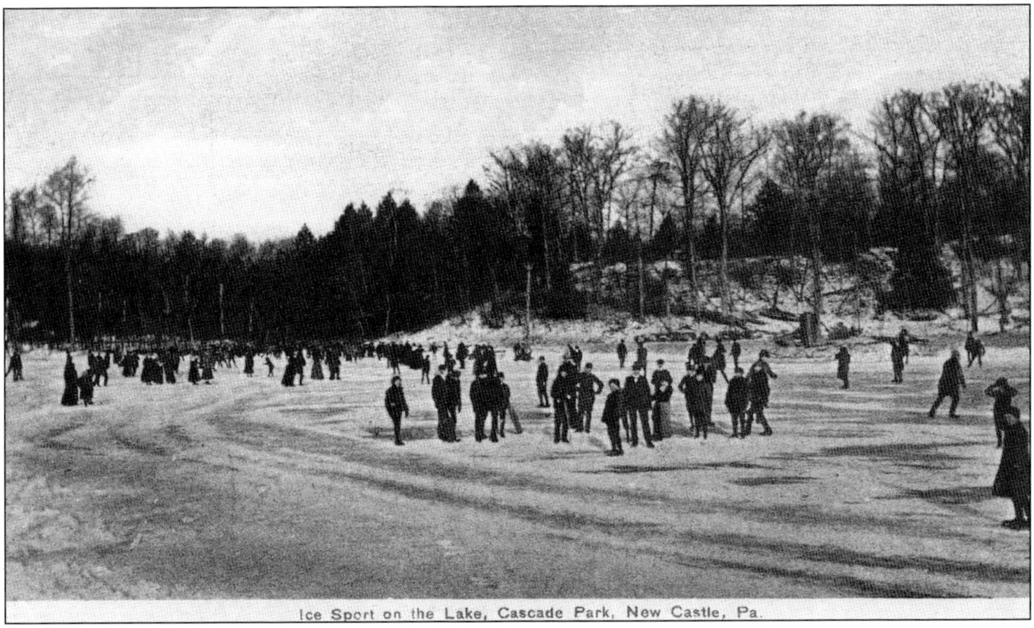

WINTER FUN, EARLY 1900S. This postcard shows how popular ice-skating was for both young people and adults. The women in the background are wearing long skirts. This is a time for a good game of Crack the Whip or some racing. For those who do not skate, a snowball fight will do.

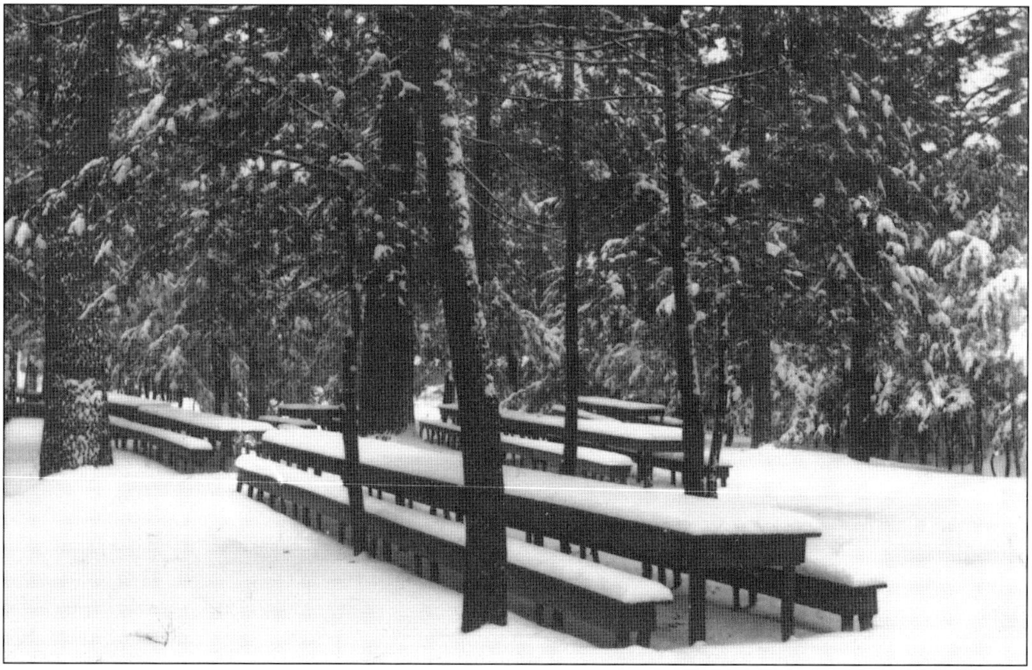

SNOW-COVERED PICNIC TABLES, EARLY 1900S. The snowy branches of the pine trees in the grove make a backdrop for the picnic tables. The thick cover of snow on the tables and benches is undisturbed. The snow is a deterrent to picnickers in the grove, but the tables are ready should any turn up.

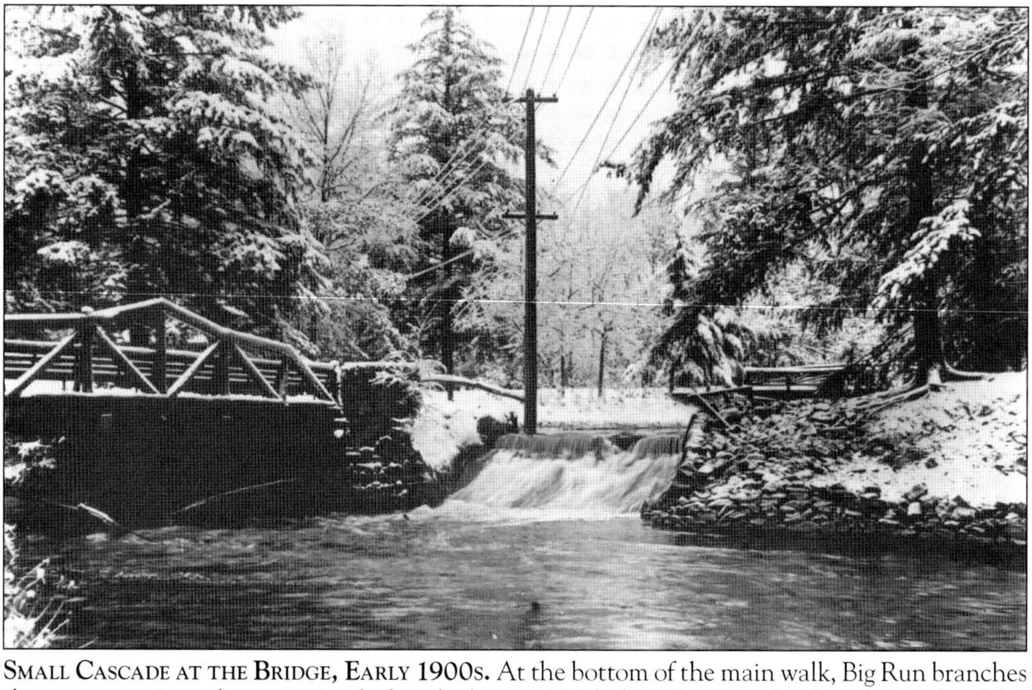

SMALL CASCADE AT THE BRIDGE, EARLY 1900S. At the bottom of the main walk, Big Run branches then meets again at the grove, just before the lagoon. Rocks have been used to line the banks of the picturesque cascade. The entire scene is framed by the snow-laden plumes of pine branches.

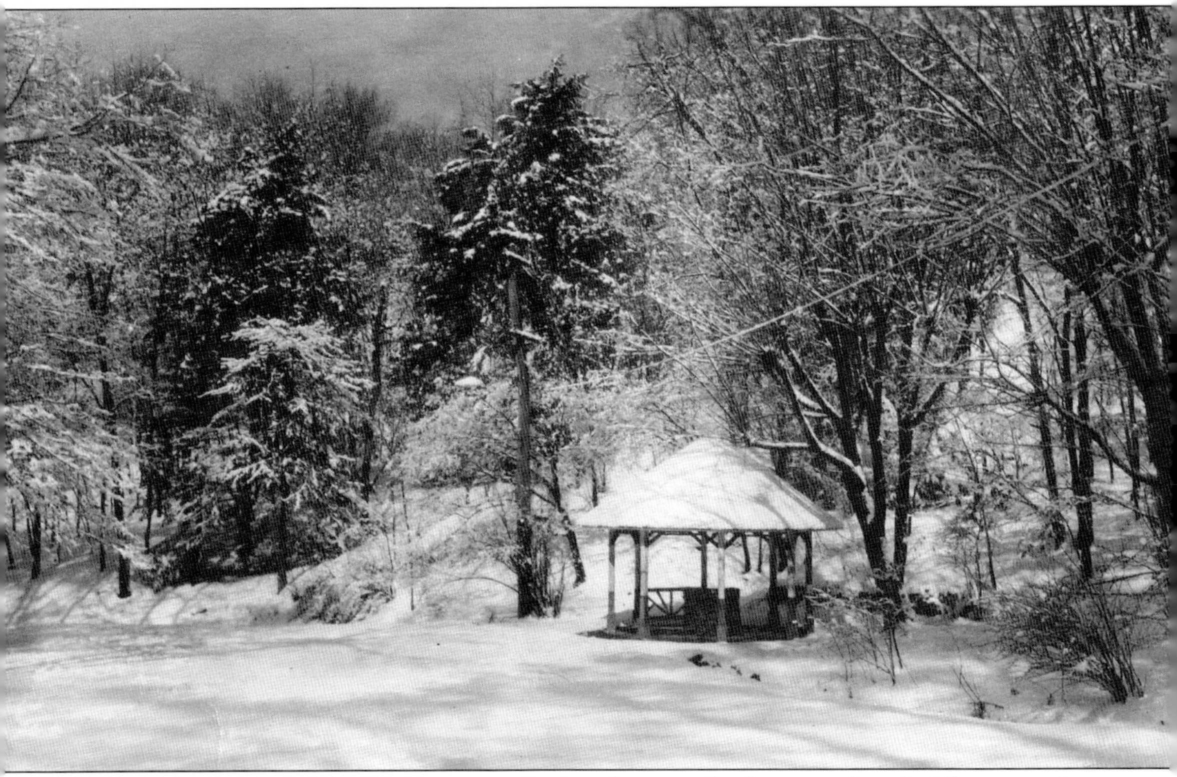

Mineral Spring in Winter, Early 1900s. In this photograph, the conical roof of the mineral spring's gazebo is emphasized by snow piled on it. Cascade Park is said to have nine springs. This one, located at the bottom of the main walk, was once rumored to have medicinal qualities. The spring's location has always been ideal. Early on, it was a refreshing stop for people arriving by streetcar or coming down from the midway and dance pavilion. Children enjoying Kiddieland rides or using playground equipment were close to the spring, and today it is handy for bocce players on the nearby courts. The snow-covered branches in this photograph tower over the spring and provide the sylvan setting the park was known for long before it became Cascade Park. (Courtesy of Pat Patterson.)

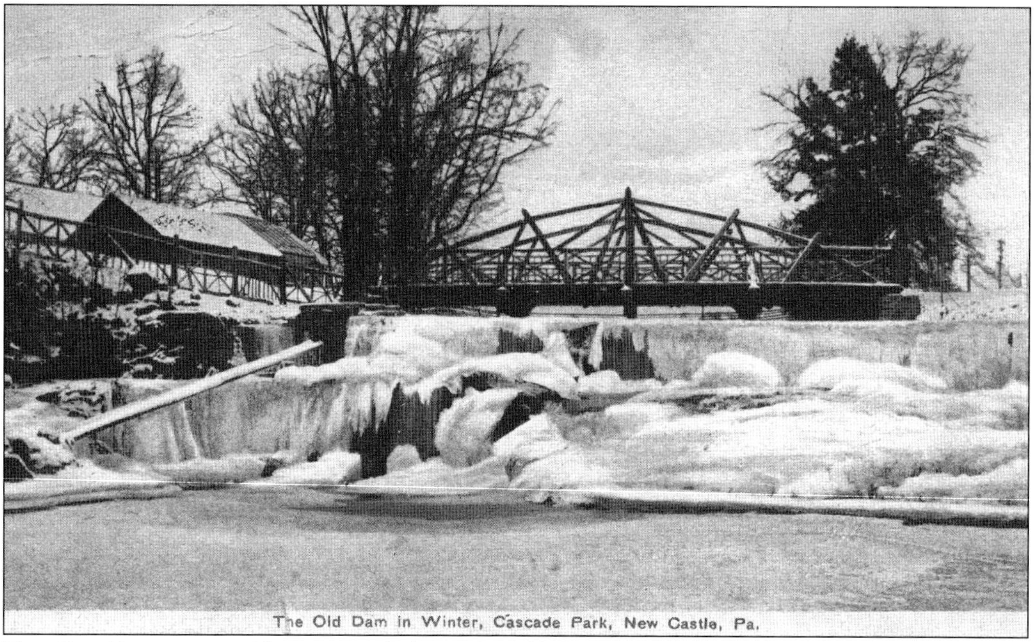

The Old Dam, 1909. This postcard shows the old dam at the upper level frozen solid. The ice-covered rocks around the dam make strange shapes under the snow. Normally a person standing on the rustic bridge would hear the sound of the falls, but the falls are silent when they turn to ice.

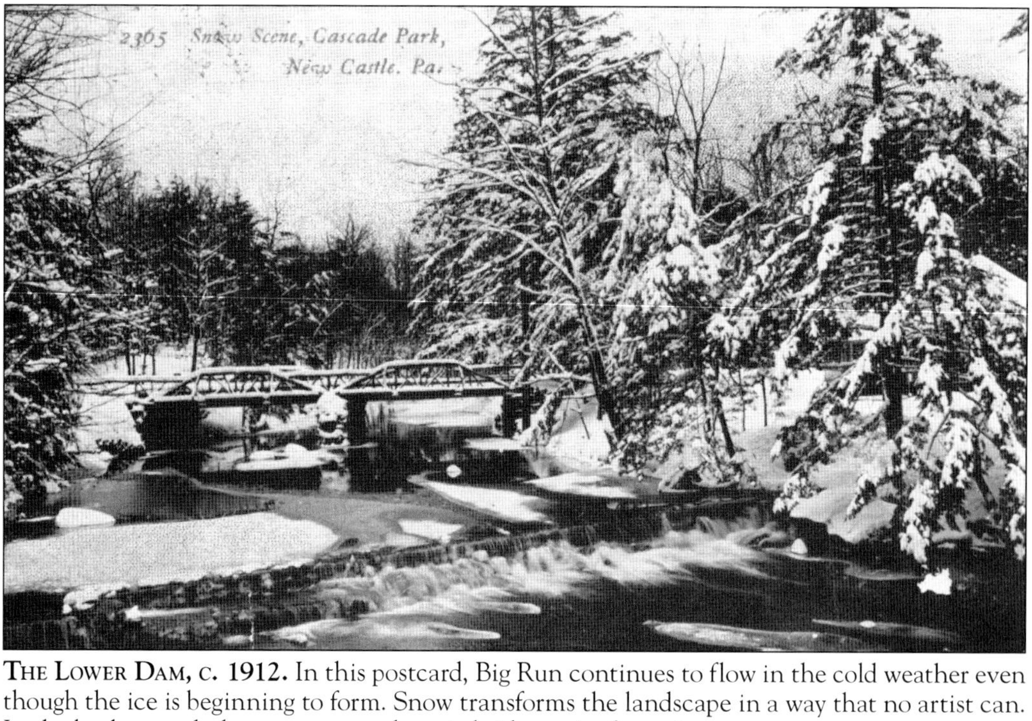

The Lower Dam, c. 1912. In this postcard, Big Run continues to flow in the cold weather even though the ice is beginning to form. Snow transforms the landscape in a way that no artist can. In the background, the snow-covered rustic bridge waits for spring.

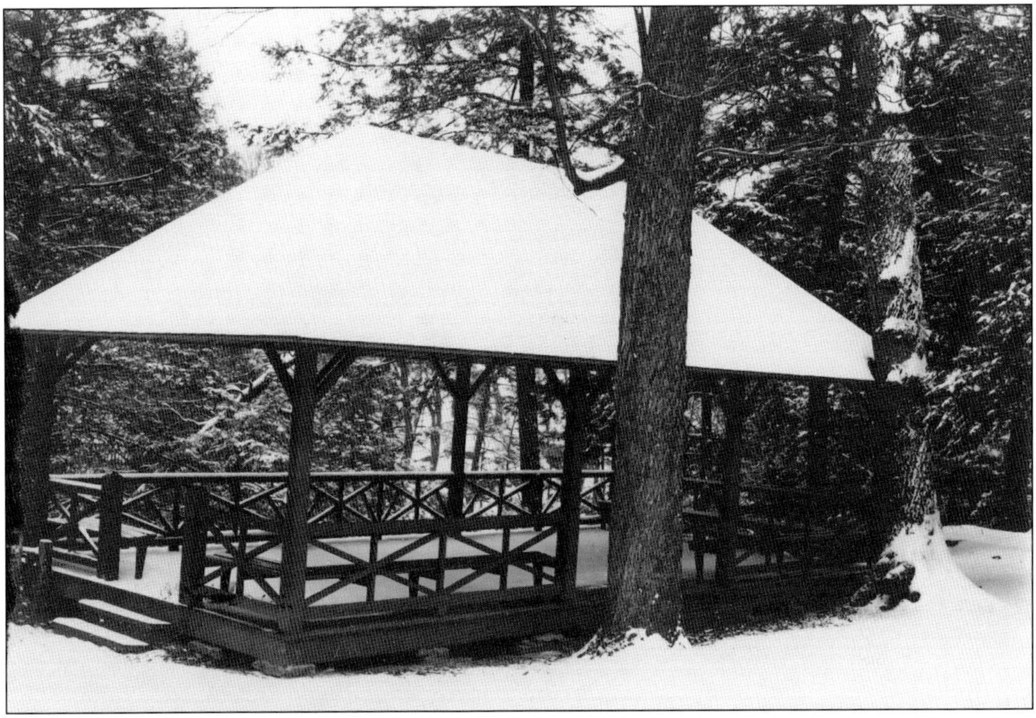

Rustic House, Early 1900s. More than half a dozen rustic houses were built on the grounds of Cascade Park for people who wanted to get away from the crowds. This private shelter waits for visitors who, in the winter season, are few and far between. The squirrels have the house to themselves.

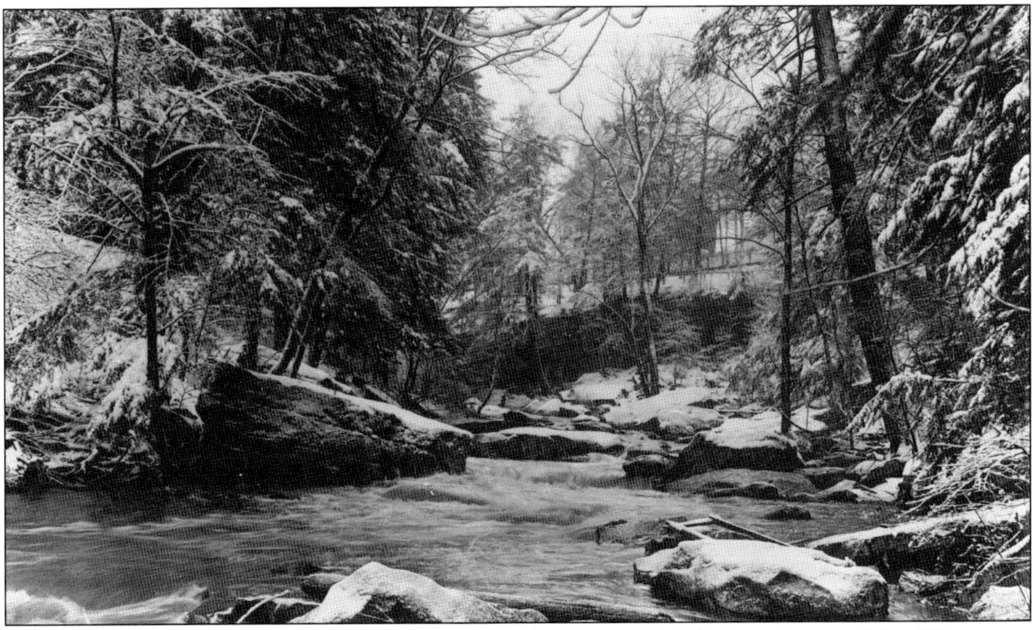

Rocks in Big Run, Early 1900. Thousands of years ago, as the ice sheets of the Wisconsin Glacier moved north, away from Cascade Park, rocks and boulders were left behind. These natural sculptures, stationary as they are, adapt to the weather and offer scenic displays that change with the season.

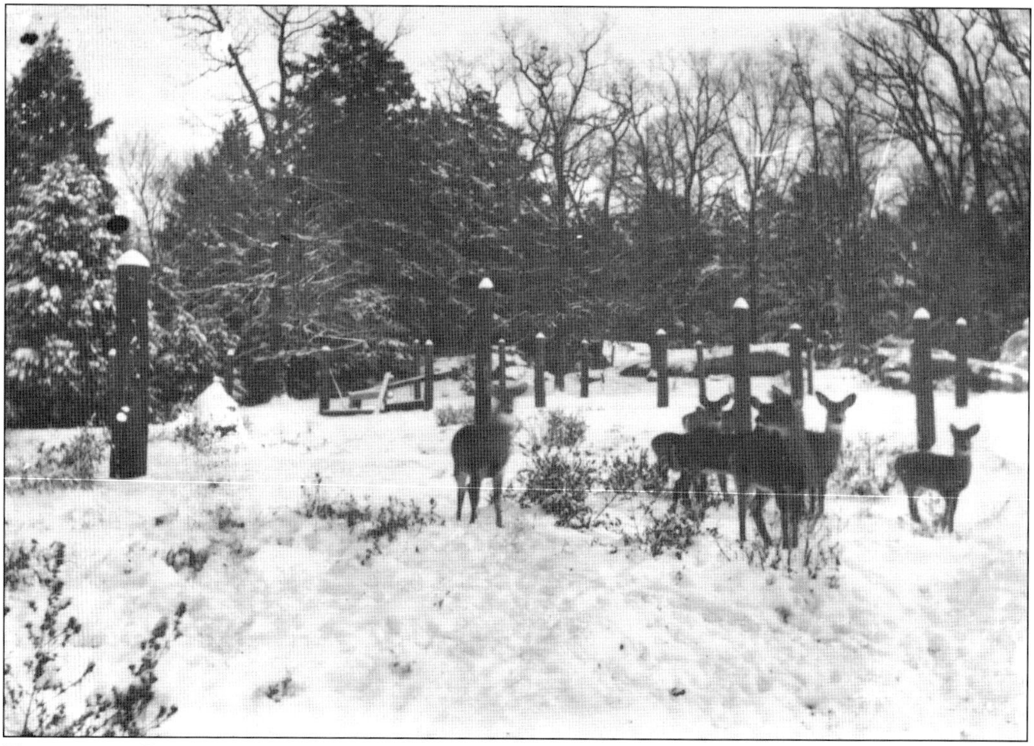

ZOOLOGICAL PARK IN WINTER, EARLY 1900S. The elk that were brought to Cascade Park in its first year arrived in the spring. In this photograph, they are enjoying winter. The zoo's bears are nowhere to be seen; they are hibernating in this snowy season. In the 1920s, the zoo was replaced by the park's first swimming pool.

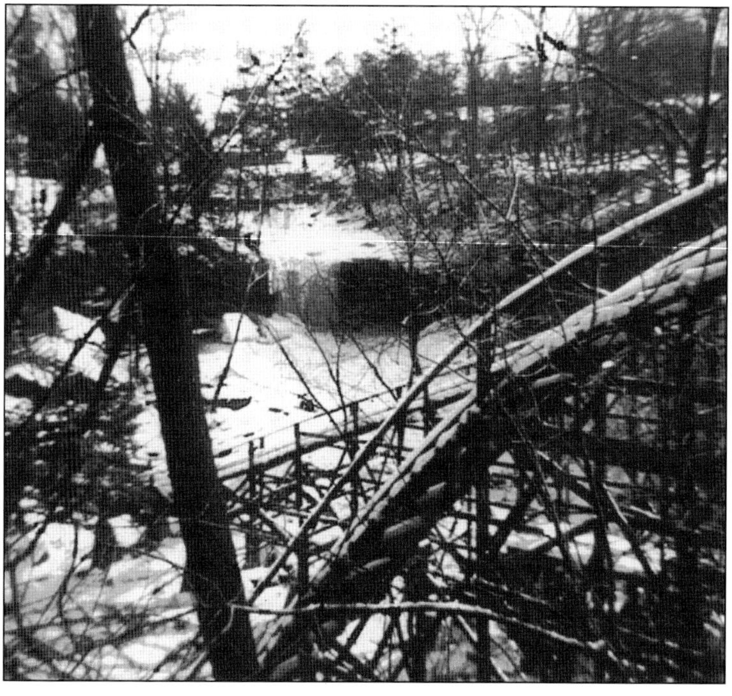

FROZEN FALLS, 1958. Big Run Falls, stilled by ice, can be seen from a distance through the rails of the Comet. Both the Gorge and the Comet were built to take advantage of the park's natural scenery, but neither of them had riders when winter scenes like this occurred. (Courtesy of Sandra Bumgardner.)

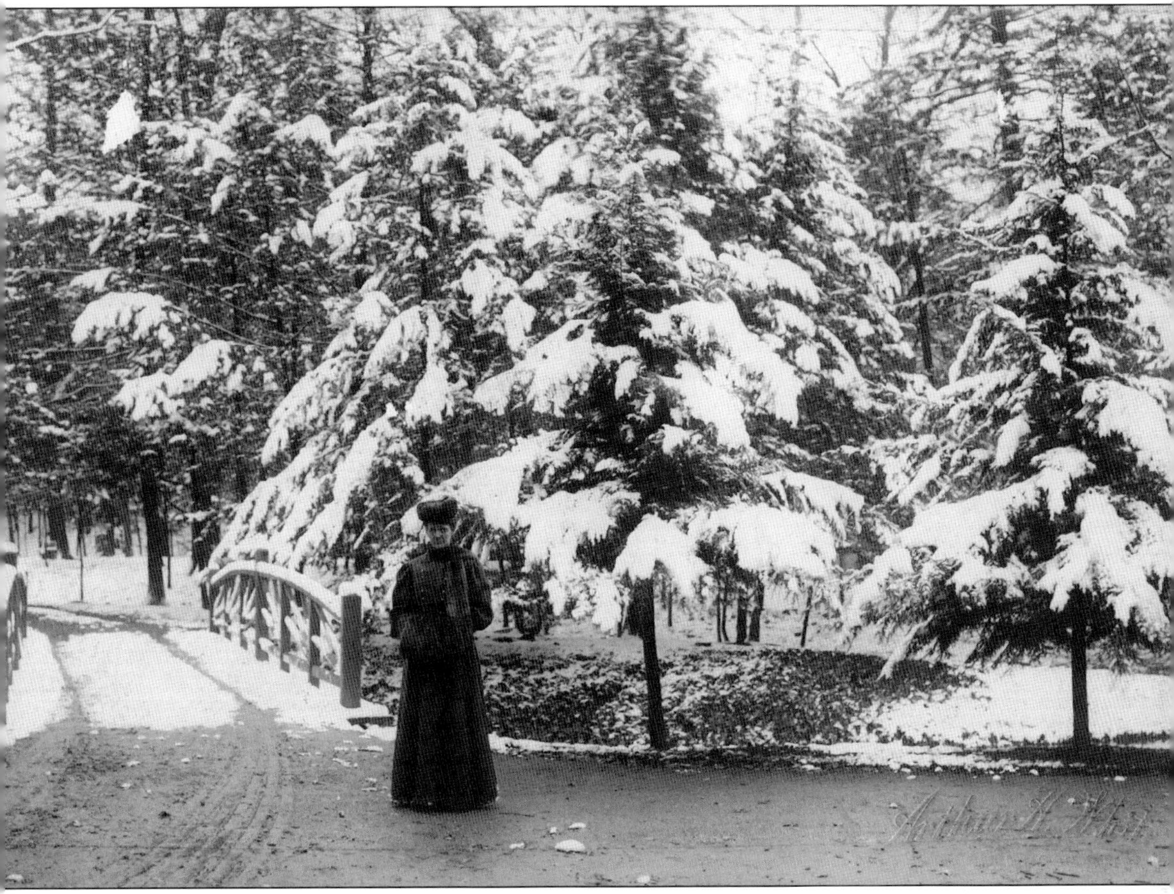

Stylish Woman at Rustic Bridge, 1910. The attractive woman in this photograph is Mary McClaren, milliner. In an era when businesswomen were few, McClaren owned a popular millinery shop in downtown New Castle at 54 ½ East Washington Street. According to a brochure of the time describing merchants and their businesses, "[Mary McClaren's] customers are among the best dressed of the town, every hat she turns out recommending her to public favor." Considered an artist, she bought her supplies at "fashion centers" and was admired for the individual touches she offered her customers. In this photograph, she is dressed for the weather, wearing a fur hat and fur scarf and carrying a fur muff to keep her hands warm. A visit to Cascade Park in the winter gave Mary McClaren an opportunity to pose in her elegant winter outfit.

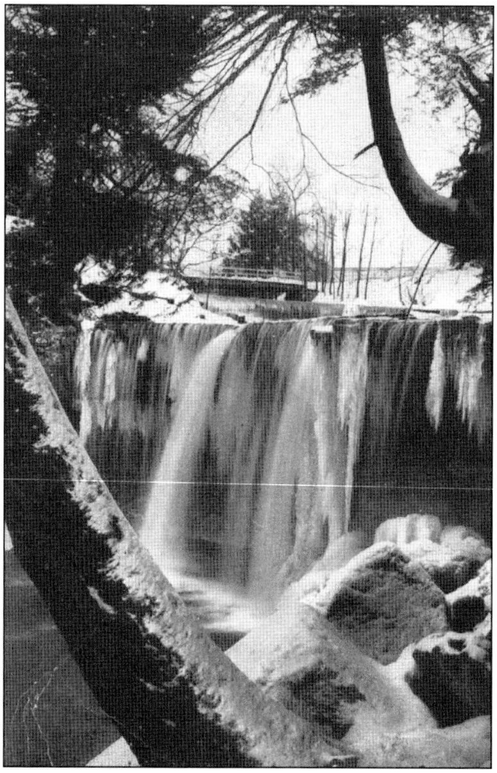

Big Run Falls, Early 1900s. In this postcard, ice is beginning to form on both ends of the falls. The flowing dam can be seen in the back, but the rush of the water is not enough to stop the freezing. The rocks and trees frame this favorite scene of winter visitors.

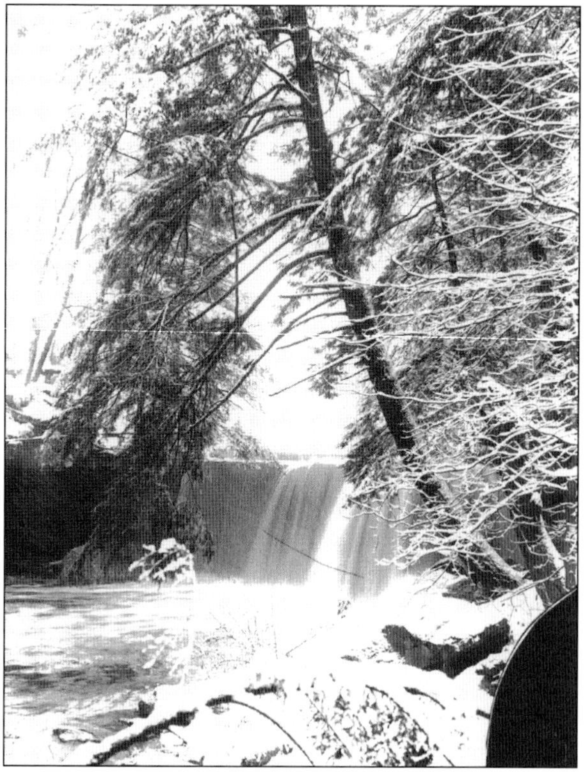

High Water in Winter, Early 1900s. Big Run was high when this photograph was taken. The falls are rushing, and the drop of the torrent is probably loud. The tree branches are thick with snow, but they are graceful as they guard the falls. (Courtesy of Pat Patterson.)

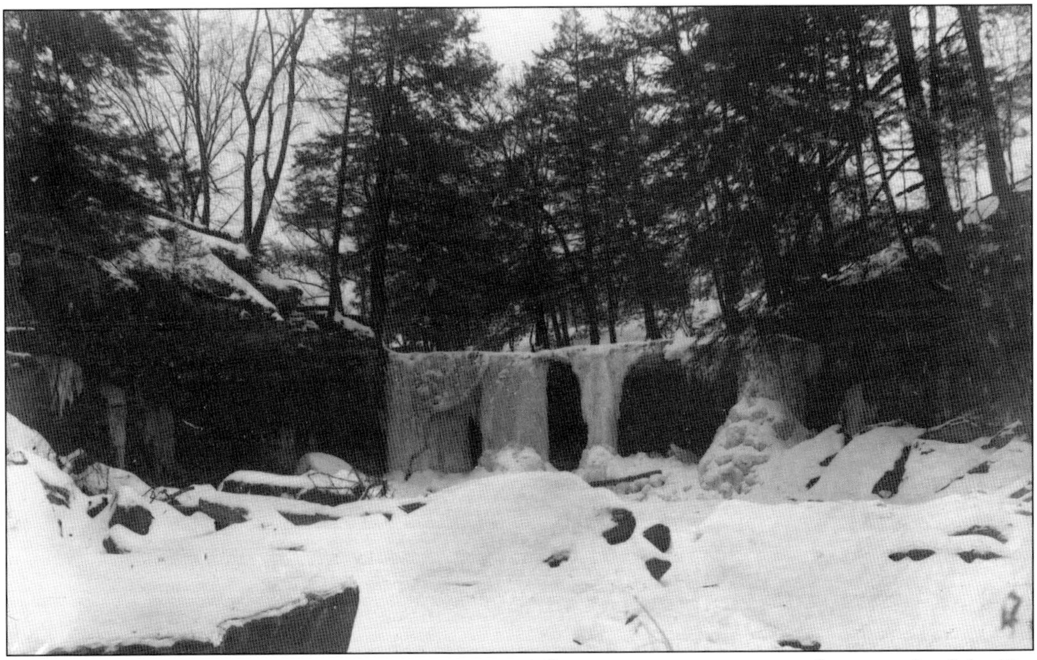

A View of Icy Falls at Big Run, Early 1900s. This is a more panoramic photograph of the Big Run Falls stationary with ice. The rocks are crusted with snow, and fallen branches are scattered along the frozen water's path. Footing must have been treacherous for the photographer.

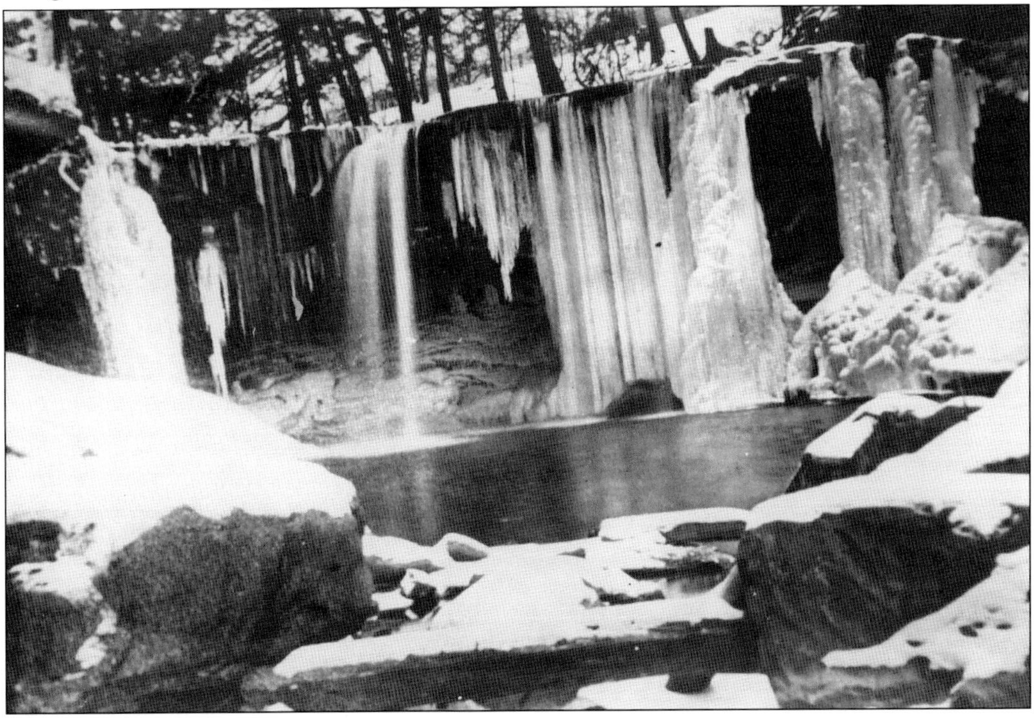

Close-up of Frozen Falls, c. 1912. In this photograph, freezing temperatures have begun to turn the falls to icicles. Big Run itself has not frozen completely, as can be seen at the bottom of the falls. The pool there appears ready to solidify, and the boulders seem frozen to each other.

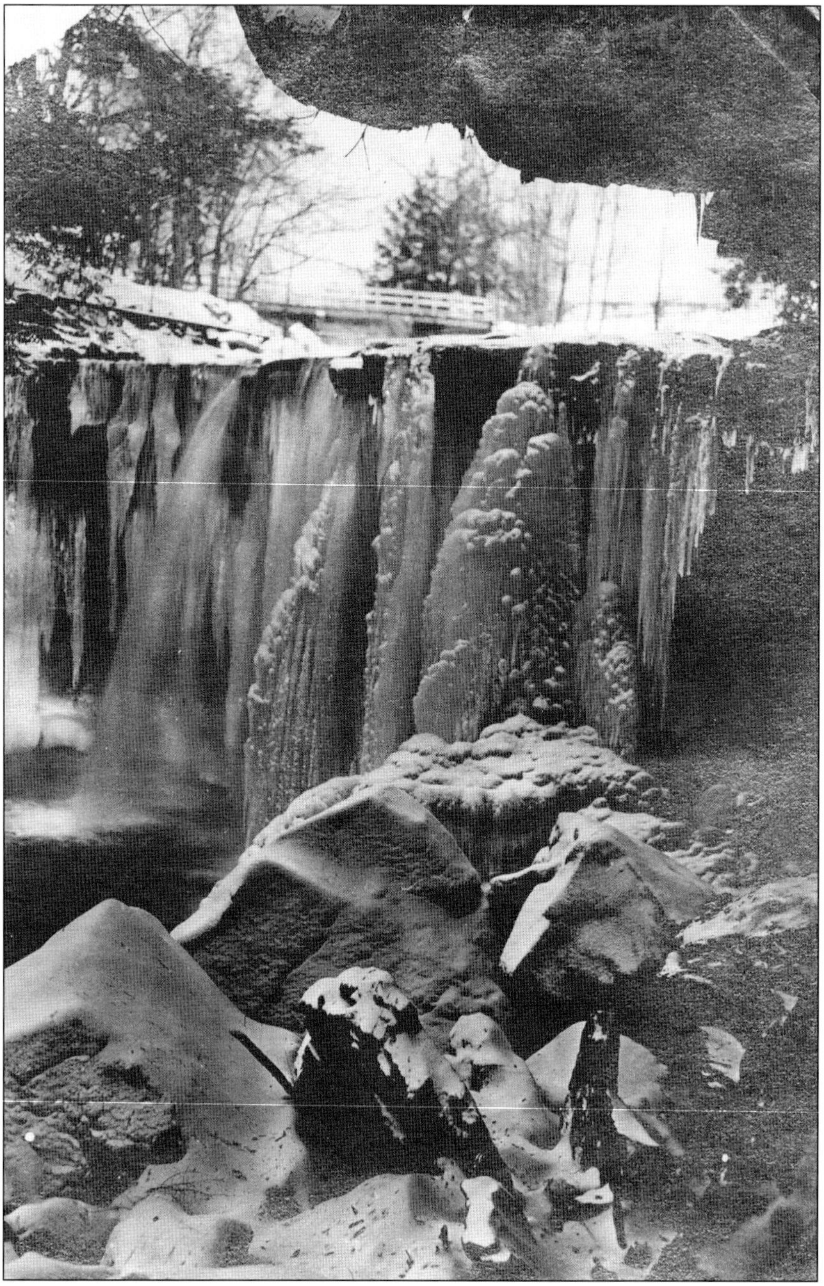

THE COLDEST DAY, C. 1912. Looking very much like stalactites, the water of Big Run Falls has frozen in ropey columns in a year that broke records for cold weather. The *New Castle News* reported that January 13, 1912, was the coldest day in the history of Lawrence County. The temperature at Cascade Park that morning was 30 degrees below zero, a temperature confirmed by the streetcar crew that traveled to the park. That temperature was surpassed by New Wilmington, which recorded 40 below zero. The coldest record before 1912 occurred in 1894, when New Castle recorded 28 degrees below zero. The 1912 freeze affected citizens of New Castle in many ways: water pipes were frozen, sewers burst, streetcars were obstructed, trains were four to five hours late, and those who walked to work were risking illness and accidents.

Nine

Scenes

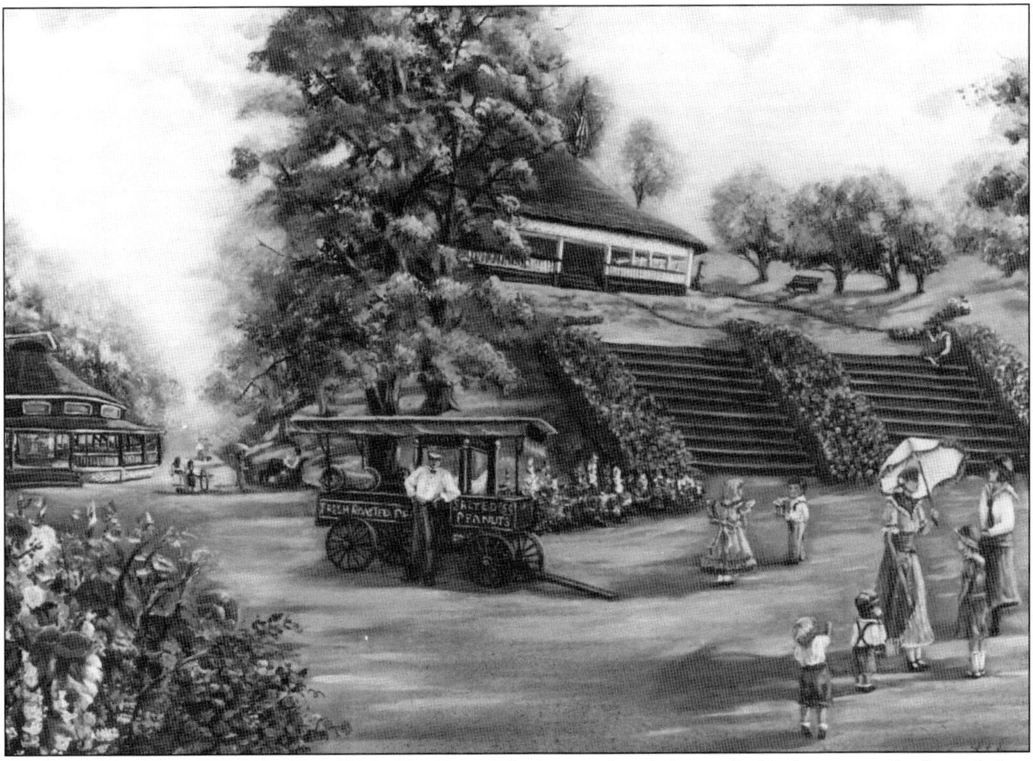

Memories of Cascade Park. Photographs and postcards of Cascade Park are easily found, but works of art are fewer. This oil painting by a local artist combines images from Cascade Park's past: the midway, the first carousel, Billy Glenn's peanut wagon, the dance pavilion, the floral steps, nasturtiums, and the luxurious gardens. (Courtesy of Barbara Tartaglione.)

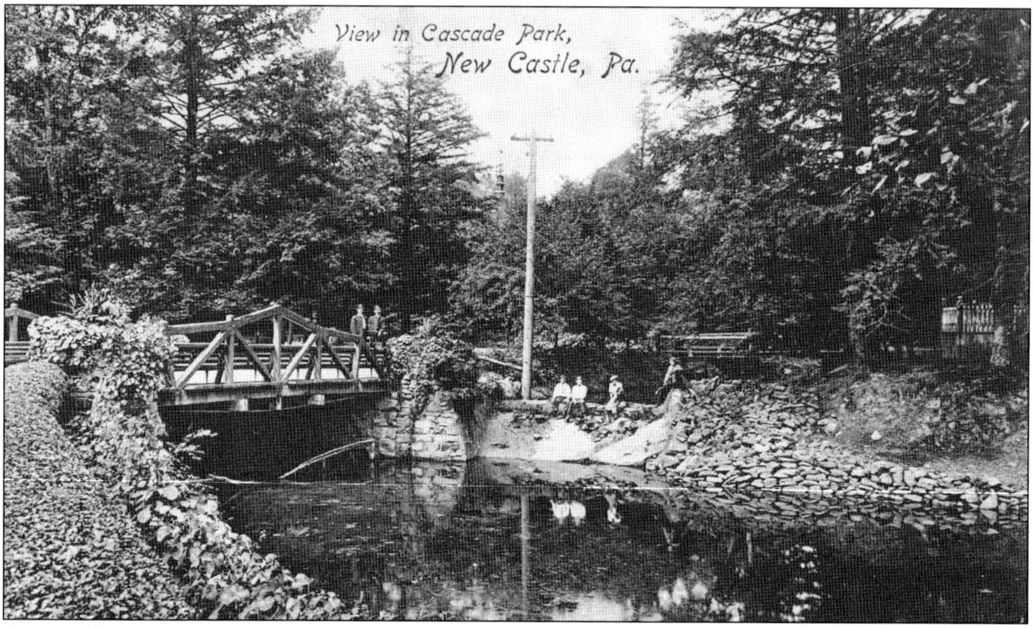

RUSTIC BRIDGE AND BIG RUN NEAR THE GROVE, C. 1912. Cascade Park's natural beauty was enhanced by plantings and gardens designed by landscape architects from Boston. Colorful flowers and lush shrubbery decorated every area. This postcard shows visitors enjoying the scenery on a typical summer day.

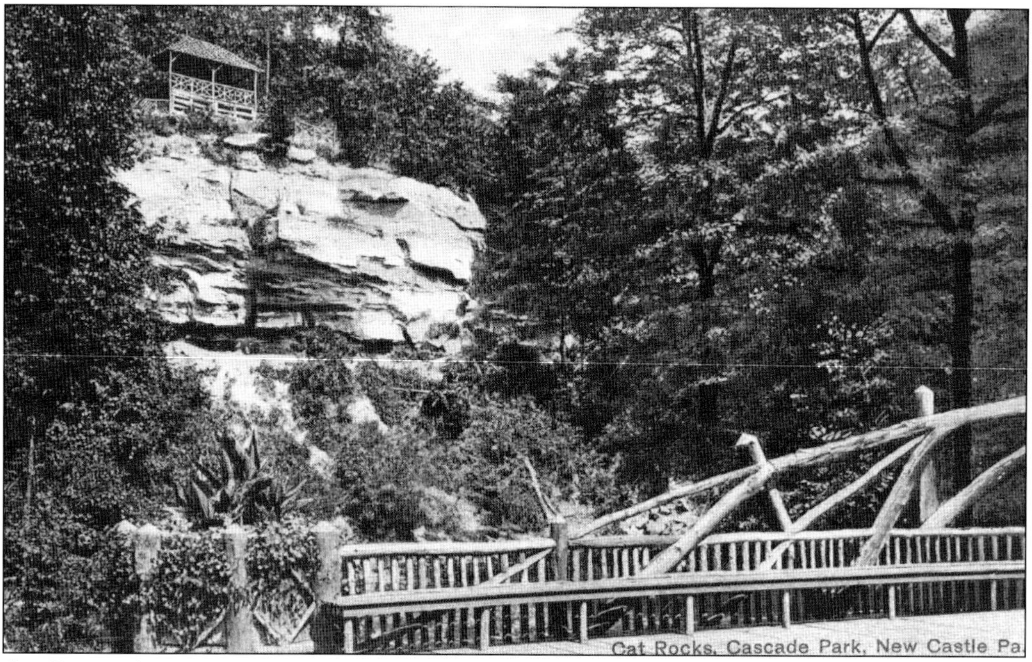

CAT ROCKS, SUMMERHOUSE, AND RUSTIC BRIDGE, C. 1910. Legends about the Cat Rocks abound—one tells of an early settler who was being pursued by a wildcat. The settler jumped from the rocks to the ravine below and escaped because the cat was afraid to jump after him. Another legend tells of the local farmers who set out to find the wildcats who were killing the farmers' small animals. The farmers located the cats in a cave and destroyed them.

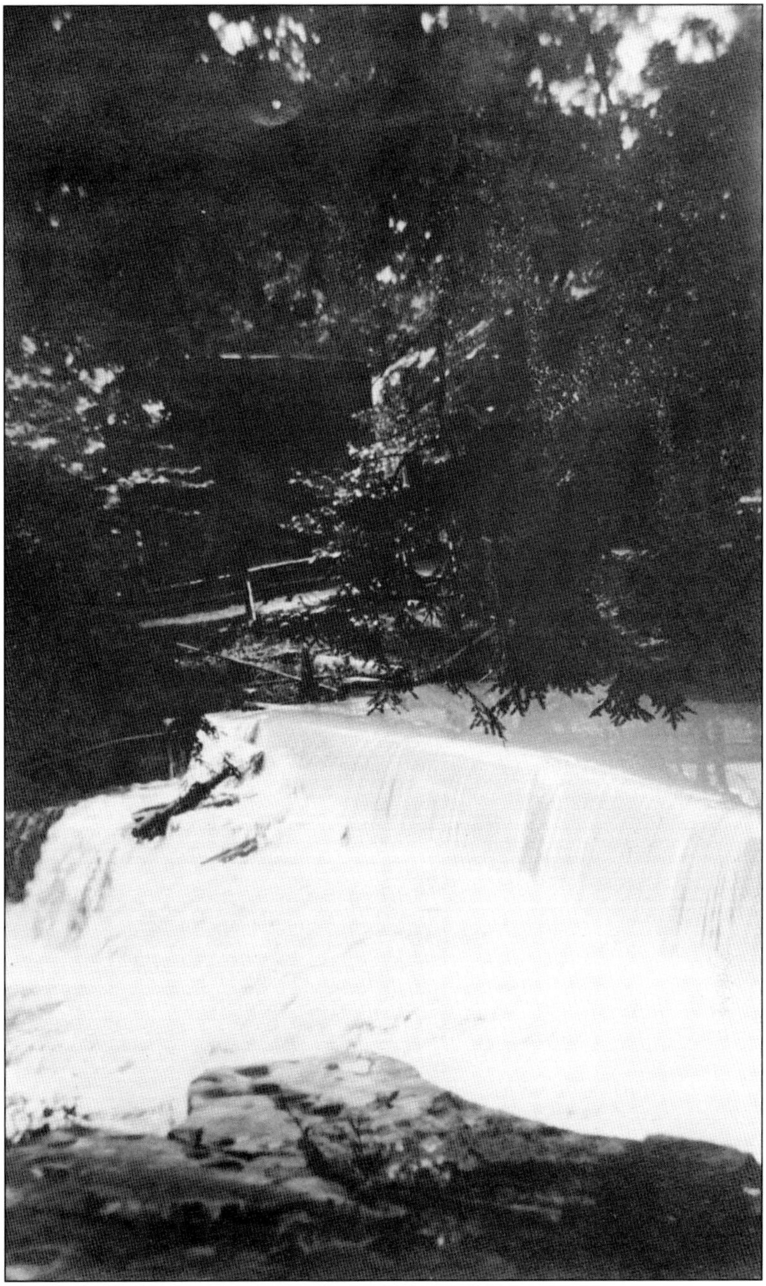

Upper Falls at High Water, 1921. These falls, like the other cascades that gave the park its name, changed from day to day and season to season. The scenery invited visitors to appreciate nature's generosity in the various natural settings of the park. The landscapes were ideal for people who were learning photography and for camera enthusiasts who were always looking for new angles for shooting their photographs. It is said that lightning bolts in electric storms emit negative ions that invigorate people. Running water, like ocean waves and waterfalls, is said to have the same effect, sending out negative ions that can increase alertness and energize bystanders. If this is so, it might explain how Big Run's cascades and falls have energized photographers and visitors over the years, probably inspiring beautiful pictures like this one. (Courtesy of Oliver Shaffer.)

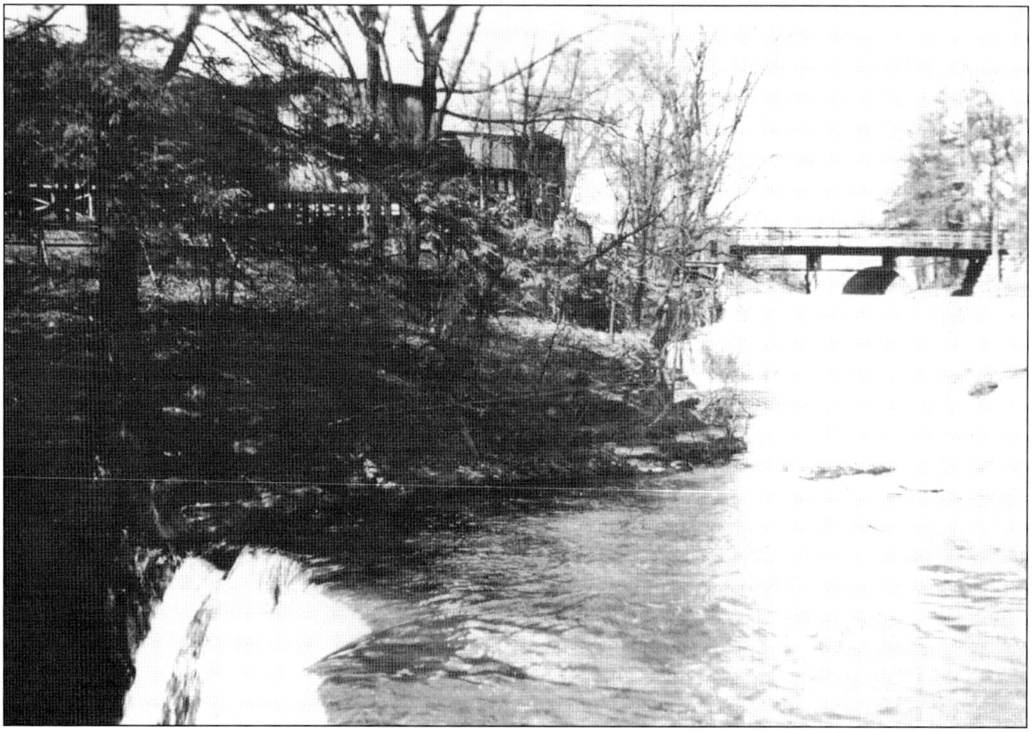

Where the Waterfall Starts, Early 1900s. The brink of the falls, where water begins to tumble downward, is barely discernible in this view. In the distance (upper right) is Big Run's stone bridge and upper dam. At lower left, the water starts flowing over the rocky shelf, falling to the waiting boulders below.

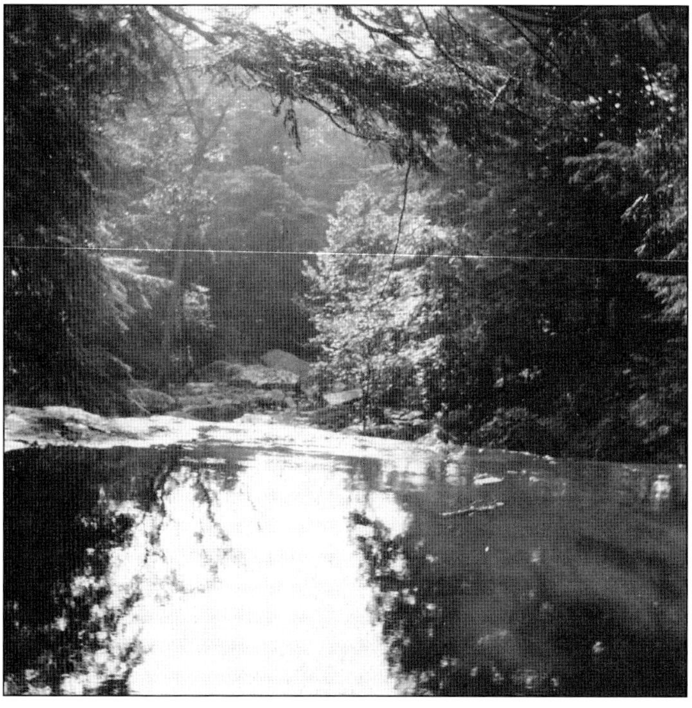

View From the Top, Early 1900s. The photographer who took this early view must have been standing in the middle of Big Run, several feet back from where the water starts to fall. Most visitors do not see this view of Big Run. Downstream, the huge boulders stand like sentinels.

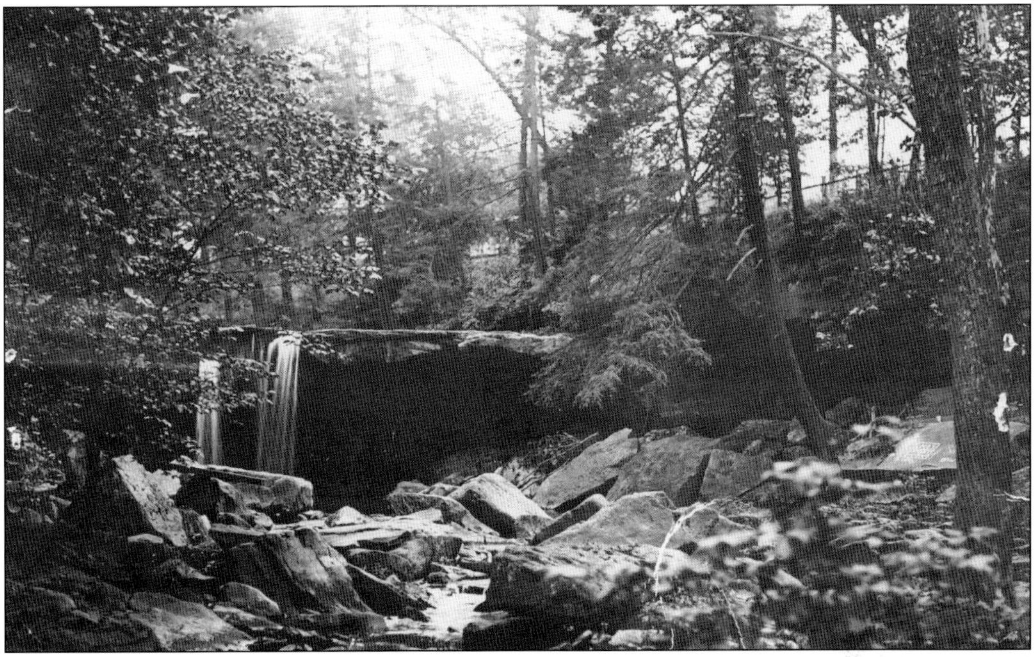

Dry Spell at Big Run Falls, Early 1900s. The falls seem to have run dry in this postcard view. They drop in two small streams at left center and trickle into Big Run. For daredevils, this is the time to investigate the cave under the falls.

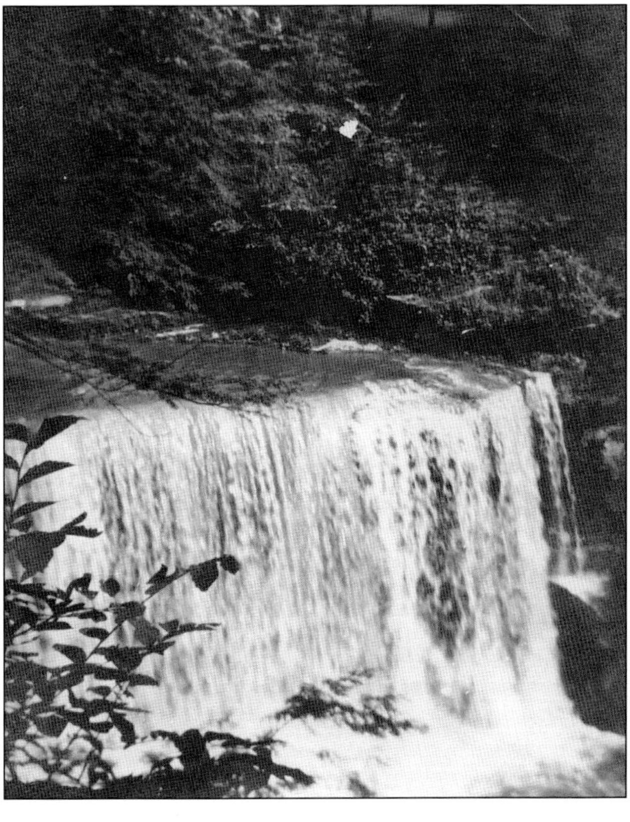

After a Heavy Rain, 1921. One can almost hear the roar of the falls as they drop, swollen from the rain. Modern technology has captured the sounds of falls, rapids, babbling brooks, and ocean waves in various recorded forms. The effect is said to be soothing for some. (Courtesy of Oliver Shaffer.)

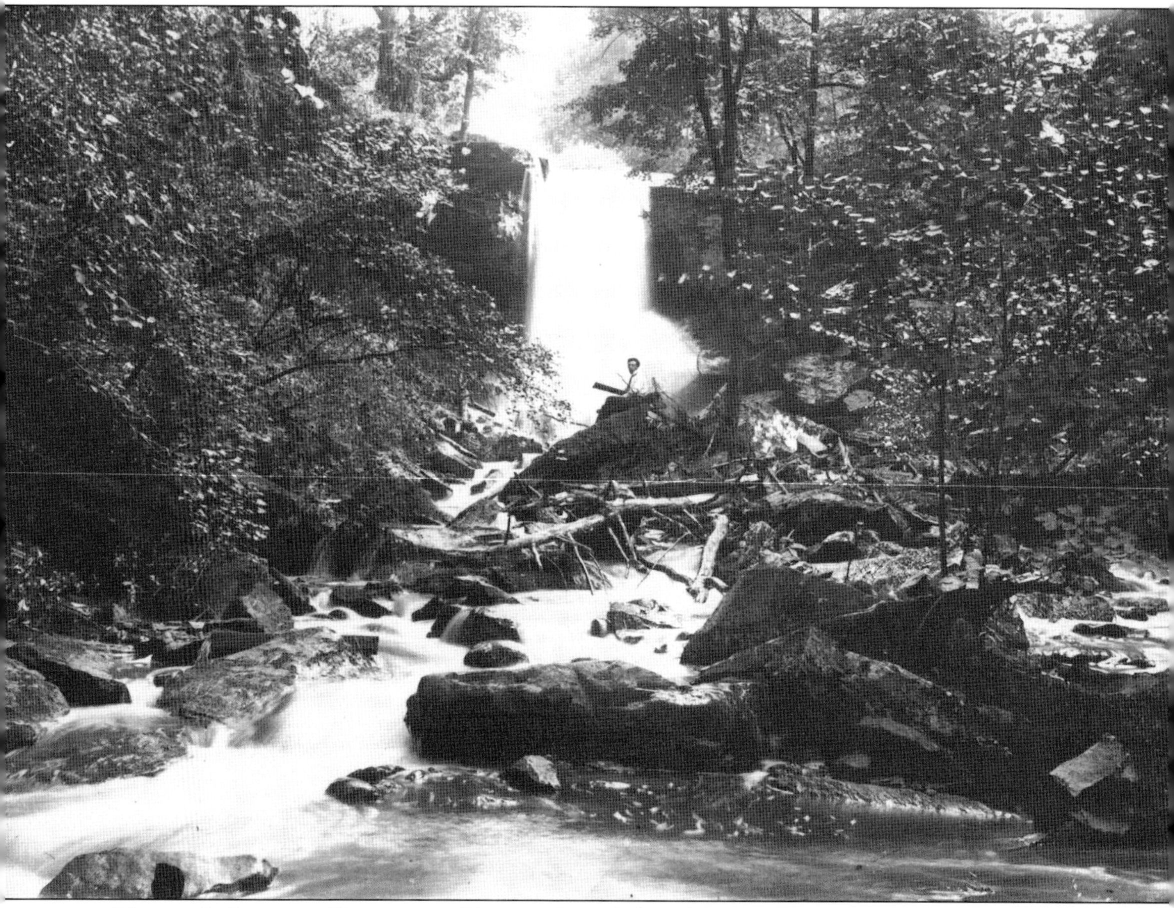

NATURE'S OUTDOOR FURNITURE, EARLY 1900S. This photograph shows a man seated on a boulder a short distance from Big Run Falls. He could be painting a picture or simply enjoying the scenery. The man's perch seems safe from inundation even though rapidly flowing water sweeps by him. The foamy white water finds its way over the rocks, and fallen branches form channels, pools, and eddies. Adventurous boys may try to race on the rocks starting from the grove and running upstream toward the falls. Jumping from rock to rock against the current is not a challenge when the water is low, but higher water poses hazards. The speed of the current, the depth of the water, and invisible obstructions lurking underfoot are not obvious. Intrepid runners may find themselves thoroughly soaked by the time they get to the falls.

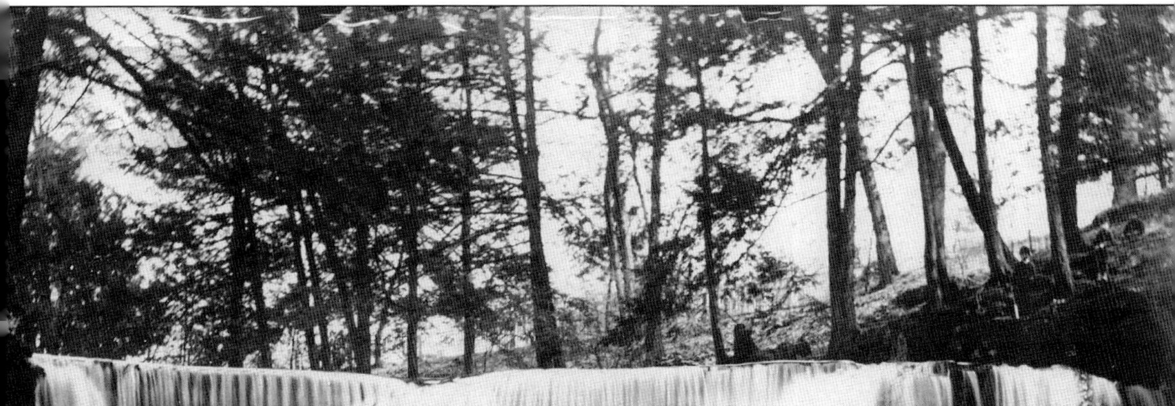

MINIATURE NIAGARA, EARLY 1900S. Historian Aaron Hazen, writing in his 1908 book, described Cascade Park's Big Run Falls as a "miniature Niagara." This photograph is a good illustration of his words. Several people stand on the bank above the falls (upper right) as though it were an observation platform. The steep slope above the water, what Hazen called "a rocky gulch," seems not to concern them. The beauty of this sheer veil of water is alluring, and the onlookers are drawn close. Views like this inspire thoughts about the magnificence of nature's artistry and the capacity of humans to enjoy the abundance of natural beauty. Unfortunately, this spectacular view was missed by A. W. Phipps, a well-known New Castle photographer, in the early 1900s. He had often visited Big Run Falls park as a favorite retreat; however, he never visited Cascade Park after it became known by that name because he felt that the changes had "robbed the area of its wild, picturesque beauty."

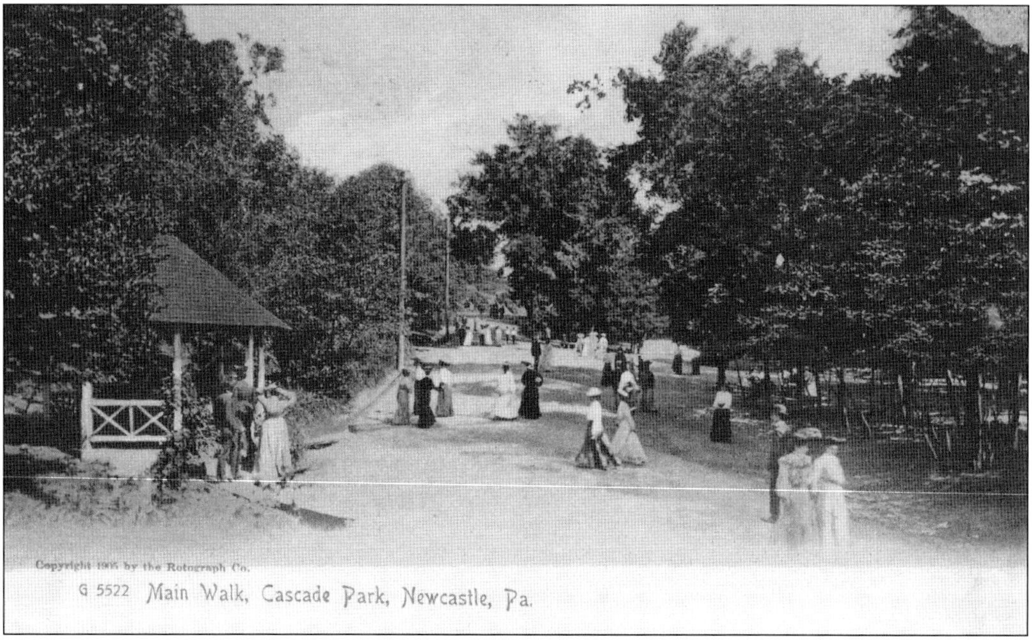

The Main Walk, 1908. In the early 1900s, elegant dress was customary for women visiting the park. Long skirts, shirtwaists, and large decorated hats were in vogue. Strolls on the main walk often limited a woman to the use of one hand, because the other hand was holding her skirt above the dust of the path.

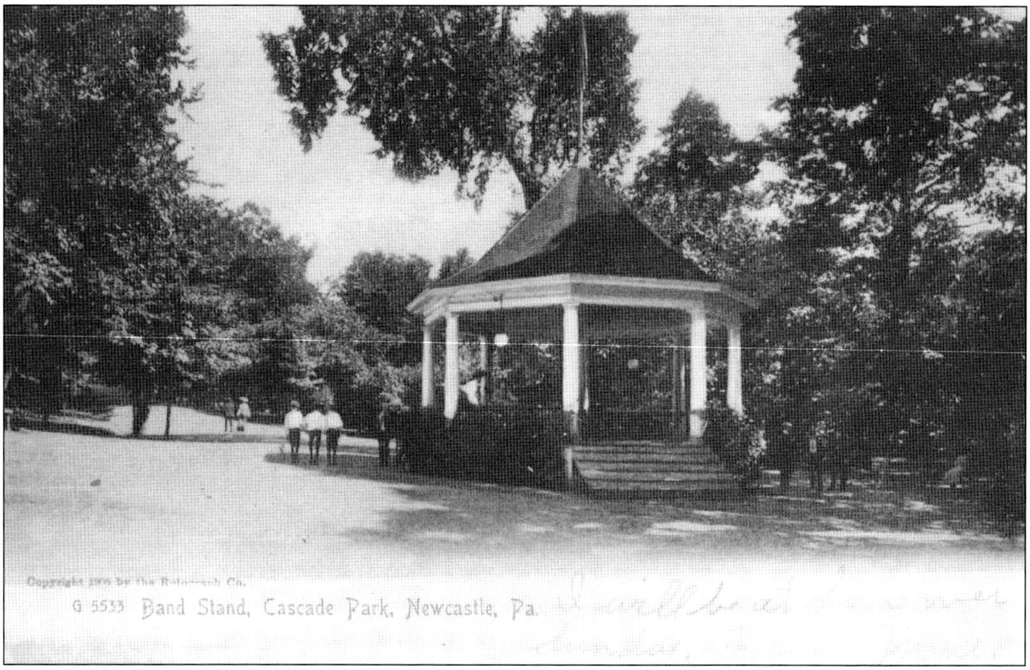

The Band Stand, 1907. Cascade Park was always festive with regular concerts in the park. Outdoor concerts are a tradition still maintained in the New Castle area, which has always been endowed with talented musicians. This gazebo, called "The Band Stand" on the postcard, was called "The Music Hall" by visitors.

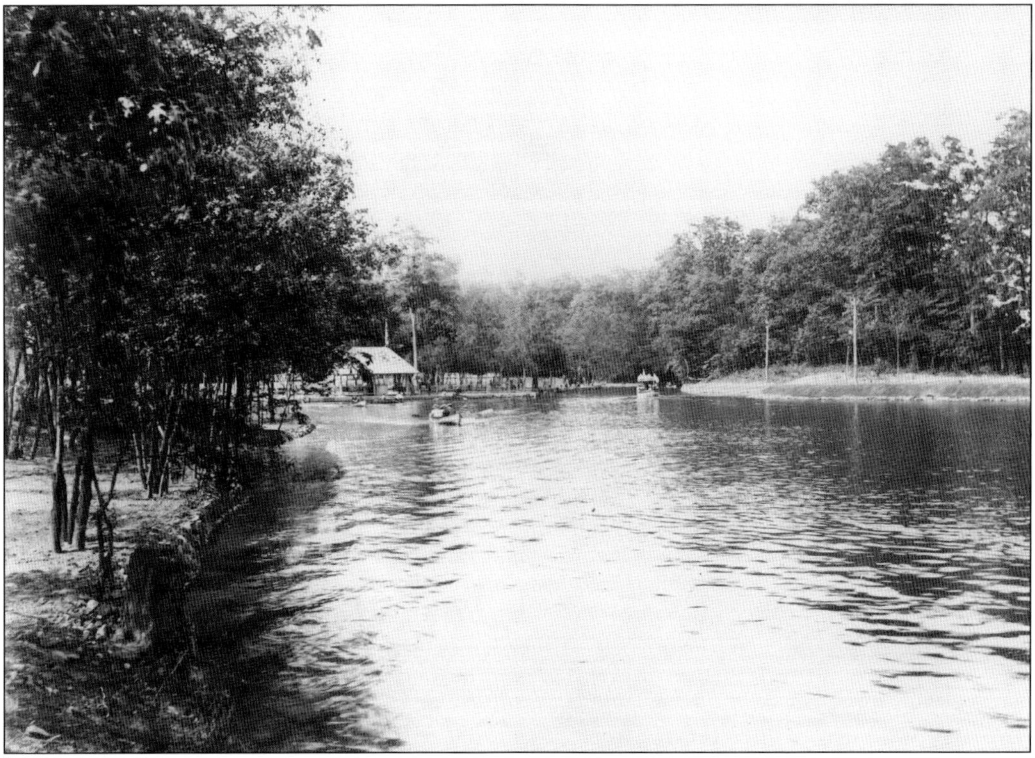

APPROACH TO THE LAKE, EARLY 1900S. The boathouse in the distance is where lake visitors could rent rowboats or buy a seat on the launch. The lake's generous expanse made either ride worthwhile. This photograph was taken from the lagoon near the terminal where streetcars made a loop to change directions.

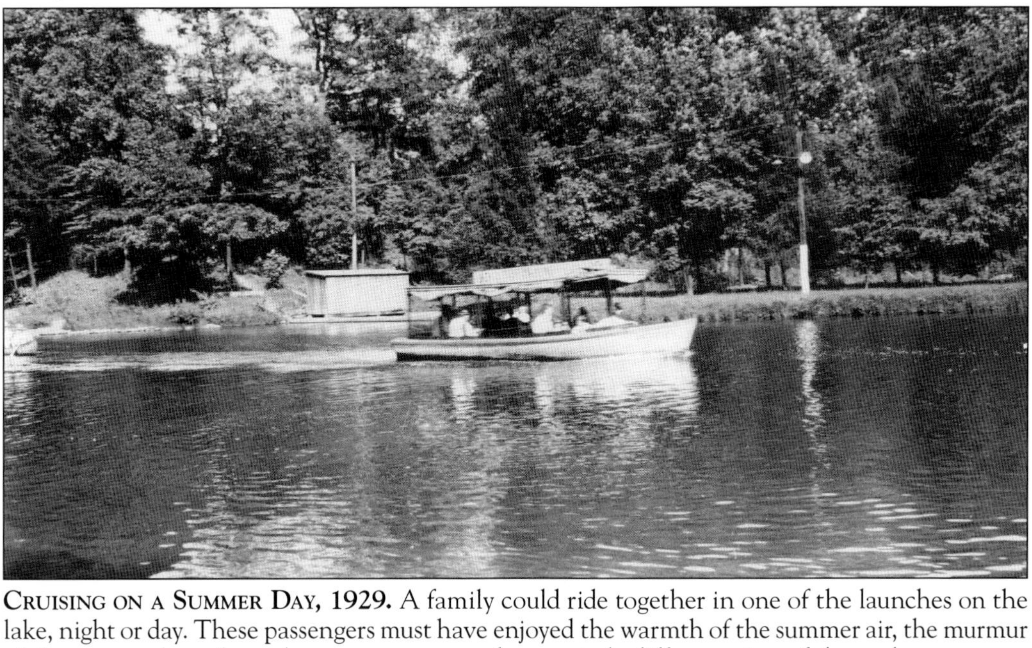

CRUISING ON A SUMMER DAY, 1929. A family could ride together in one of the launches on the lake, night or day. These passengers must have enjoyed the warmth of the summer air, the murmur of the trees, echoes from the amusements, and an entirely different view of the park.

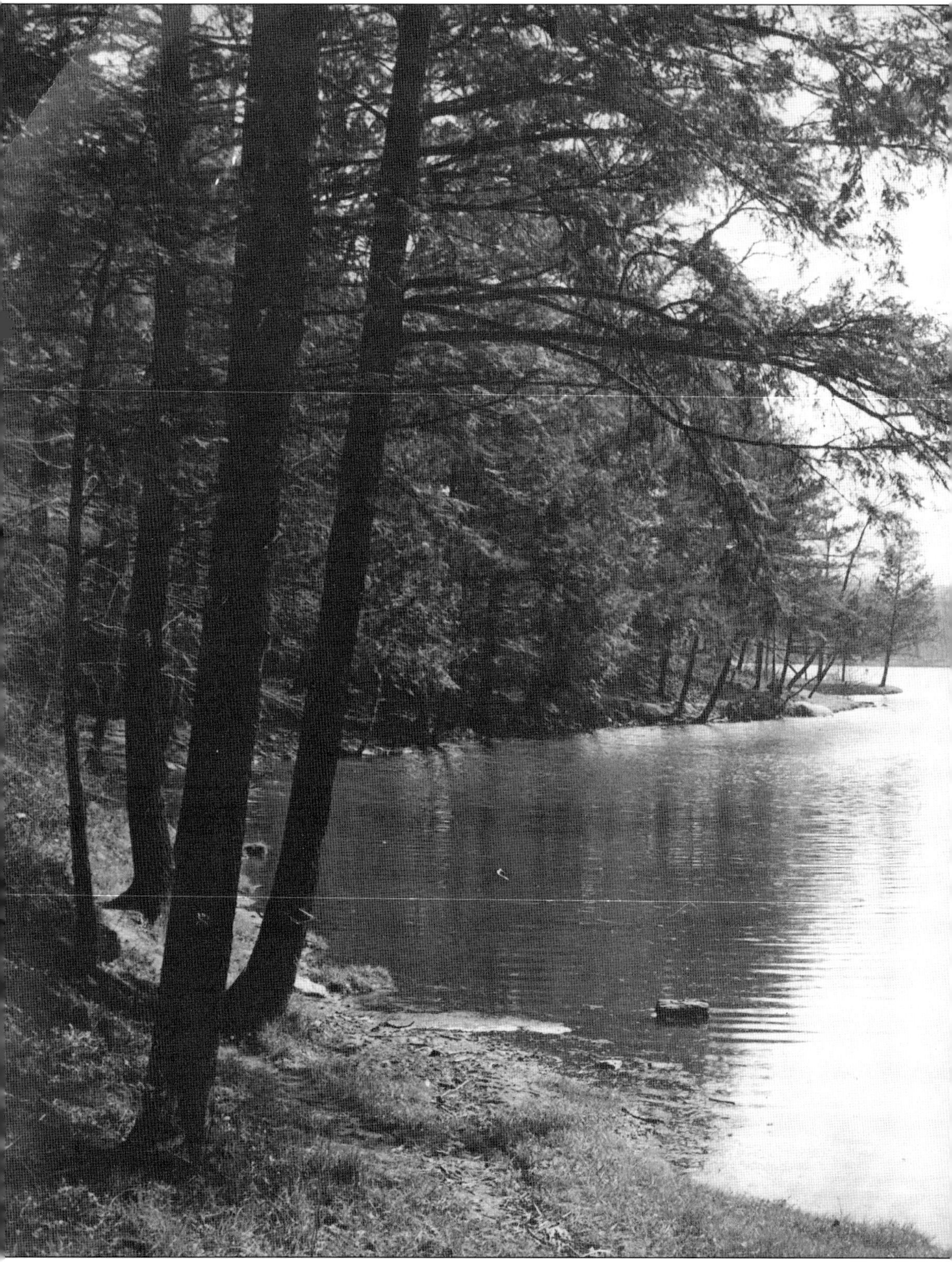

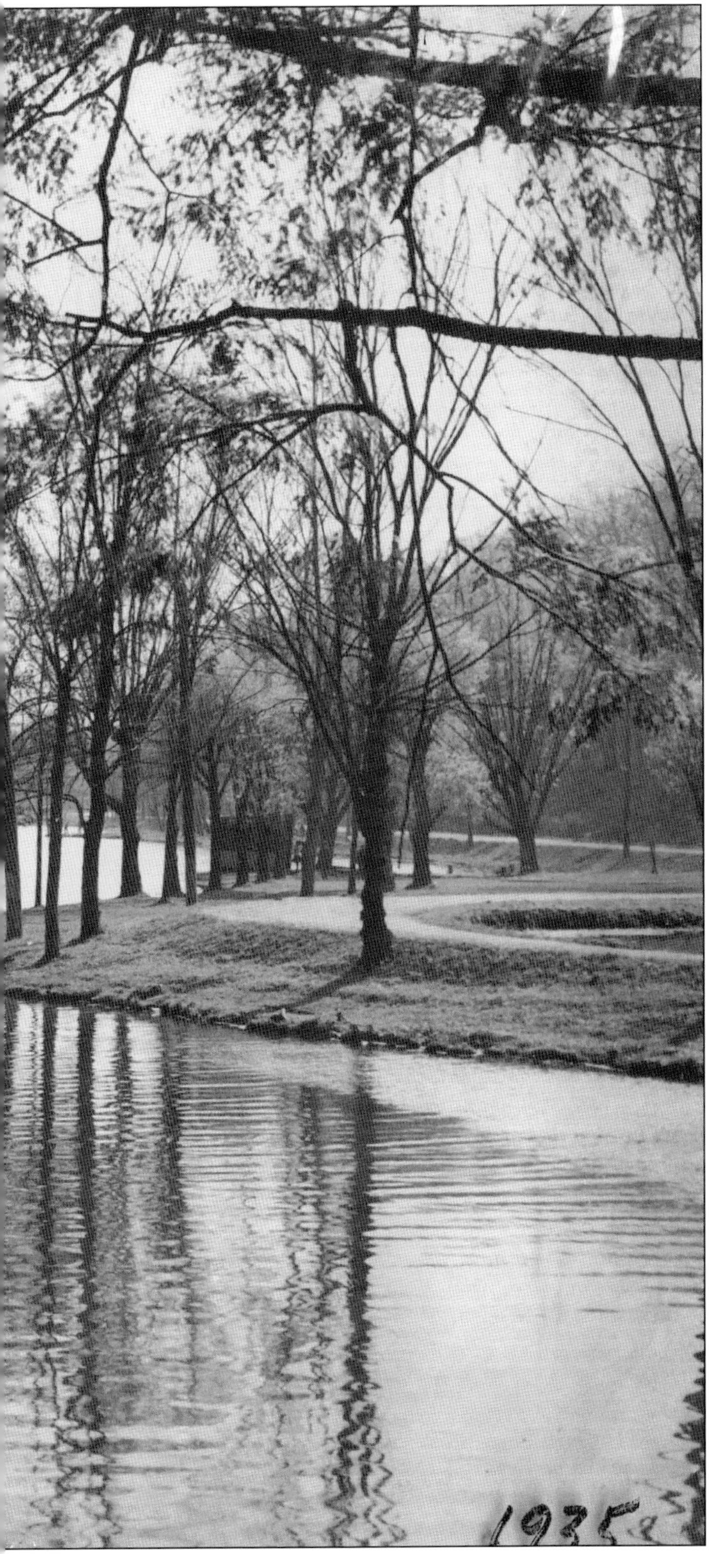

A TRANQUIL SCENE, 1935. From the beginning, Cascade Park drew thousands of people. Excursion trains came from Pittsburgh and Youngstown; employee picnics, family reunions, and special days like the Fourth of July attracted crowds. The grove alone was said to accommodate 5,000 people. Many of them were drawn to the lake, where one could be quickly refreshed. Seldom was the lake as quiet as it looks in this photograph. During the summer, when the trees were full, a boat ride past the lagoon would be under a green canopy and passengers would glide into the open sunshine and wide expanse of what used to be called Crystal Lake. Early morning would draw the fishermen, many with sons and grandsons. The lake provided recreation for the young and not so young, and it provided beauty and pleasure to all who took time to look.

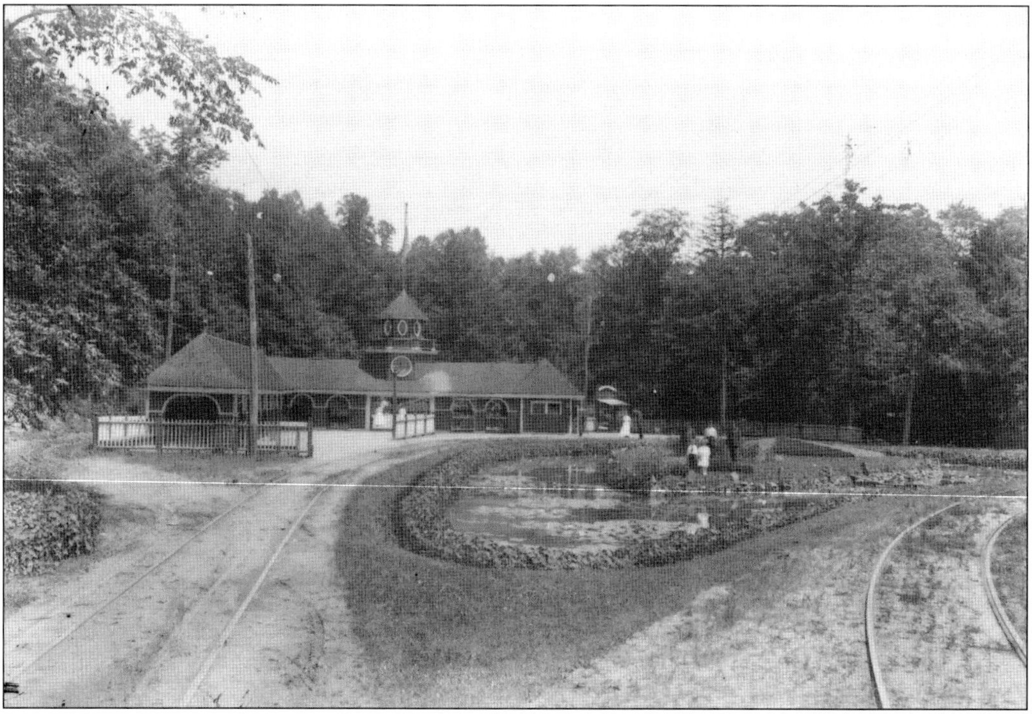

Posing in the Lagoon, Early 1900s. This was the first entrance to Cascade Park. The arriving streetcars would turn right, loop around the lagoon, and be positioned to leave. The plantings in the lagoon changed from year to year, but they were water lilies most often. A group of visitors stand in the center of the lagoon to pose for a photograph.

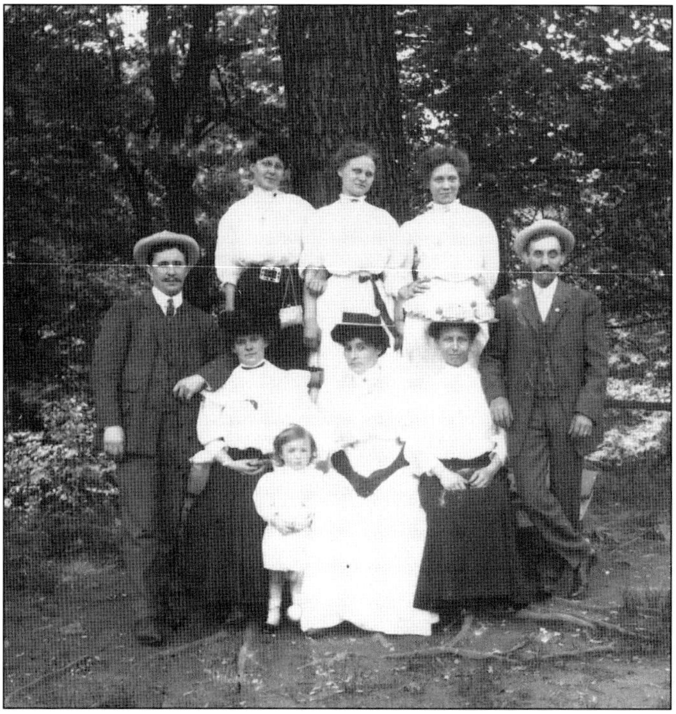

Posing among the Trees, Early 1900s. This photograph shows a handsome group: women in their popular shirtwaists, men in full suits and boaters. They are posed against a tree, where a park bench is probably providing the seating. Women sewed most of their clothing, as custom tailoring was not readily affordable.

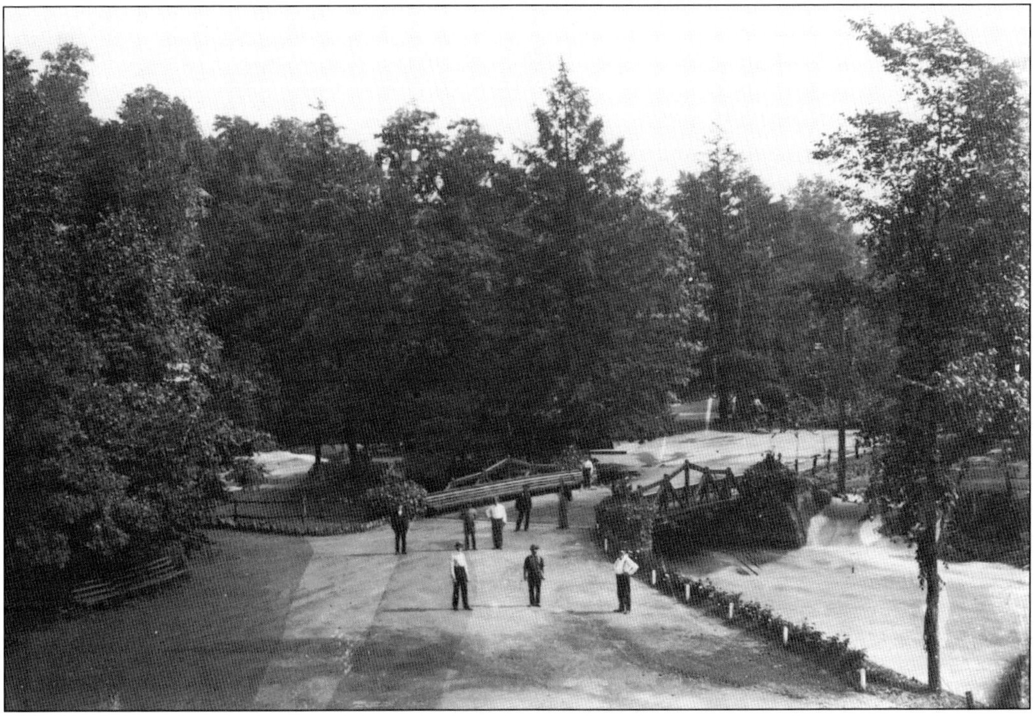

POSING IN THE LOWER PARK, EARLY 1900S. The men posing in this photograph appear to be workmen. They are standing on and around one of the rustic bridges, looking at the photographer. Cameras were not yet generally available in the early 1900s, so having a picture taken was an occasion.

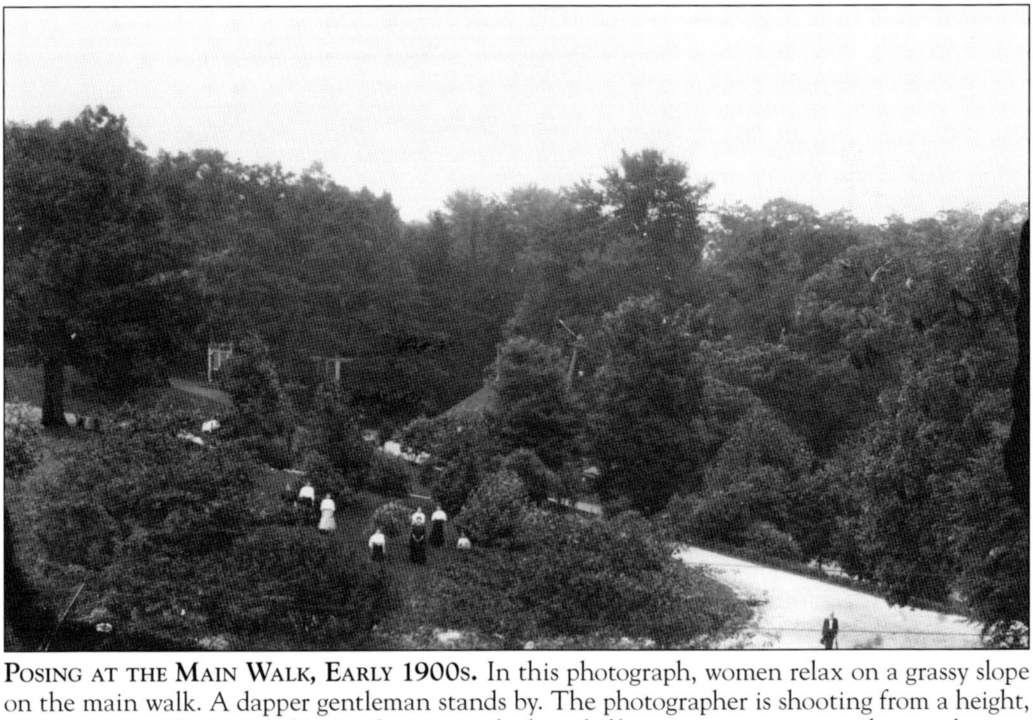

POSING AT THE MAIN WALK, EARLY 1900S. In this photograph, women relax on a grassy slope on the main walk. A dapper gentleman stands by. The photographer is shooting from a height, perhaps a tree. He is probably too far away to be heard if he wants to rearrange the people.

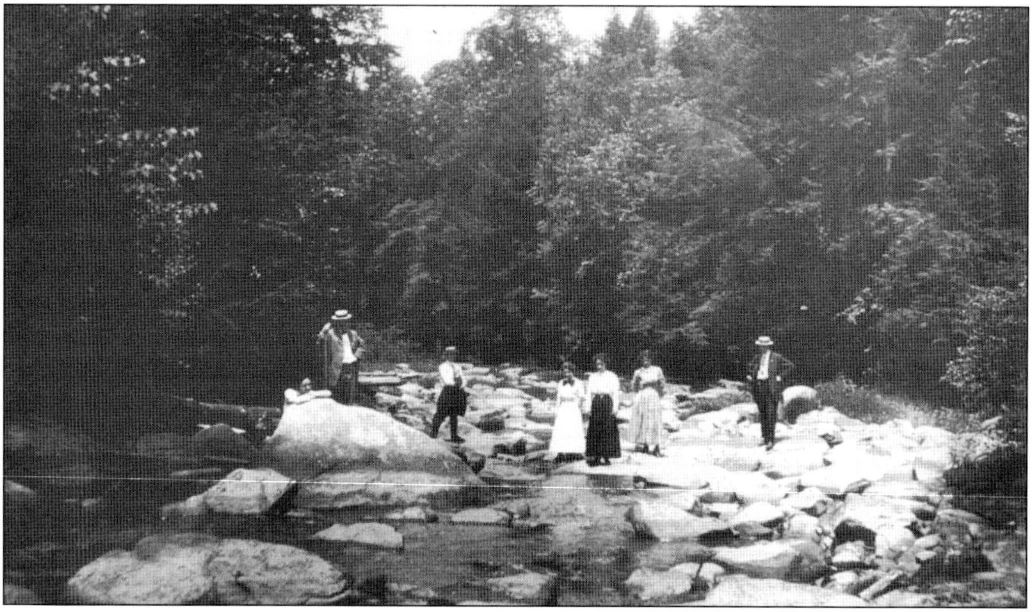

Posing on the Rocks in Big Run, c. 1910. The women in this photograph seem to be considering whether to jump across Big Run. The water is not deep at this point, but the irregular shapes and sizes of the rocks and boulders seem to deter them. (Courtesy of Sandra Bumgardner.)

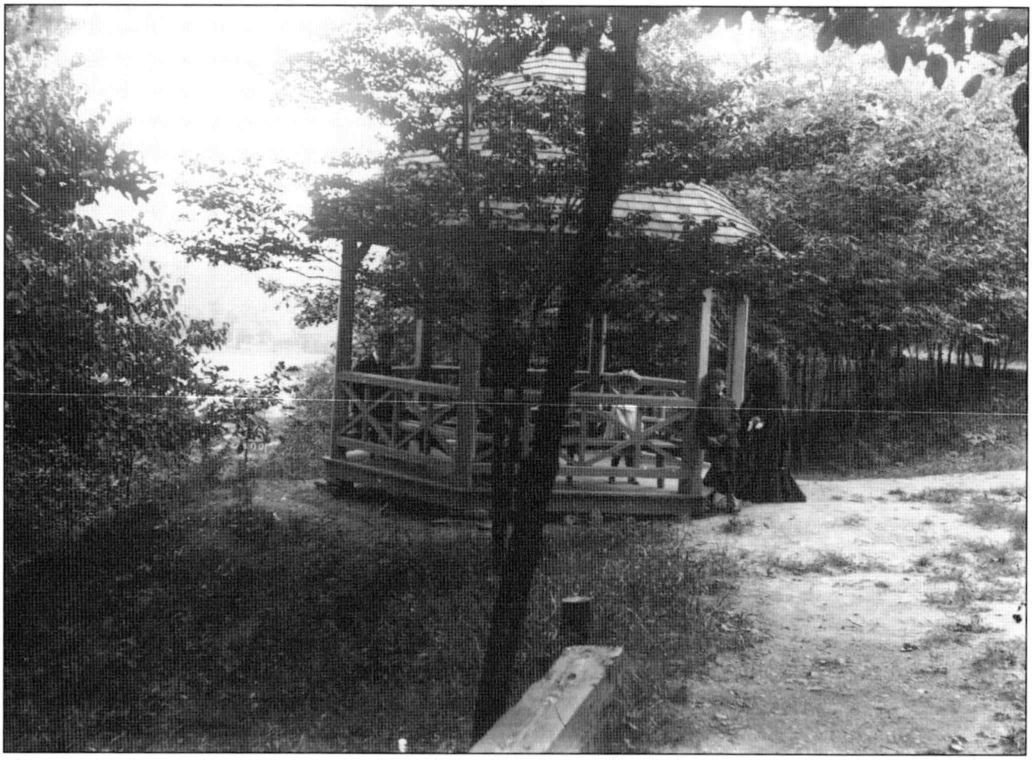

Posing at a Rustic House, Early 1900s. The well-dressed occupants of this rustic house command a view of the lake (left, through the trees). The house is not far from the ridge overlooking the falls. It is a welcome resting place for any visitors who climb up from the grove.

Posing in the Woods, 1906. This rustic house shows another use of twig architecture, a style similar to that of Cascade Park's rustic bridges. The conical roof is characteristic of the Queen Anne style of architecture fashionable in the Victorian era. The gentleman standing next to the hut is also fashionable, wearing a derby, or bowler, hat.

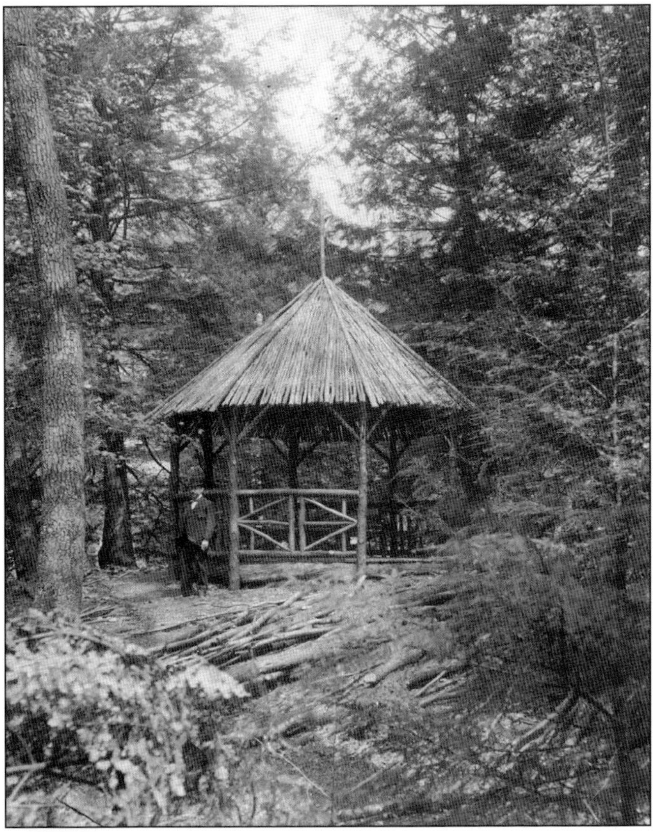

Posing at the Floral Steps, Early 1900s. The people in this photograph appear to be arranged by the photographer. When Cascade Park opened in 1897, the landscape designer installed lush plantings throughout the park. Flowers, shrubbery, and a variety of plants continued to be maintained after the opening and seem to flourish in this photograph along the floral steps.

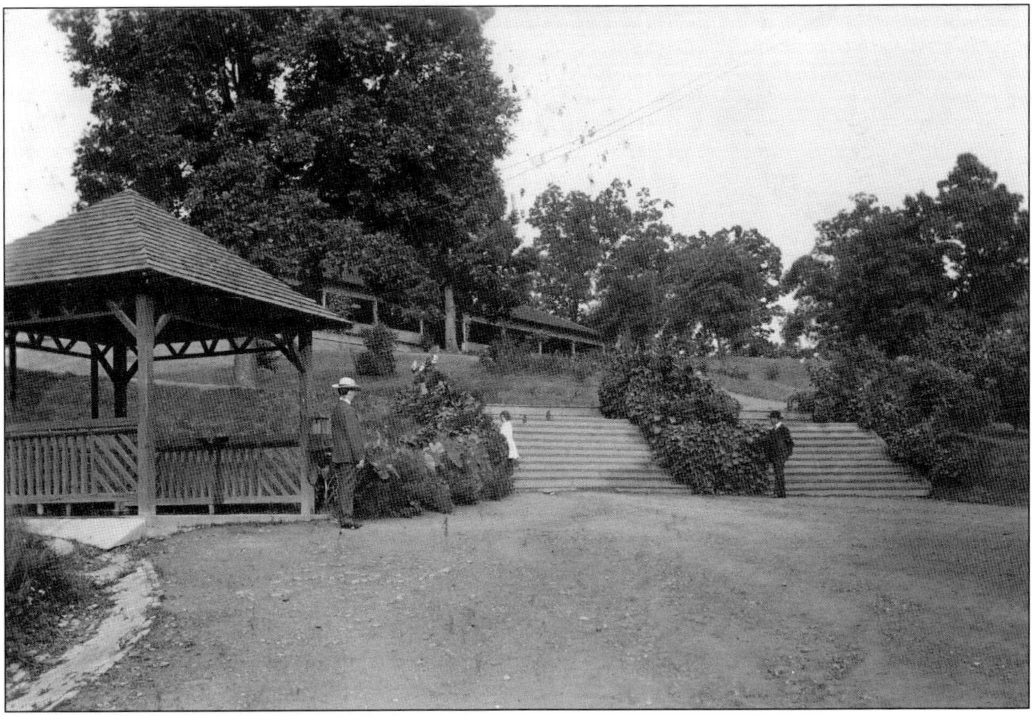

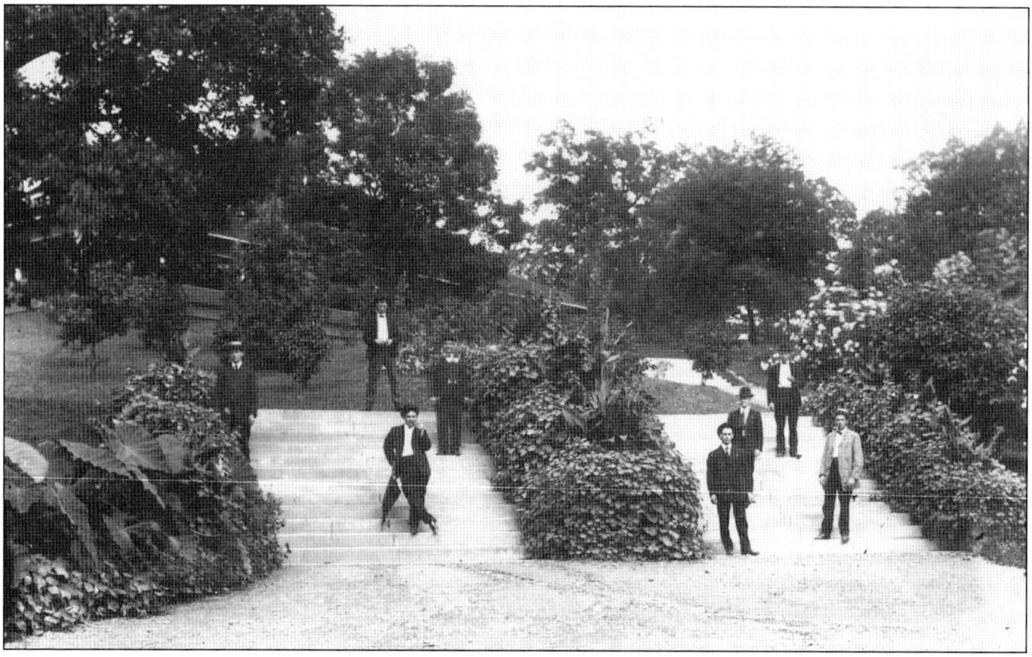

A Number of Men at the Floral Steps, Early 1909. When the floral steps were first built in 1898, they led up to the first roller coaster next to the dance pavilion, as well as to the dance pavilion itself. Today they serve as a shortcut to the parking lot or to the front entrance of the dance pavilion. The men in this photograph appear to be posed in a tableau for the pleasure of onlookers.

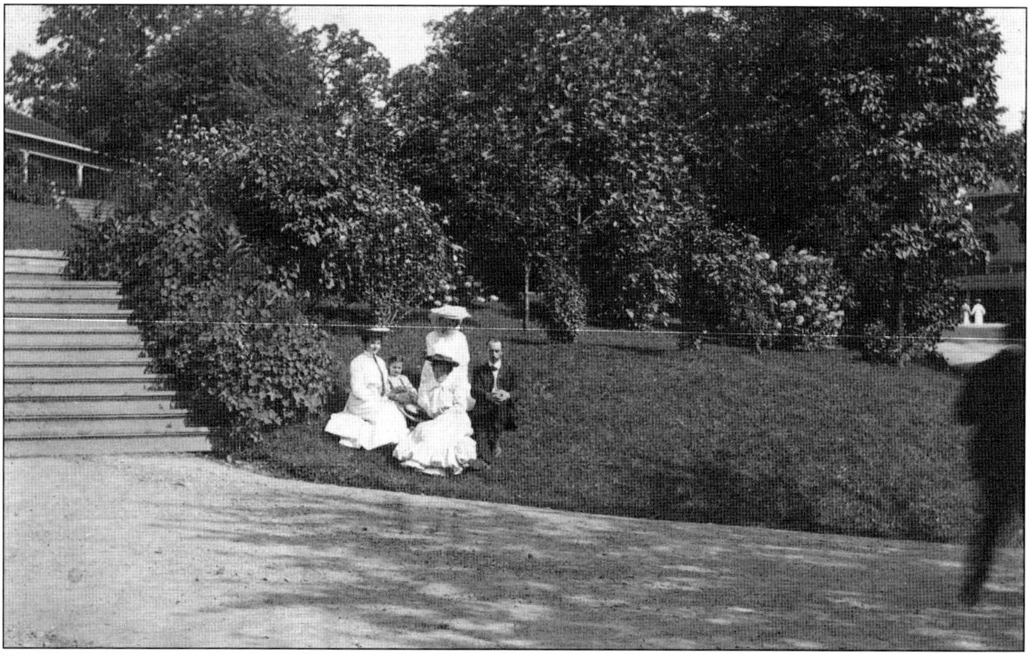

Posing on the Lawn, Early 1900s. Rather than sit on the floral steps, this family chose to sit on the lawn next to the main walk and the shrubs that are in full bloom. Part of the midway can be seen in the background. Although it was customary for men to wear hats in public, for some reason this man does not wear one.

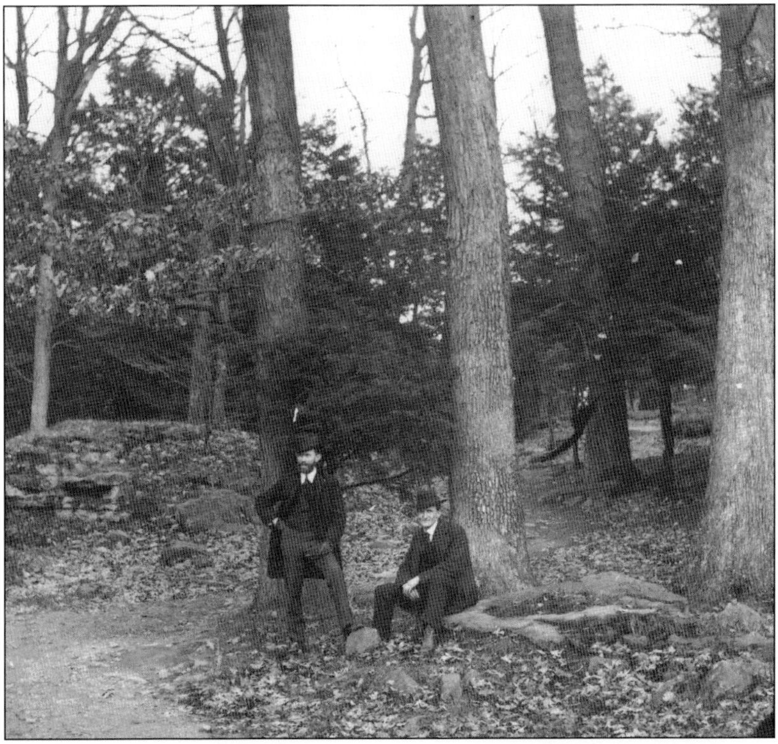

Two Men Pause, Early 1900s. A walk through Cascade Park was usually a leisurely stroll with friends or family. In this photograph, two men have left the path and pose for a picture. The trees appear to be losing their leaves, and a fallen branch provides seating for one of the men.

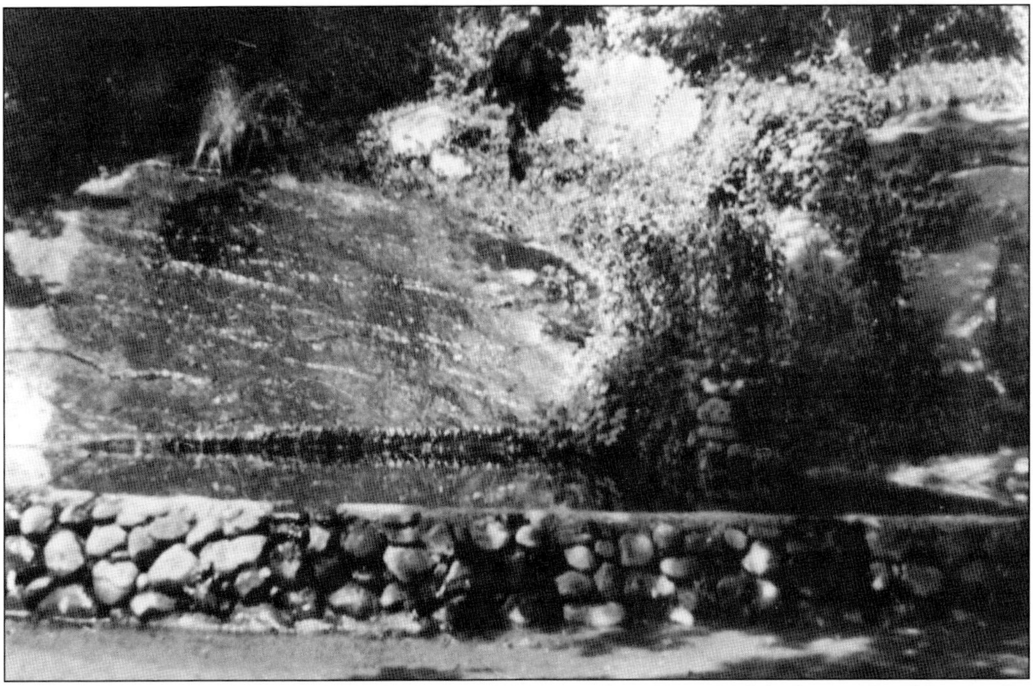

Large Boulder and Flowing Water, Early 1900s. This was one of the largest boulders in the park. Water constantly flowed in a thin sheet across its front surface. Occasionally water spurted upward from the top like a fountain. The water collected at the boulder's bottom, held by a stone wall. Once located near the bottom of the main walk, the boulder has been removed.

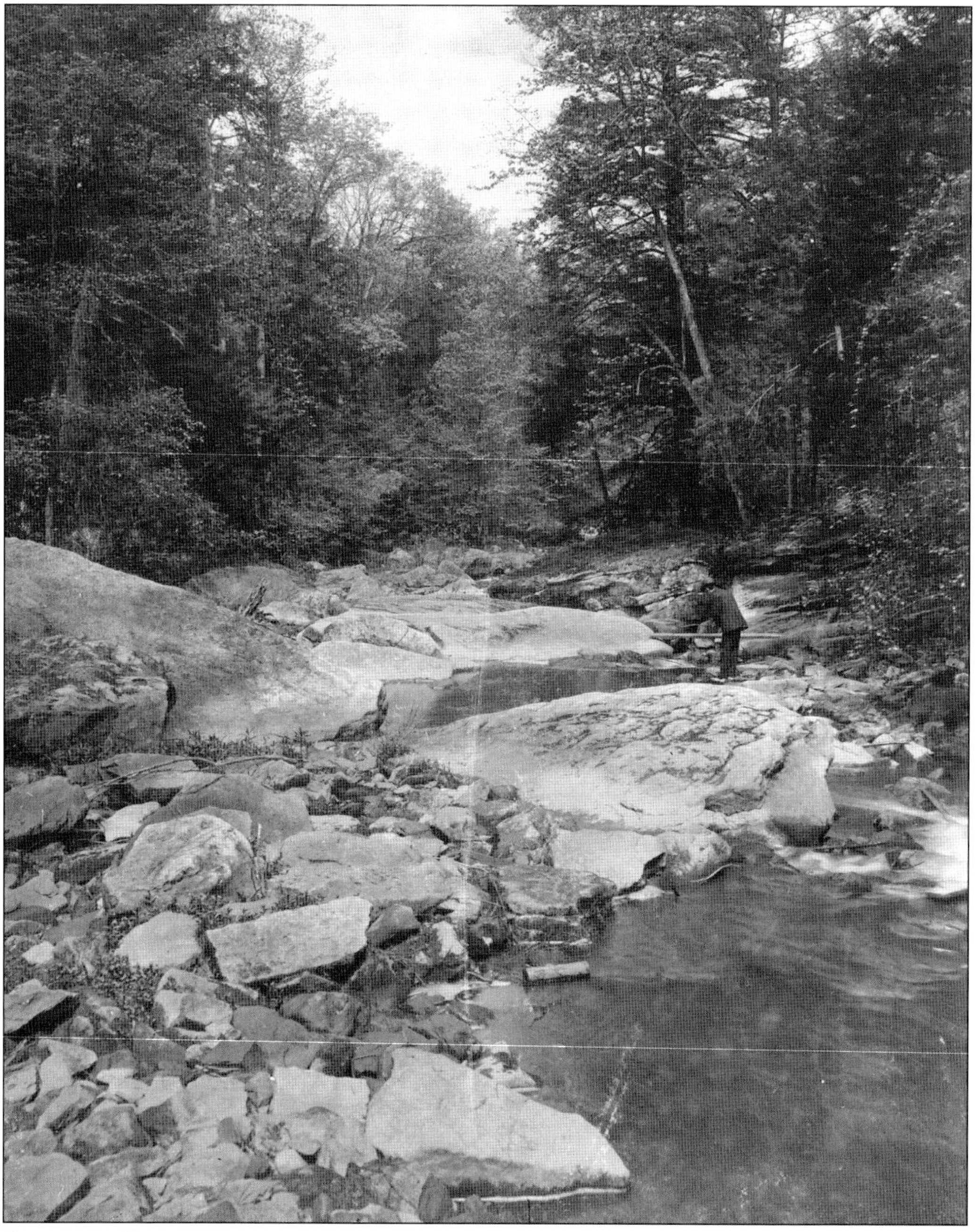

ROCKS AND POOLS IN BIG RUN, EARLY 1900S. At right center, a man is standing on the rocks holding what appears to be a fishing rod over a pool. In front of him, a board between two boulders seems to be a barricade. The rocks fit together like a gray mosaic, showing a variety of grooves and textures. Some flat surfaces are inscribed by visitors who want to be permanently identified with Big Run or Cascade Park. The little rocks are transient. They will probably move on when the water gives them a push. For now, it appears that this is a place for quiet solitude, but at high water, this stretch of Big Run is probably dangerous. When this photograph was taken, there were no cell phones for emergencies. Nevertheless, this lone fisherman appears to be undaunted.

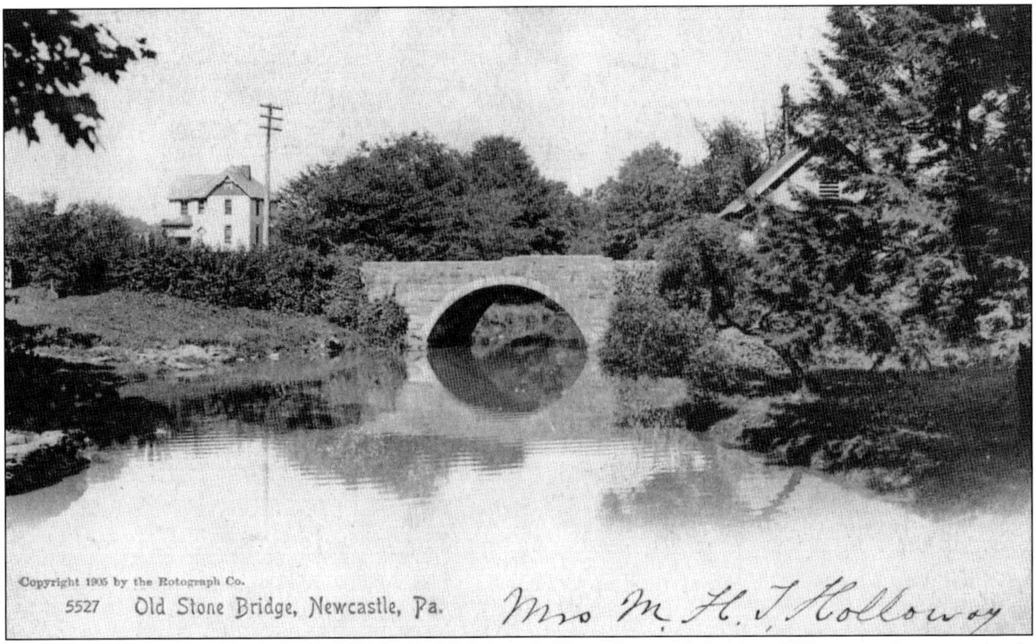

OLD STONE BRIDGE, 1905. One of Cascade Park's boundaries is East Washington Street, which crosses over Big Run. This postcard shows the Old Stone Bridge when East Washington Street was called Pittsburg Street. This bridge was built in 1861, replacing a bridge that had washed out in the heavy rains of that year.

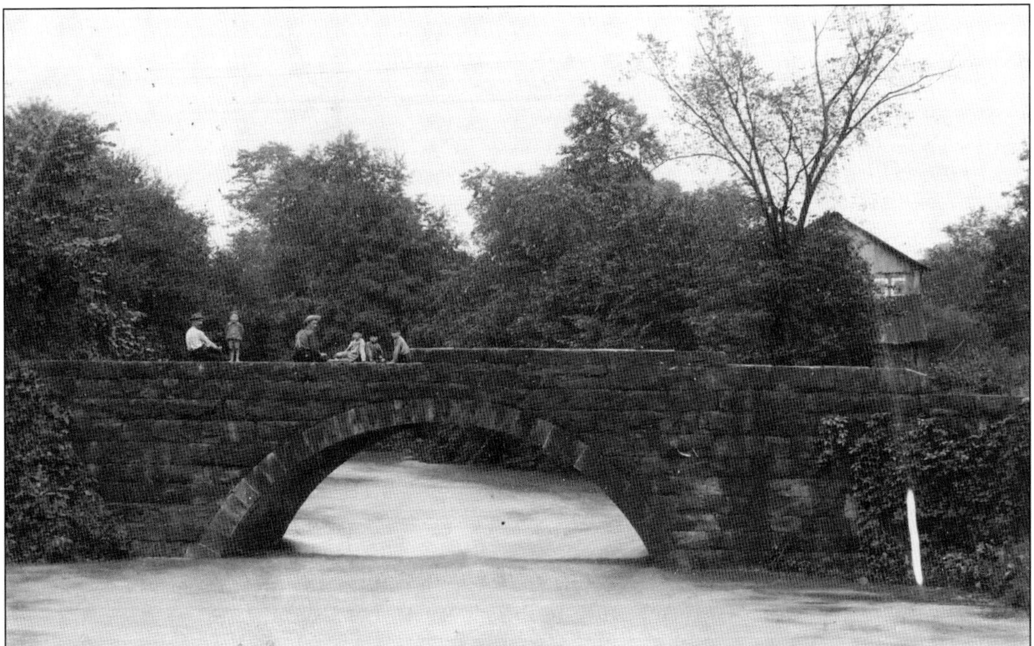

OLD STONE BRIDGE, EARLY 1900S. In 1902, the Old Stone Bridge was the only stone bridge in Lawrence County. In 1907, it was widened by 12 feet. By 1927, the volume of traffic on East Washington Street had increased and another extension was necessary. The extension buried the Old Stone Bridge.

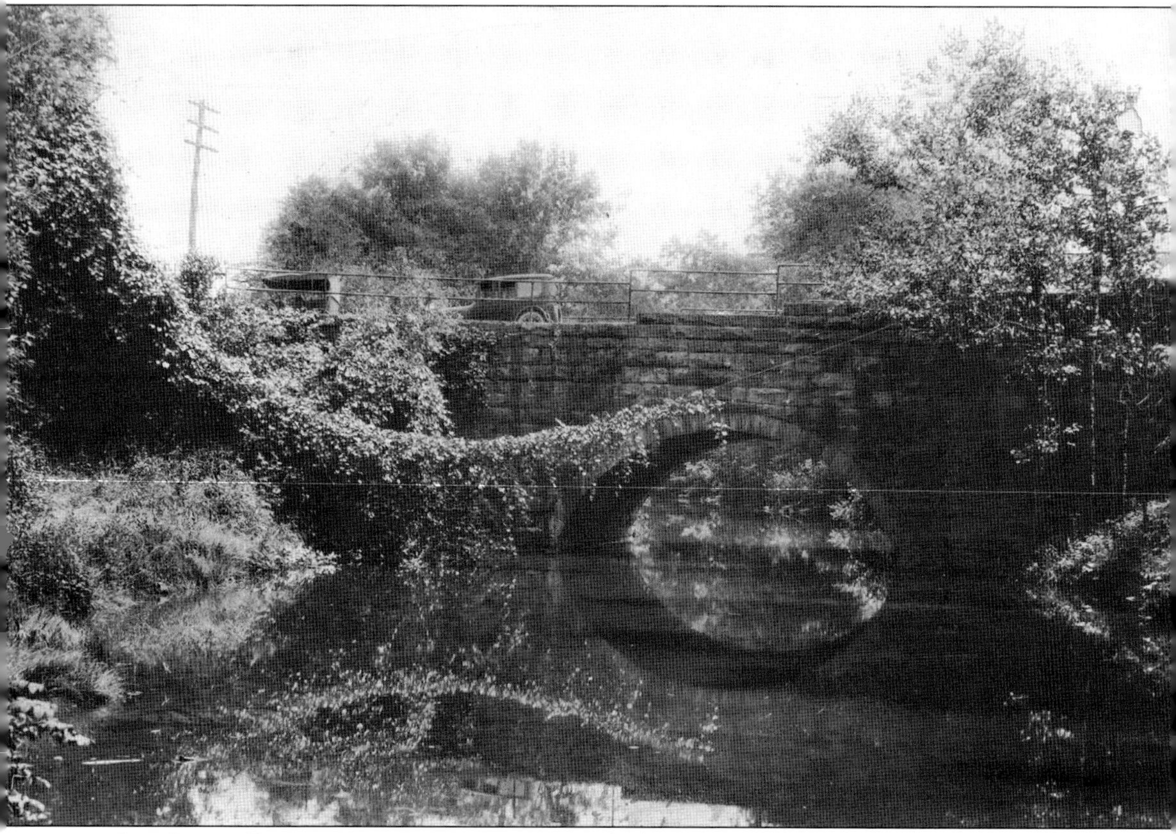

Old Stone Bridge, c. 1920. As years passed, the greenery that was so abundant in Cascade Park from its first days reached the Old Stone Bridge. By 1930, the greenery was gone. The bridge had disappeared and the greenery with it. That was the result of work started in 1927 to widen the bridge and build a newly graded approach to the crossing over Big Run. In the course of that work, a 5-foot pedestrian walk was added. The result of the new grading was that the Old Stone Bridge sat far beneath the new grade, gradual as it was, and most of the old bridge was no longer visible. In June 1927, the paving was completed, detour signs were removed, and traffic resumed. Big Run still crosses under East Washington Street, but the charming bridge is gone. (Courtesy of the New Castle Public Library.)

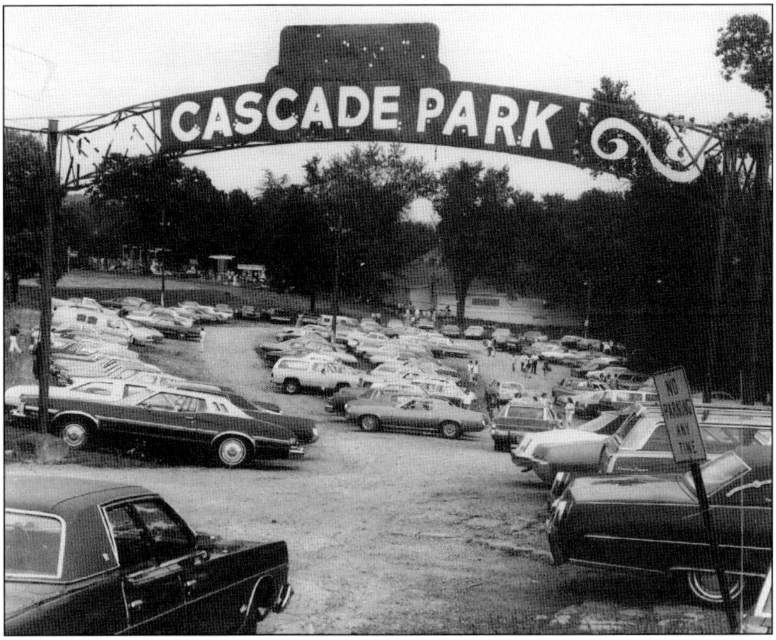

Full Parking Lot, c. 1980. Although the sign in the parking lot says "no parking at any time," parked cars filled the area around it. The lot just was not big enough for the crowd at Cascade Park the day this photograph was taken. In the background (upper left) is the miniature golf concession, which was removed in 1999. The dance pavilion is at right center.

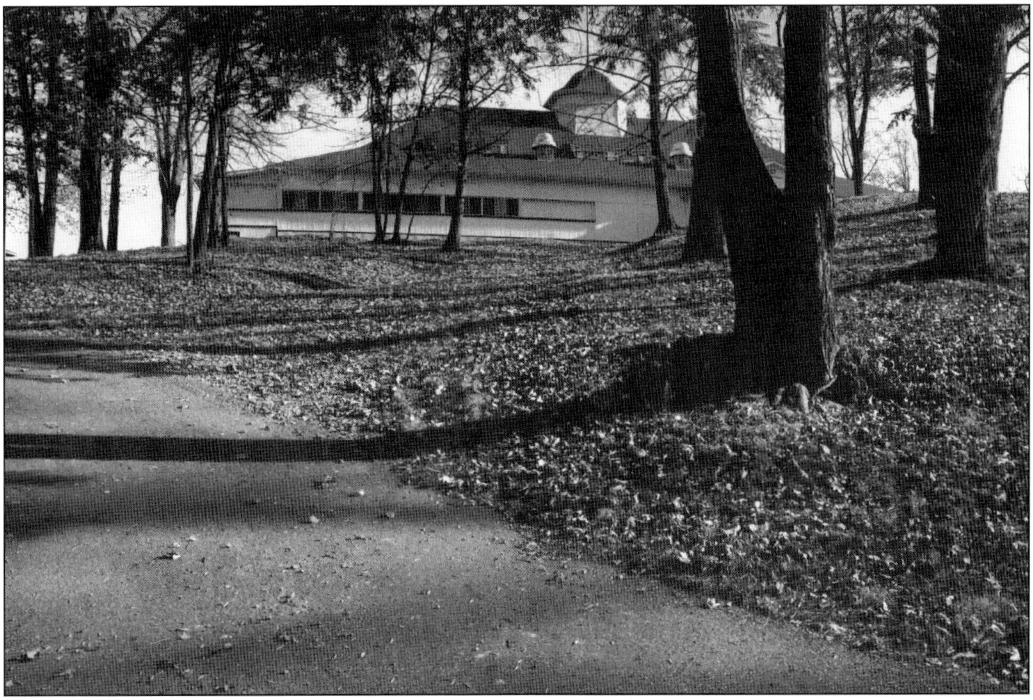

Dance Pavilion in Autumn, 2009. Well past 100 years old, the dance pavilion looks regal, sitting on a promontory in this quiet scene. It still welcomes Old Timers Day, the Paws and Taws, the Saturday night dances, and many other events that make it a community meeting place. With new windows for cold weather, it can look forward to new events. (Courtesy of Adam Pivovar.)

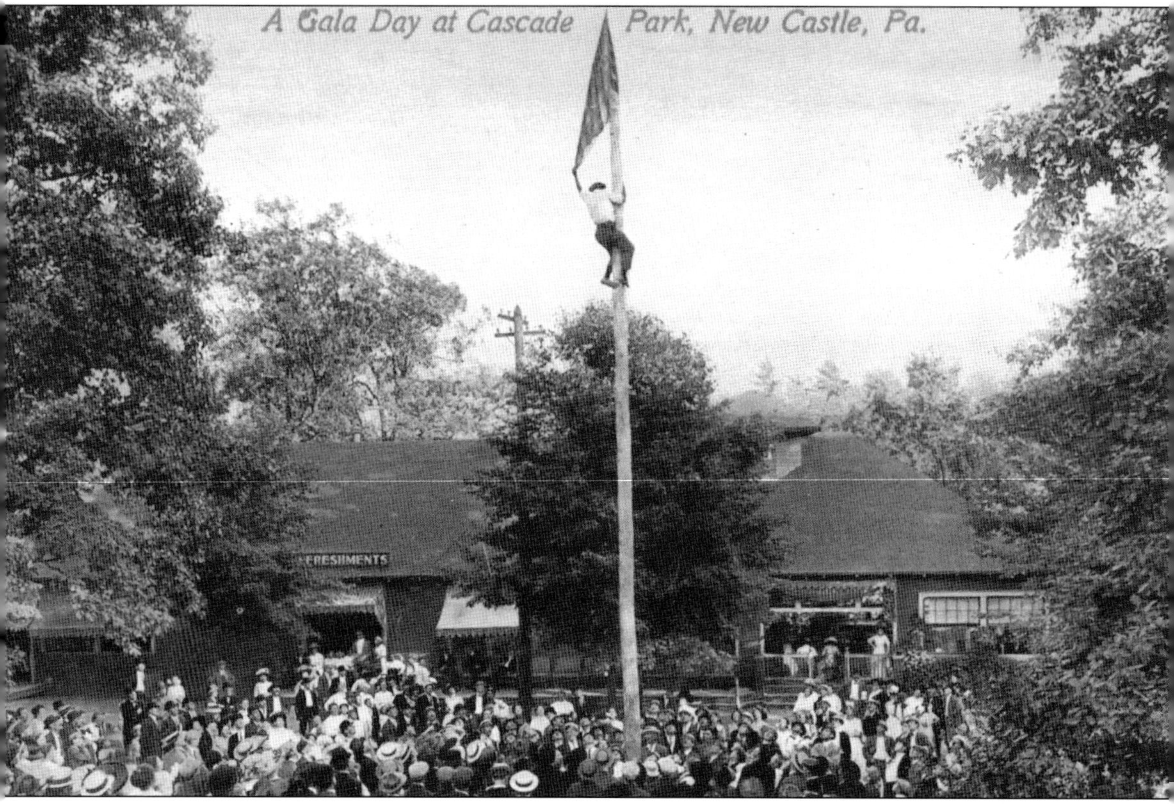

Gala Day at Cascade Park, c. 1912. This postcard shows a happy crowd cheering for the fellow who climbed the flagpole. In the background is the restaurant, a building that seldom appears in postcards and photographs. Festivities of the kind shown here were frequent at Cascade Park. The Fourth of July always had the largest crowd of the season, and business was always brisk. According to the *New Castle News*, in 1900, people by the thousands began to line up early for the streetcars at the corner of Mill and Washington Streets. Twenty-four cars carrying 80 people each were making roundtrips every 40 minutes. The traction company calculated attendance was 21,000 that day, close to the limit of 25,000 they claimed the park could hold. In 1917, the *New Castle News*, reporting on the Fourth of July celebration that year, said, "Cascade Park Gets Monster Throng." No matter what year, the crowds always stayed all day because it ended with fireworks.

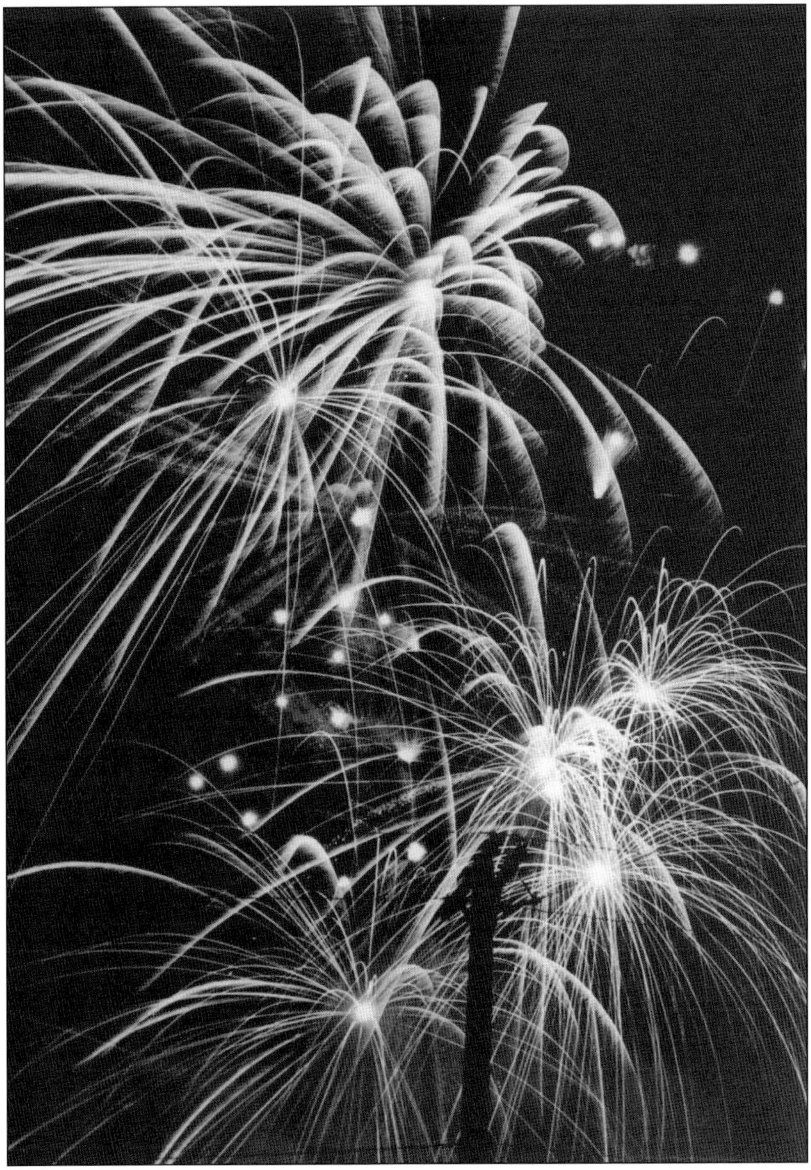

Fireworks at the Park, c. 1948. Cascade Park fireworks were usually set up on a small island in the lake. Occasionally they were at the ball grounds. Onlookers could count on spectacular Fourth of July and Labor Day displays, but often, groups such as the International Order of Odd Fellows (IOOF) would celebrate with fireworks. In 1909, when the IOOF had their fourth annual outing, the program listed 33 different pyrotechnical pieces, among them aerial bombs, roman candles, pinwheels, rockets, set pieces, fountains, and torpedoes. In 1925, the park observed the centennial of New Castle's incorporation as a borough with fireworks shows on three different nights during the weeklong celebration. In 1948, the city marked its founding in 1798 with a sesquicentennial week of celebrations and programs, and the park's "mammoth" display of fireworks. Fireworks displays have always been frequent in New Castle, where they have been manufactured. The first fireworks factory in the city was started in 1886 by Leopold Fazzoni, an Italian immigrant. Other fireworks companies followed with names like Rozzi, Conti, Zambelli, and Vitale. Zambelli and Pyrotecnico (Vitale) still operate local companies. (Courtesy of Adam Pivovar.)

BIBLIOGRAPHY

Art Work, Beaver and Lawrence Counties, Pennsylvania. Chicago: W. H. Parish and Company, 1894.

Atlas of the County of Lawrence and the State of Pennsylvania. Philadelphia: G. M. Hopkins and Company, 1872.

Cascade Park, New Castle, Pennsylvania. Marjorie Vesco, 2005. DVD.

Hazen, Aaron. *20th Century History of New Castle and Lawrence County*. Chicago: Richmond-Arnold Publishing Company, 1908.

Richards, Bart. Transcript of tape recorded interview. 4 May 1977.

Richards, Bart. *Lawrence County*. New Castle, PA: New Castle Area School District, 1968.

Samuelson, Dale. *The American Amusement Park*. St. Paul, MN: MBI Publishing Company, 2001.

Souvenir Program of New Castle's Centennial Celebration, 1825–1925. New Castle, PA: 1925.

Cascade Park Memories. Dir. Marjorie Vesco. The Video Standard, 2005. VHS.

Zona, Beverly. *All the Summers Were Golden: A History of Cascade Park*. New Castle, PA: Lawrence County Historical Society, 2001.

INDEX

Discover Thousands of Local History Books Featuring Millions of Vintage Images

Arcadia Publishing, the leading local history publisher in the United States, is committed to making history accessible and meaningful through publishing books that celebrate and preserve the heritage of America's people and places.

Find more books like this at
www.arcadiapublishing.com

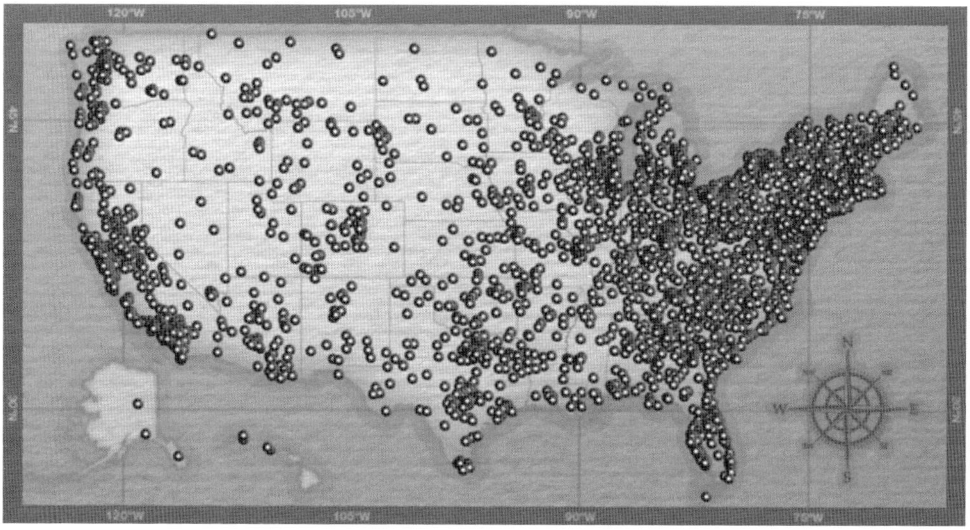

Search for your hometown history, your old stomping grounds, and even your favorite sports team.

Consistent with our mission to preserve history on a local level, this book was printed in South Carolina on American-made paper and manufactured entirely in the United States. Products carrying the accredited Forest Stewardship Council (FSC) label are printed on 100 percent FSC-certified paper.

MADE IN THE USA